Summary of Contents

W9-CNB-078

ANGULARJS: NOVICE TO NINJA

BY SANDEEP PANDA

AngularJS: Novice to Ninja

by Sandeep Panda

Copyright © 2014 SitePoint Pty. Ltd.

Product Manager: Simon Mackie **English Editor**: Paul Fitzpatrick
Technical Editor: Golo Roden **Cover Designer**: Alex Walker

Published by SitePoint Pty. Ltd.

48 Cambridge Street Collingwood
VIC Australia 3066
Web: www.sitepoint.com
Email: business@sitepoint.com

ISBN 978-0-9922794-5-5 (print)

ISBN 978-0-9924612-6-3 (ebook)
Printed and bound in the United States of America

About Sandeep Panda

Sandeep Panda is a web developer and writer with a passion for JavaScript and HTML5. He has over four years' experience programming for the Web. He loves experimenting with new technologies as they emerge and is a continuous learner. While not programming, Sandeep can be found playing games and listening to music.

About SitePoint

SitePoint specializes in publishing fun, practical, and easy-to-understand content for web professionals. Visit http://www.sitepoint.com/ to access our blogs, books, newsletters, articles, and community forums. You'll find a stack of information on JavaScript, PHP, Ruby, mobile development, design, and more.

To my Mom and Dad who taught me to love books. It's not possible to thank you adequately for everything you have done for me. To my grandparents for their strong support. To my brother Preetish for being a constant source of inspiration. And to my awesome friends Ipseeta and Fazle for always believing in me.

Table of Contents

Chapter 6   Developing Single Page Blogger ... 113

Chapter 7   Understanding AngularJS
Forms 129

Preface

AngularJS is an open source JavaScript framework that lets you create amazing AJAX-based web apps. Generally, the complexity involved in building large-scale and complex AJAX apps is tremendous. AngularJS aims to minimize this complexity by offering a great environment for development, as well as the means to test your apps.

As a client-side MVW (Model-View-Whatever) framework, one of the most powerful features of AngularJS is its ability to bring structure to your web apps. Another nice thing about AngularJS is that it extends the HTML vocabulary to make it suitable for building web apps, enabling you to create them declaratively; the resulting code is clean and very readable.

AngularJS ships with many great features out of the box, which you'll use in your day-to-day programming. It supports two-way data binding, nice templating, easy REST interaction, custom component creation, multiple views, routing, and much more. AngularJS also plays well with other libraries and frameworks. For example, you can combine jQuery and AngularJS together to create awesome web applications. AngularJS also demands no commitment. You can include Angular in your web page and use as many features as you like. If you need only the two-way data binding, but no REST interaction, you can employ that feature alone.

AngularJS favors Test Driven Development very much, and features great support for both unit and end-to-end testing. But it also takes debugging very seriously. In 2012, the AngularJS team released a Chrome plugin called Batarang which makes the debugging process a breeze. As a result, the products you develop with AngularJS are very robust and maintainable.

For these reasons (and many more that we'll discuss during the course of this book), AngularJS is one of the top choices when it comes to Single Page App development. You're going to enjoy working with AngularJS!

Who Should Read This Book

This book is suitable for intermediate level web designers and developers. Experience of HTML, CSS, and JavaScript is assumed.

Conventions Used

You'll notice that we've used certain typographic and layout styles throughout this book to signify different types of information. Look out for the following items.

Code Samples

Code in this book will be displayed using a fixed-width font, like so:

```
<h1>A Perfect Summer's Day</h1>
<p>It was a lovely day for a walk in the park. The birds
were singing and the kids were all back at school.</p>
```

If the code is to be found in the book's code archive, the name of the file will appear at the top of the program listing, like this:

```
                                                          example.css
.footer {
  background-color: #CCC;
  border-top: 1px solid #333;
}
```

If only part of the file is displayed, this is indicated by the word *excerpt*:

```
                                                     example.css (excerpt)
  border-top: 1px solid #333;
```

If additional code is to be inserted into an existing example, the new code will be displayed in bold:

```
function animate() {
  new_variable = "Hello";
}
```

Also, where existing code is required for context, rather than repeat all it, a ⋮ will be displayed:

```
function animate() {
    ⋮
    return new_variable;
}
```

Some lines of code are intended to be entered on one line, but we've had to wrap them because of page constraints. A ➡ indicates a line break that exists for formatting purposes only, and that should be ignored.

```
URL.open("http://www.sitepoint.com/responsive-web-design-real-user-
➡testing/?responsive1");
```

Tips, Notes, and Warnings

Hey, You!

Tips will give you helpful little pointers.

Ahem, Excuse Me ...

Notes are useful asides that are related—but not critical—to the topic at hand. Think of them as extra tidbits of information.

Make Sure You Always ...

... pay attention to these important points.

Watch Out!

Warnings will highlight any gotchas that are likely to trip you up along the way.

Supplementary Materials

http://www.learnable.com/books/angularjs1/
The book's website, containing links, updates, resources, and more.

https://github.com/spbooks/angularjs1/
The downloadable code archive for this book.

http://community.sitepoint.com/category/javascript

SitePoint's forums, for help on any tricky web problems.

books@sitepoint.com

Our email address, should you need to contact us for support, to report a problem, or for any other reason.

Want to Take Your Learning Further?

Thanks for buying this book. We appreciate your support. Do you want to continue learning? You can now get unlimited access to courses and ALL SitePoint books at Learnable for one low price. Enroll now and start learning today! Join Learnable and you'll stay ahead of the newest technology trends: http://www.learnable.com.

Chapter 1

Falling In Love With AngularJS

So, you're a web developer. Let me ask you a question: What do you usually do when you're asked to build a web application? If it's a client-side app, you most likely set up a project structure quickly, and grab your favorite JavaScript library, or just use plain vanilla JavaScript, to get started. If the application involves back-end logic, your favorite server-side language helps you.

Well, things are changing. Let me share a little secret with you: Pure HTML can now be used to build full-blown web applications! We all know HTML is great for creating static documents, but for developing a dynamic web app, standalone HTML is not really the best tool. This is where AngularJS comes in. **AngularJS** is what HTML would have been had it been designed for building web applications.

AngularJS is a framework that extends HTML by teaching it new syntax, making it suitable for developing really great web applications. With AngularJS you can introduce new HTML elements and custom attributes that carry special meaning. For example, you can create a new HTML element `<date-picker/>`, say, which adds a date picker widget, or a `<drop-zone/>` element, which can support drag-and-drop actions.

In this chapter, I'll outline all the great features of AngularJS that'll make it your new best friend. Then we'll briefly cover the download and installation process, followed by a discussion of a typical AngularJS app's anatomy. We'll also examine why Test Driven Development (TDD) is a must for any ninja developer. In fact, the AngularJS framework has been designed from ground up with TDD in mind. So, we'll see how to perform Unit and End-to-End testing during development, and also set up a test environment.

Throughout this book, we'll be working through the creation of a real-world AngularJS web app. Over the course of the book, we will develop the app and keep improving it. So, your mission, should you choose to accept it, is to become an AngularJS ninja by the end of the book and have a real-world app ready for deployment. Let's start our journey!

The Power Features of AngularJS

In this section, we'll explore some of the most compelling features of AngularJS which make it stand out from the crowd.

- **Magical two-way data binding:** The two-way data binding is probably the coolest and most useful feature in AngularJS. Put simply, data binding is automatic synchronization of data between your view (HTML) and model (simple JavaScript variables). In AngularJS we create templates and bind different components with specific models. So, whenever the model value changes, the view is automatically updated, and whenever the value of any view component changes (e.g the value of input text) the bound model is also updated. In other words you can carry out operations on the model, change their values, and AngularJS guarantees that the view will be updated to reflect the changes. This frees you from writing tons of boilerplate code and DOM manipulations just to get started. We'll explore two-way data binding in full in Chapter 2.

- **Structure front end code**: As web developers we don't care about any structure or pattern while writing client-side code. It's just us and the browser refresh button until we get things working. But this approach is bad in the long run, and if you are doing this, no doubt you'll get yourself into trouble very soon. With no structure your life will only get harder when the app becomes complex. Also it leaves no scope for good testing. But if you use AngularJS you're going to build solid, well-structured, and fully testable apps in no time. This not only saves you from maintenance nightmares, but makes your (and your Project Manager's) life much easier.

 Model View Whatever?

> AngularJS is an **MVW framework** (Model-View-Whatever) where **Whatever** means **Whatever Works for You**. The reason is that AngularJS can be used both as Model-View-Controller (MVC) and Model-View-View-Model (MVVM) framework. But what's important to us is that we can build solid web apps with great structure and design with minimum effort. We'll discuss more about this while examining some AngularJS code later in this chapter.

Routing Support: Single Page Apps (SPAs) are everywhere nowadays. With the advent of HTML5 and its related APIs, we don't want to redirect our users to a new page every time they click on something. Instead, we want to load the content asynchronously on the same page and just change the URL in the browser to reflect it. Lots of other popular websites are already doing this, such as Twitter and the Chrome app store. It makes the user feel as if they are interacting with a desktop app. With AngularJS we can implement a Single Page App very easily with minimum effort. In fact, AngularJS was built with these things in mind; you can basically create different views for different URLs. AngularJS will then load the appropriate view in the main page when a specific URL is requested. The routing feature also fosters maintainability. This is because we are logically dividing our app into different parts and thereby making it more maintainable. We will see how to implement Single Page apps with multiple views and routing in Chapter 4.

Templating done right with HTML: AngularJS uses plain old HTML as the templating language. The workflow becomes much simpler with plain HTML as the templating language, as the designers and developers don't have to depend on each other. Designers can create UIs in usual way and developers can use declarative binding syntax to tie different UI components with data models very easily. For example, you can use an expression like {{name}} to display a name model in HTML. Chapter 4 provides extensive coverage of templating in AngularJS.

Enhanced user experience with form validation: Forms are the most important part of any CRUD (Create, Read, Update, Delete) app. Providing feedback to the user while the form is being filled provides a great user experience. With that in mind AngularJS forms incorporate real-time form validations, custom validators, formatters and much more. It also offers several CSS classes that indicate which state the form controls are in—most importantly valid or invalid. You can quickly write CSS rules against these classes to customize the look and feel of the form controls in different states. Chapter 7 is all about forms and data validations.

■ **Teach HTML new syntax with directives:** A directive in AngularJS is what tricks HTML into doing new things that are not supported natively. This is done by introducing new elements/attributes and teaching the new syntax to HTML. For example, an HTML page doesn't know how to create a date picker widget. With directives you can create a new element called `<date-picker/>` and use it in HTML. This makes the UI creation process simple and intuitive. The concept of directives is unique to AngularJS and is great for developing declarative UI. Chapter 10 provides an in-depth guide to learning and implementing directives.

■ **Embeddable, testable, and injectable:** One of the nice things about AngularJS is that it's a good team player. You can easily embed an AngularJS app within another app. AngularJS never requires full commitment. You can use it along with other technologies very easily. I have already mentioned testing. When you're unit testing your app during development, you are fixing bugs right away, which you would have otherwise encountered unexpectedly further down the line. Being a modern framework, AngularJS favors Test Driven Development and offers out of the box support for unit and End-to-End testing. There is really no excuse not to test your app. As the book progresses, we'll be developing a demo app and unit testing isolated pieces of code. Each component in an app might not be independent; to function properly it might need some other services or components. **Dependency Injection** means that our code is not in charge of obtaining its dependencies. Rather its dependencies are injected automatically by a dependency injection container. With this approach each component of the app is loosely coupled to the others and the developer can test each one in isolation. AngularJS provides full support for Dependency Injection, and this makes our app more testable and maintainable.

■ **Powered by Google and an active community:** Whenever we adopt a new technology we always look for a good community support. AngularJS is currently being maintained by the awesome developers at Google. Being open source software the code is released under the MIT license and is available for download at GitHub. You can download the source and see if you can improve something. The documentation is also pretty good, and you can always ask questions on StackOverflow or the SitePoint forums to clear any doubts. AngularJS is under rapid development and keeps improving with each version. As a result, the number of developers using it is also increasing and you can find great tutorials on AngularJS all over the web. So, rest assured there is plenty of good information available to help you through.

Did these features excite you? Are you all set and geared up to start developing awesome AngularJS apps? Let's get started and see how to download and install AngularJS.

 Why is it Called AngularJS?

In case you are wondering why the name of the framework is AngularJS: Well, HTML uses angle brackets. Hence, the name!

Download and Installation

Downloading and installing AngularJS is very simple. You just need to point your `<script>` tag to the AngularJS script file and you are good to go! Either you can download the script to your server and serve it from there, or you can use a CDN. When you are in production mode I recommend you to use a CDN. Let's look at both ways to install AngularJS.

Installing via CDN

Just put the following script in the `<head>` of your HTML to get started:

```
<script type="text/javascript" src=" http://ajax.googleapis.com/
►ajax/libs/angularjs/1.2.16/angular.js"></script>
```

At the time of writing this book, AngularJS 1.2.16 was the latest stable release. So that's the version we'll be using throughout this book.

Angular Version Numbering

Even-numbered AngularJS versions are stable releases, while the odd-numbered versions are for developers only. For example, versions 1.0.x, 1.2.x, etc. are stable while the versions 1.1.x,1.3.x, etc. are unstable releases.

The above script points to the non-minified version of AngularJS. You should use this version in the development phase as the script is human-readable, contains comments and offers better error reporting.

As soon as you move into the production phase, you should use the minified version of AngularJS. This greatly improves the loading speed of your application. It's also compiled with the Closure compiler to make sure the script is optimized and downloads faster. To get the minified AngularJS via CDN just use the following `<script>`:

```
<script type="text/javascript" src=" http://ajax.googleapis.com/
➥ajax/libs/angularjs/1.2.16/angular.min.js"></script>
```

What's a Closure Compiler?

Wondering what the heck a Closure Compiler is? Read more about it here[1].

Hosting on Your Server

If you don't want to use a CDN it's certainly possible to serve the AngularJS script from your server. In fact it's not uncommon to host the libraries locally. Many companies do it because the CDNs might be blocked in the users' network. So, if you want to host the files yourself just head over to `http://code.angu-larjs.org/1.2.16/` and there you can find both `angular.js` and `angular.min.js`. Just download those to your server (your local machine for now) and include it in the HTML as usual.

Here is how you can include the files:

Non-minified:

---

[1] https://developers.google.com/closure/compiler/

```
<script type="text/javascript" src="angular.js"/>
```

Minified:

```
<script type="text/javascript" src="angular.min.js"/>
```

In addition to the main files above, there are several extra Angular scripts we are interested in:

- **angular-route.js:** Adds routing support. As we will be building a real-world single-page app in the book we will need this.

- **angular-animate.js:** This is useful for creating nice CSS3 animations.

- **angular-mocks.js & angular-scenarios.js:** This is useful for testing purposes.

- **angular-resource.js:** Provides better support for interacting with REST APIs.

Fortunately, you don't need to download all these right now. The Angular Seed project that we will download shortly offers these scripts out of the box.

Required Tools

To write better software we need to use the right tools, and there are some great tools and editors available for AngularJS. But when learning a new technology it's often better not to use any IDE. This way you will get to know the nitty-gritty of the technology. Once you are well-versed, IDEs can be used to boost your productivity. As you are just going to be working with plain JavaScript and HTML files, any text editor will do just fine. Personally, I use TextMate, a simple editor for Mac.

Now, let's check out several other options.

1. Jetbrains WebStorm[2]: This is a great commercial IDE from Jetbrains. It also has a nice AngularJS plugin and offers good support. Just note that WebStorm requires you to purchase a commercial/personal license and is available for Windows, Mac and Linux based systems. The commercial license costs $99 USD while the personal license costs $49 USD. You can also opt for a 30-day evaluation copy.

---

[2] http://www.jetbrains.com/webstorm/

2. Sublime Text 2 & 3[3]: Sublime Text is a pretty good editor with nice AngularJS support via plugins. While Sublime Text is free to evaluate, a license is needed for continued usage. The cost is $70 USD. Sublime is available for PC, Mac, and Linux-based systems.

3. TextMate[4] (For Mac users only): TextMate is a simple and elegant editor with good AngularJS plugins. It's free to use, but it is only available for Mac users.

4. NetBeans[5]: Netbeans (available for PC, Mac, and Linux) is an open source editor that is also a good option for AngularJS development.

Keep in mind that many AngularJS features like routing, REST interaction etc. won't work if you access the files locally (via `file://`). For that, you'll need a development server. But don't worry about that for now; in a moment, we'll discuss the Angular Seed project, and will learn how to set up a complete AngularJS development (and testing) environment with very little effort. This also includes a tiny development server written in Node.js to access files with `localhost`.

AngularJS Batarang

But wait! What about debugging? Don't fret, the AngularJS team have got you covered. They have released an awesome Chrome plugin called the **Batarang** to debug Angular-JS apps. It also addresses any performance bottlenecks there might be. It's a beautiful tool and I recommend you install it.

You can download it directly from the Chrome App Store[6]. After installing, open your browser's developer tools and you can find a new tab called **AngularJS**. It will look something like Figure 1.1.

---

[3] http://www.sublimetext.com/
[4] http://macromates.com/
[5] https://netbeans.org/
[6] https://chrome.google.com/webstore/detail/angularjs-batarang/ighdmehidhipcmcojjgiloacoafjmpfk?hl=en

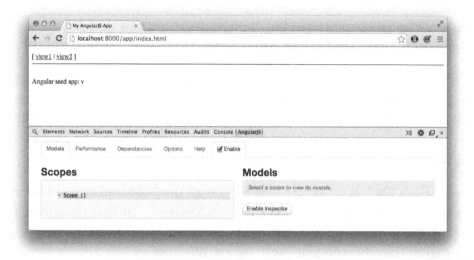

Figure 1.1. The AngularJS Batarang

Don't forget to check the **enable** option. Later on, we'll explore all the features of Angular Batarang.

The Angular Seed Project

Every project should have a structure to organize the files. The Angular Seed project provides a good skeleton structure for AngularJS apps so that you can quickly bootstrap the app and start developing. In addition to providing a fixed structure, it also offers a pre-configured test environment, a set of useful scripts, and a ready-to-use web server. The Angular Seed is not itself another framework. It just gives you a great head start on AngularJS development, and offers a nice project structure to easily organize the files. With Angular Seed you also get AngularJS itself, and other related scripts. You can either serve these scripts from your server, or use a CDN if required.

To download the version of Angular Seed used in this book, point your browser to: https://github.com/angular/angular-seed/tree/69c9416c8407fd5806aab3c63916dfcf0522ecbc. Once you are on the page, just click on **Download Zip** and this should download the project files as a zip archive. After extracting the zip you will get a folder called **angular-seed-master**. Place it anywhere on your local machine. The **app** folder, present inside **angular-seed-master**, is the folder that is going to be deployed. This means when moving to production we will just take this folder and nothing else. The rest of the folders are there for various configurations and tests. But during development we are going to use the entire contents of the **angular-seed-master** folder.

If you open up the **app** folder inside **angular-seed-master** you will find several folders which have reasonably self-explanatory names. For example, all your CSS files go inside the **css** folder, and all the images are placed inside **img**. Similarly, the **lib** folder contains all the AngularJS scripts. We are mainly interested in `angular.js` script and will be using only this initially.

There is also a **js** folder inside **app** which holds all the JavaScript files of your application. Initially, there are five `.js` files which represent different modules of your app. For instance, whenever you will create a `controller` it should go inside **controllers.js**. The other components in the **app** directory are:

- **directives.js**

- **filters.js**

- **services.js**

Okay, we've discussed the development aspect, but that is only half of the story. The next step is setting up a test environment. But for the time being, let's just focus on developing a simple AngularJS app. I will show how to set up a test environment later on in this chapter.

The Anatomy of an AngularJS app

Before building your first AngularJS app, you should be aware of the different components of AngularJS. Here I will outline some of the important components that you should absolutely know before moving further.

1. **Model:** The data shown to the users. The model data are simple POJOs (Plain Old JavaScript Objects).

2. **View:** This is what the users see when they visit your page, that is to say after the raw HTML template involving directives and expressions is compiled and linked with correct scope.

3. **Controller:** The business logic that drives your application.

4. **Scope:** A context that holds data models and functions. A controller usually sets these models and functions in the scope.

5. **Directives:** Something that teaches HTML new syntax. It extends HTML with custom elements and attributes.

6. **Expressions**: Expressions are represented by {{}} in the HTML. They are useful for accessing scope models and functions.

7. **Template:** HTML with additional markup in the form of directives (`<drop-zone/>`) and expressions {{}}.

Well, enough talking! Let's create a short and simple app.

Objective: To create an HTML page that asks users their annual salary and the percentage of that they want to spend buying gadgets. There should be two input text fields: one for salary and the other for percentage. There is also a `<span>` tag which displays the result of calculation. As soon as the value of any field changes the result is updated.

Implementation: Just imagine how you would implement this in plain JavaScript or jQuery. First you would create the required input fields and result `<span>`. You'd then register callbacks for `keyup` event on the input fields. Inside the callback, you'd read the values from input fields, calculate the result and finally `innerHTML` the value into the `<span>`.

But with AngularJS none of the above is required. In fact, you won't need to write even a single line of JavaScript for this app! Have a look at the following snippet which implements the same thing in AngularJS. You can create a file called **test.html** inside the **app** directory of **angular-seed-master** and paste the following snippet.

```
<!doctype html>
<html lang="en" ng-app>

<head>
  <title>My First AngularJS App</title>
</head>

<body ng-init="salary=0;percentage=0">

  Your Salary?
```

```
    <input type="text" ng-model="salary">
    <br/>How much should you invest in gadgets?
    <input type="text" ng-model="percentage">%
    <br/>The amount to be spent in shopping will be:
➡ <span>{{salary*percentage*0.01}}</span>
    <script src="lib/angular/angular.js"></script>
</body>

</html>
```

Now to access the page we need a web server. To run the web server that ships with Angular Seed you'll need Node.js. Head over to http://nodejs.org/ and download the latest release. At the time of writing the latest Node.js version was 0.10.26. Just download and install it in your machine. Once you are done open up the terminal (for Mac) or Command Prompt (for Windows), type node and hit enter. If the command is found, you know you have successfully installed node.

 Using the Command Prompt

If you are unsure about how to handle the command prompt or terminal, please check out the following links:

Windows Command Prompt: http://www.makeuseof.com/tag/a-beginners-guide-to-the-windows-command-line/

Mac Terminal: http://guides.macrumors.com/Terminal

The next step is running the server. In your command prompt or terminal move to **angular-seed-master** and run the following command: node scripts/web-server.js. This will start the server at port 8000. So, to access the newly created **test.html** point your browser to http://localhost:8000/app/test.html.

Surprised by the small amount of code required to pull this off? This is what makes AngularJS best suited for rapid web app development. Let's examine what's happening here:

1. An AngularJS application bootstraps with the ng-app attribute (actually, it's a directive).

2. ng-init initializes your data models: the data to be presented on the UI.

3. `ng-model` binds an input field with model data. This establishes a two-way binding, which means the data model will be updated automatically whenever the input field value changes and vice versa.

4. `{{}}` is called an **expression**, which is composed of one or more data models. The main purpose of an expression is binding the model data to the view uni-directionally; that is, syncing from model to view. You can also perform operations like multiplication, division etc. on the models, as shown in the example above. AngularJS evaluates this expression and replaces it with the calculated value. The beautiful thing is that the expression is re-evaluated each time any of the data models it depends on changes. In our case, whenever a user types anything into input fields the data-models are updated. As a result the expression `{{salary*percentage*0.01}}` is re-evaluated automatically which, in turn, updates the DOM for us.

What is MVW?

It's 2014. Front end code is just as important as back end logic. To keep your app maintainable and well-structured in the long run it's important to follow a pattern. Fortunately, AngularJS can be used to develop apps based on both the MVC or MVVM patterns. That's the reason it's been declared as an MVW (Model-View-Whatever) framework. But before jumping into the details, let me give you a primer on MVC and MVVM.

MVC

Model-View-Controller (MVC) is an architectural pattern that fosters improved code organization by promoting **separation of concerns**. The UI (View) is separated from business data (Model) of the app through a Controller which handles inputs, delegates the tasks to business logic and coordinates with the model and view.

You can read more about MVC here: http://alexatnet.com/articles/model-view-controller-mvc-javascript

MVVM

Model-View-ViewModel (MVVM) is a design pattern to build declarative UIs. In MVVM, a **ViewModel** exposes your application's business data (the Model) to the View in a way the View can understand it. In other words the ViewModel is a pure code representation of your business data. For instance, if you are creating a notes editor, your ViewModel should hold a list of notes and expose methods to add/edit/delete them.

You can read more about MVVM here: http://addyosmani.com/blog/understanding-mvvm-a-guide-for-javascript-developers/

It's your call to decide which way you want to use AngularJS. However, we'll follow the MVC pattern through this book. So, let's take a look at how to use AngularJS to introduce MVC to our app.

Structuring Our Code With MVC

In the world of MVC, everything has its own place. The major benefit is that the business logic is decoupled from the UI (the view). The next benefit is that, if you want to fix a bug in a component or modify its functionality, you know exactly where the component goes, which makes maintenance much easier. It also helps you structure your code into several loosely coupled modules which can be loaded and tested independently.

Here's what each component does:

1. **Controller:** The Controller handles inputs, calls the code that performs business rules and shares data with view via $scope. The business logic is what your app is known to do. In case of a weather app the business logic is all about obtaining the weather data (probably from a REST web service). In AngularJS we perform this logic inside a service and inject it into the controller. Using the service our controller obtains the data and sets it on a $scope object so that the view can display it. In this way the controller is just aware of the $scope and not the view. Tomorrow you can change the whole UI from a web view to mobile view and the business logic will be the same because the controller is completely separated from the view.

2. **Model:** The Model represents the business data that drives your UI. Your UI is a projection of the model data at any given time through the view.

3. **View**: The view is only concerned with displaying the data and is decoupled from the business logic. It should update itself whenever the underlying data model changes. In AngularJS the view reads model data from the $scope which

has already been set by our controller and displays it. This helps the front end development to progress in parallel with the back end activity.

 The Scope is the Glue

Think of the scope as a glue between Controller and View. This way our Controller and View are not aware of each other, but still they can share data. This means if tomorrow your manager asks you to change the current UI to something else you can do that pretty easily without touching the business logic.

Now we've discussed the basics, let's modify the previous code accordingly. Again we will use Angular Seed structure to bootstrap development.

JavaScript — **apps.js** Paste this inside **/app/js/apps.js**.

```
angular.module('myApp', [
  'myApp.controllers'
]);
```

myApp is our main module that's loaded when the app bootstraps. This module depends on the `controllers` module which has the `FinanceController` controller, which will be created next.

JavaScript — **controllers.js**

```
angular.module('myApp.controllers', []).
➥controller('FinanceController', function($scope) {
  $scope.salary = 0;
  $scope.percentage = 0;
  $scope.result = function() {
    return $scope.salary * $scope.percentage * 0.01;
  };
});
```

A `$scope` object is passed to the `FinanceController` constructor function. We set different properties like `salary` and `percentage` on this scope, which are made available to the view. We also set a function `result()` on this `scope` that calculates the final result and returns it. This function is accessed in the view.

HTML — This should go into **/app/test.html** of your Angular Seed project:

```
<!doctype html>
<html lang="en" ng-app="myApp">

<head>
  <title>Finance Meter</title>
</head>

<body ng-controller="FinanceController">

  Your Salary?
  <input type="text" ng-model="salary">
  <br/>How much should you invest in shopping?
  <input type="text" ng-model="percentage">%
  <br/>The amount to be spent on gadgets will be:
➥<span>{{result()}}</span>

  <script src="lib/angular/angular.js"></script>
  <script src="js/app.js"></script>
  <script src="js/controllers.js"></script>
</body>

</html>
```

In HTML `ng-controller` instantiates the `FinanceController` passing a `$scope` object. In this case, the controller is applied to the entire `<body>` element. As a result all the `$scope` properties set by our controller can be referred directly anywhere inside `<body>` and `</body>`. If you look at the code you can see we're referring to the model properties in `ng-model`. These models are updated every time the input field value changes. We are also calling the `$scope` function `result()` inside expression `{{}}` which is re-called every time `salary` or `percentage` models change. As a result the DOM is always updated with the correct result.

With a few additional steps we have structured our code in much better way.

 Naming Your Controllers

Please note that whenever you register a controller in a module its name should follow **PascalCase**; in other words, it should be camelCase with its first letter in uppercase. According to JavaScript conventions every constructor function should be named in PascalCase so that users know they need to use **new** on the function to obtain an instance. Since, in AngularJS, the controllers are nothing but constructor functions, we should follow PascalCase while naming them. On the other hand, the module name should be in camelCase.

Playing with Filters

Want to try something cool? Replace `{{result()}}` in the previous HTML snippet with `{{result() | currency}}` and see the result automatically formatted as currency (with $ symbol and commas). This is called afilter, which we'll be covering later in this book.

As we have finished developing the app let's have a look at the testing process briefly. In the next section we'll discuss what unit and End-to-End tests really are. Then we'll have a quick overview of testing with Karma & Jasmine, and set up a testing environment in Angular-Seed project we downloaded.

Unit and End-to-End Testing in AngularJS

Unit testing is a technique that lets developers validate isolated pieces of code. The unit is the smallest testable part of your code. So, while you're coding it's always a good idea to validate and ensure that your code works as expected. For example, when you write a controller it's smart to unit test it first before moving to next thing. This way, if you need to add some more functionality to the controller, you can do so and also validate that you haven't broken any of the previous functionalities in this process.

End-to-End testing helps ascertain that a set of components, when integrated together, work as expected. End-to-End tests should be carried out when user stories are being generated. For instance, an End-to-End test can be done to ensure when a user enters correct username, password and hits login button he is taken to the admin panel. End-to-End tests differ from unit testing in that they take two or more pieces of unit-tested code and ensure that they work as expected when integrated together.

We'll be unit testing our code as we start developing our demo app.

Setting up the test environment is simple, but requires the following of a series of steps. Assuming you have already downloaded Angular Seed, let's outline the pre-requisites to set up test environment.

1. Firstly, we need Node.js and npm (Node Package Manager) to install various tools.

2. We are going to download the Jasmine library as this is the test framework we will use.

3. We will also need the Karma test runner (formerly Testacular) to run the tests.

That's all. Now that we are aware of the tools needed we are good to go. Just follow the steps below and setting up the test environment for your app will be a breeze.

1. We have already installed Node.js. There is no need to install npm (Node Package Manager) separately as it comes bundled with the Node.js release.

2. The next step is downloading the Karma test runner. To do that, navigate to the `angular-seed-master` directory in terminal/command prompt. On a Windows machine you can simply move to the directory in command prompt via the `cd` command. On Mac, you can just drag the `angular-seed-directory` and drop it onto the terminal icon in the dock. Now run `npm install karma`. This will install the Karma test runner. As a result, a new directory called `node_modules` will get created under `angular-seed-master` which holds Karma.

3. Now we need two plugins. The first one is the Jasmine library. The second one is `karma-chrome-launcher/karma-firefox-launcher/karma-safari-launcher/karma-opera-launcher` (which one you need depends on the browser you use). These launchers help us see the test results directly in the browser. You can just change test specs and refresh the browser page to see the updated test results. To install the plugins use the following commands: `npm install jasmine` and then the command to install the appropriate plugin for your browser:

```
npm install karma-chrome-launcher
npm install karma-firefox-launcher
npm install karma-safari-launcher
npm install karma-opera-launcher
```

4. To perform End-to-End tests we will need Protractor. To install it, just run the following command: `npm install protractor`.

Running these commands will install the plugins into node_modules directory inside angular-seed-master. Congratulations! You have successfully created a test environment for yourself. Now take a moment, grab a drink, and come back to explore a couple of important points.

Where to Put Your Tests

All your unit tests go into **angular-seed-master/test/unit** and all the End-to-End tests go inside **angular-seed-master/test/e2e**. If you open up the **angular-seed-master/test/unit** directory you will find four different .js files: **controllersSpecs.js, filtersSpecs.js, directivesSpecs.js, servicesSpecs.js**. You'll write the unit tests for your controllers inside **controllersSpecs.js**. Similarly, the unit tests for other components will go into their corresponding files.

Inside **angular-seed-master/test/e2e** directory you can find **scenarios.js**. All your End-to-End tests will go here.

How to Run Tests

To run tests, first, move to **angular-seed-master** in the terminal/command prompt.

For Unit Tests

If you are on Mac, use the command: sh scripts/test.sh . On Windows, double-click on test.bat inside the scripts directory. This will start the Karma server and bring up your browser. Just click on the **debug** button in the browser, which will take you to a different tab, as shown in Figure 1.2.

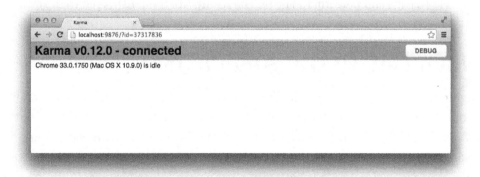

Figure 1.2. Running a unit test

Then just open your browser's web developers tool and go to **console**. There you can find the results of your test cases. Whenever you make any changes to the tests or modify an existing one just hit refresh and the console shows you the updated result, as shown in Figure 1.3.

Figure 1.3. Updated results

For End-to-End Tests

If you are on Mac use the command: `sh scripts/e2e-test.sh` . On Windows, double-click on **e2e-test.bat** inside the **scripts** directory. Before running this, be sure to start the test server as described above. This will bring up the browser, open up your HTML page and perform the tests. The results are then displayed in the terminal.

When Not To Use AngularJS

AngularJS was designed with data-driven apps in mind. It's also an excellent choice if your app interacts with a lot of RESTful web services. But if your app needs heavy DOM manipulations where model data is not the focus, you might want to use a library like jQuery instead, as that is better suited for this kind of task. If you want to develop a web app which is basically a game or involves heavy graphics manipulation, AngularJS is not the way to go. In short, AngularJS is best if your UI is data-driven.

Conclusion

As a ninja developer you are expected to complete any task assigned to you on the fly in best possible way. This is exactly where AngularJS helps you. Looking at our first app we can conclude that AngularJS helps us overcome three major obstacles in web app development:

1. **The plumbing** —Removes the need for a significant amount of coding just to get started.

2. **DOM manipulations** — The data model is the single source of truth. If you update just the model the DOM is automatically updated. That's why most of the AngularJS based apps don't need to programmatically manipulate the DOM. But you are free to do so if needed.

3. **JavaScript coding for simple tasks** — No more JavaScript for every simple or small task. The data models and two-way data binding reduce the amount of JavaScript code needed to achieve simple objectives.

On the other hand, Angular also brings us the following major benefits:

1. **Greatly reduces the number of lines of code**. Less code means fewer maintenance nightmares, and makes your life so much easier.

2. **Great testability and maintainability** come with well-structured code and separation of concerns.

3. **Awesome testing support**. Application testing is as important as application development.

By now you should be well on your way to being an AngularJS disciple. In the next chapter we will be exploring the two-way data binding feature of AngularJS.

Modules, Controllers & Data Binding

Structuring your code is the key to writing maintainable software. The good news is that with AngularJS you can easily divide your front-end source code into reusable components, called **modules**. An AngularJS module is basically a container that groups together different components of your application under a common name. If you look at the Angular Seed project that we downloaded in Chapter 1, you can see that there are different modules defined in the files **controllers.js**, **directives.js**, **filters.js** , **services.js**, etc. In our main JavaScript file, **app.js**, we have a module myApp which depends on the above modules (yes, modules can depend on other modules). Finally, in the HTML we tell AngularJS to start bootstrapping our app using myApp module as the starting point. This is done by writing ng-app='myApp' in the HTML.

Built-in Modules

AngularJS has several built-in modules. The ng module defines many directives, filters, services for our use. We have already used some of the directives from this module such as ng-model, ng-controller, etc. Similarly, you can also create your own module and use it in your app.

AngularJS needs to know about the different components of our app and how they are wired together. To tell that story to AngularJS we divide our app into reusable modules and declaratively specify their dependencies on each other. Let's see how to create a simple module.

Creating Our First Module

To create a module, we call the `angular.module()` function. The first argument to the function is the module name. The second argument is an array that specifies the additional modules upon which this module depends. If there's no dependency you just pass an empty array.

```
angular.module('firstModule',[]);
➥//defines a module with no dependencies

angular.module('firstModule',['moduleA','moduleB']);
➥//defines a module with 2 dependencies
```

Once you have a module, you can attach different components to it. Just think of `angular.module()` as a global API for creating or retrieving modules and registering components. The call to `angular.module()` returns a reference to the newly created module. This is how we can attach a controller to the above module:

```
var firstModule=angular.module('firstModule',[]); //define a module

firstModule.controller('FirstController',function($scope){
➥// register a controller
    //your rocking controller
});

firstModule.directive('FirstDirective',function(){ // register a
➥directive
    return {

    };
});
```

The above snippet has one big flaw. When we store the newly created module in a variable it's added to the JavaScript global scope—and it's not good practice to pollute the global scope unnecessarily.

One way to overcome this is to wrap the above code in an IIFE[1] as follows:

```
(function() {
  var firstModule = angular.module('firstModule', []);
➡//firstModule is not global here

  firstModule.controller('FirstController', function($scope) {
➡// register a controller
    //your rocking controller
  });

  firstModule.directive('FirstDirective', function() { // register
➡a directive
    return {

    };
  });
})();

//firstModule undefined here
```

The function executes as soon as it's created. And inside, where you wrote `var firstModule = angular.module('firstModule', []);`, the variable `firstModule` is not added to the global scope, meaning we're no longer polluting the global scope.

Fortunately, to keep things simple AngularJS has another great mechanism, which is superior to this approach. When you call `angular.module()` with two arguments (the last argument for dependencies) AngularJS creates a new module. Subsequently when you call `angular.module()` with a single argument (just the module name), AngularJS retrieves the already created module and returns it. Isn't that great? With this in mind, let's modify our above snippet:

```
angular.module('firstModule',[]); //specify dependency list here

angular.module('firstModule').controller('FirstController'
➡,function($scope){ //just use it
    //your rocking controller
});

angular.module('firstModule').directive('FirstDirective'
```

---

[1] http://en.wikipedia.org/wiki/Immediately-invoked_function_expression

```
➥,function(){ //just use it
   return {

   };
});
```

Alternatively, if you really want to be smart, you could use:

```
angular.module('firstModule',[]).controller('FirstController'
➥,function($scope){
       //your rocking controller
}).directive('FirstDirective',function(){ //your directive
   return {

   };
});
```

The above code works because each function you call on the `angular.module()`
(such as `controller()`, `directive()` etc.) returns a reference to the module itself.
So, the calls can be chained together, and you can keep attaching different components in this way.

Be Careful When Calling angular.module() Multiple Times

Only the first call to `angular.module()` should specify the second argument.
All the subsequent calls to `angular.module()` should just pass a single argument
which retrieves an already created module. If you call `angular.module()` multiple times with two arguments you are just redefining the dependency list, not
retrieving an existing module.

Using angular.module()

You can also use `angular.module('moduleName')` in a different source file
to retrieve an existing module and attach components to it.

Modular Programming Best Practices

When you divide your source code into different modules you have two choices:

■ **Modularization by layers**

Modularization by features

First, let's get into the **app/js** directory of the Angular Seed to find out which pattern is used here. If you open up the directory you will see the following five source files, each representing a module:

1. **app.js**

2. **controllers.js**

3. **directives.js**

4. **filters.js**

5. **services.js**

This is called **modularization by layers**.

Each type of component goes into a particular module. Finally, the main app module is defined in **app.js**, which depends on the other four modules. This is specified by passing a dependency list to `angular.module()` as the second argument. You just refer to this main module in `ng-app` in HTML. This type of modularization can be useful in many scenarios. For example, if you encounter a bug in a particular type of component, say a service, you know where to look for it.

But when your app grows in terms of size and complexity it may not be good to modularize by layer. Instead you can achieve this **by feature**. For example, your website might have a login module, a comment module and a posts module. All these modules exist independently and are loosely coupled. Usually, you'd create a separate directory for each module and place all the relevant JavaScript files inside the relevant folders. This fosters code re-usability because you can just take the entire folder for a particular module and use it in a different project. Also separate dev teams can work on different modules simultaneously as they are not tightly coupled to each other. Furthermore, unit testing becomes a piece of cake since you need to load only the required modules and can test each module in isolation easily.

We can tweak the Angular Seed Project a bit to use this pattern. For example, a blogging system could use the following file structure:

```
/app
    /img -- application level images
    /css -- application level css
    /js
        app.js -- the main app module
    /modules
        /login
            /js
                controllers.js  --controllers for login module
                directives.js   --directives for login module
            /views -- views for login module
            /css
            /img
            loginModule.js -- Main login module definition
        /comment
            /js
                controllers.js  --controllers for login module
                directives.js   --directives for login module
            /views -- views for comment module
            /css
            /img
            commentModule.js -- Main comment module definition

        ...

        ...
    index.html
```

Inside each of these files, we define our modules. For the login module, the definitions are as follows:

/app/modules/login/js/controllers.js

```
angular.module('mainApp.login.controllers',[]);
```

/app/modules/login/js/directives.js

```
angular.module('mainApp.login.directives',[]);
```

/app/modules/login/loginModule.js

```
angular.module('loginModule',['mainApp.login.controllers',
➥'mainApp.login.directives']);
```

For the comment module, the definitions are as follows:

/app/modules/comment/js/controllers.js

```
angular.module('mainApp.comment.controllers',[]);
```

/app/modules/comment/js/directives.js

```
angular.module('mainApp.comment.directives',[]);
```

/app/modules/comment/loginModule.js

```
angular.module('commentModule',['mainApp.comment.controllers',
➥'mainApp.comment.directives']);
```

The main module is defined in **/app/app.js** like this:

```
angular.module('mainApp',['loginModule','commentModule']);
```

Finally, inside **index.html** we bootstrap the app by writing:

```
ng-app='mainApp'
```

As you can see, the modules `loginModule` and `commentModule` don't know about each other, but they are brought together by the app's main module `mainApp`. In HTML, when AngularJS encounters ng-app, it bootstraps the application by loading the specified module. In this case, AngularJS bootstraps the app by loading the module `mainApp`. But AngularJS sees that the module `mainApp` depends on two other modules `loginModule` and `commentModule`. So, it starts loading those modules as well. But these modules also have dependencies on other modules (`controllers`, `directives`, etc.), which are also loaded by AngularJS. In this way, AngularJS starts your app by loading all the necessary modules.

Using Dot Notation in Module Names

The dot notation used in the module names is there simply to mimic namespaces, and doesn't hold any special meaning in AngularJS. You could just as easily use a comma or a colon instead of a dot, but it seems most logical to namespace module names with a dot.

Modularization by features clearly keeps your app maintainable and testable in the long run. It also gives different teams the freedom to focus on different parts of your project independently. So, we'll stick with this pattern while developing our demo application in this book.

Controllers

The Role of a Controller

The task of a controller is to augment the scope by attaching models and functions to it that are subsequently accessed in the view. A controller is nothing but a constructor function which is instantiated by AngularJS when it encounters ng-controller directive in HTML. We'll explore AngularJS scopes in next chapter. As I mentioned in Chapter 1, the scope is just the glue between the controller and the view, so that your controller can add properties to the scope and the view can access those.

Attaching Properties and Functions to Scope

As the next step, let's write a controller that passes the current date, time, and a name to the view via a scope.

Controller:

```
angular.module('myApp',[]).controller('GreetingController'
➡,function($scope){
  $scope.now=new Date(); //set the model 'now' on scope
  $scope.greeting='Hello';    //set the name model on scope
});
```

You register a controller on a module by calling controller() on angular.module(). The controller() function takes two arguments: The first one is the name of the controller, and the second is the constructor function that'll be called when `ng-controller` directive is encountered in HTML. Notice the argument `$scope` to the constructor function? When you declare `$scope` as a parameter to the controller's constructor function, you're saying that your controller is dependent on `$scope` object. The parameter name `$scope` has a special meaning. AngularJS infers the dependencies of your controller from the parameter names in the constructor function. In this case, when AngularJS finds `ng-controller='GreetingController'` in HTML, it creates a new `scope` for your controller and passes that as an argument to the constructor function while instantiating the controller. This is called *Dependency Injection*, which is an important and core part of AngularJS. We'll discuss Dependency Injection at length later in the book.

 Multiple Dependencies

You can have multiple dependencies for your controller and can declare all those as parameters to the controller's constructor function. In addition to `$scope`, each AngularJS app has a `$rootScope`. Let's assume you have a custom service that interacts with a back end via XHR. You can declare these two as dependencies for your controller, like this:

```
angular.module('myApp',[]).controller(
➥'ControllerWithDependency',
➥function($rootScope,customService){
  //use the dependencies here
});
```

While instantiating your controller, AngularJS reads the parameter list, and from these names it knows which services/objects to inject. Also, you should note that AngularJS prefixes its own services and objects with $ as a naming convention. So you should not prefix your custom services with $.

Now that we have our `DateTimeController` ready it's time to use it in the view.

HTML

```
<!DOCTYPE html>
<html ng-app="myApp">

<head>
  <script type='text/javascript' src="https://ajax.googleapis.com/
```

```
➥ajax/libs/angularjs/1.2.16/angular.js"></script>
  <script src="app.js"></script>
</head>

<body ng-controller="GreetingController">
  {{greeting}} User! The current date/time is <span>{{now | date:
➥'medium'}}</span>.
</body>

</html>
```

Here, we have attached ng-controller directive to body. This means everything in <body> and </body> is under this controller's scope. Each time ng-controller is detected, AngularJS creates a new scope for this particular controller and instantiates it. So, when ng-controller="GreetingController" is encountered the constructor function of GreetingController runs, which sets two models on scope object: greeting and now. In the view we can access these models by using expressions {{}}. When we write {{greeting}} AngularJS replaces it with the value of the greeting property that has been set on the scope by the controller. The same is true for the model now as well. Whatever you write inside {{}} resolves against the controller's scope.

Using Built-in Filters

date: 'medium' is a built-in filter that formats a date object.

When you run the HTML in the browser you should see something like:

```
Hello, User! The current date/time is <current date & time here>.
```

Try Out Code Snippets Quickly

To try these small code snippets you don't always need to open up your editor and start the server. Here's a simple trick. To try out the above code, open up http://plnkr.co/edit/ in your browser. On the top select New->AngularJS->AngularJS 1.2.x. This will create an AngularJS project for you. Copy and paste our controller definition to app.js in the left sidebar. Paste the HTML into index.html in the left sidebar. To view the output click on the Live Preview (a tiny eye icon) on the right sidebar. Now whenever you make any changes to the source the output will automatically refresh.

Adding Logic to the Controller

Apart from handling user inputs and setting scope models, a controller often sets functions to the $scope. These functions perform some kind of logic and often interact with services that encapsulate business data of the app.

To understand this, let's add a function to the $scope that returns the greeting text hello in a random language. Here's how we modify our controller definition:

```
angular.module('myApp', []).controller('GreetingController'
➥, function($scope) {
  $scope.now = new Date();
  $scope.helloMessages = ['Hello', 'Bonjour', 'Hola', 'Ciao',
➥'Hallo'];
  $scope.greeting = $scope.helloMessages[0];
  $scope.getRandomHelloMessage = function() {
    $scope.greeting = $scope.helloMessages[parseInt((Math.random()
➥* $scope.helloMessages.length))];
  }
});
```

Here, we added a model helloMessages to $scope, which is an array of strings. This represents the text hello in five different languages. We also set a function getRandomHelloMessage() on the $scope that selects a message randomly and sets the value to scope model greeting. As a result of data binding when $scope.greeting is updated the expression {{greeting}} changes in the view.

Now, the corresponding view would be:

```
<!DOCTYPE html>
<html ng-app="myApp">

<head>
  <script type='text/javascript' src="https://ajax.googleapis.com/
➥ajax/libs/angularjs/1.2.16/angular.js"></script>
  <script src="app.js"></script>
</head>

<body ng-controller="GreetingController">
```

```
  {{greeting}} User! The current date/time is <span>{{now | date:
➥'medium'}}</span>.
  <br/>
  <button ng-click="getRandomHelloMessage()">Random Hello Message
➥</button>

</body>

</html>
```

Here, we added an HTML `button` which responds to the `click` event by calling the function `getRandomHelloMessage()` on the controller's scope. This method, in turn, changes the value of the `greeting` model and, consequently, the change is reflected in the view.

Admittedly, this example is very simple. But we've learned the basics of a controller and how it should be used. Now let's discuss what a controller should *not* do:

- No DOM manipulation. This should be done in `directives`.

- Don't format model values in controllers. Filters exist for this purpose. We have already seen filters in action with the built-in date filter.

- Don't write repeatable code in controllers. Rather encapsulate them in services. For example, you might need to fetch some data from server at multiple places. So, instead of repeating that code in the controllers, you should wrap the code in a service and inject it to the controllers when required. After all the controller's task is handling user inputs, setting properties/functions to `$scope` and interact with services to perform the business logic.

Controllers *should* be used to:

- Set the initial state of a scope by attaching models to it.

- Set functions on the scope that perform some tasks.

 Naming Controllers

In many online resources you might encounter controller names that end with `Ctrl`. I recommend that use a full name, like `DemoController` and not `DemoCtrl`. This makes your code more readable.

Adding Instance Functions and Properties to Controllers

Although controllers usually set functions and properties to the scope, you can also create instance functions and properties of the controller. Remember, AngularJS instantiates your controller by calling the constructor function that you provide. This means you have the freedom to create instance variables and functions. Let's modify our previous controller to use instance variables instead of scope models.

Controller

```
angular.module('myApp', []).controller('GreetingController',
➡function($scope) {
  this.now = new Date();
  this.helloMessages = ['Hello', 'Bonjour', 'Ola', 'Ciao', 'Hallo'];
  this.greeting = this.helloMessages[0];
  this.getRandomHelloMessage = function() {
    this.greeting = this.helloMessages[parseInt((Math.random() *
➡this.helloMessages.length))];
  }
});
```

There's a small tweak in the view:

```
<!DOCTYPE html>
<html ng-app="myApp">

<head>
  <script type='text/javascript' src="https://ajax.googleapis.com/
➡ajax/libs/angularjs/1.2.16/angular.min.js"></script>
  <script src="app.js"></script>
</head>

<body ng-controller="GreetingController as greetingController">
  {{greetingController.greeting}} User! The current date/time is
➡<span>{{greetingController.now | date: 'medium'}}</span>.
  <br/>
  <button ng-click="greetingController.getRandomHelloMessage()">
➡Random Hello Message</button>
```

```
</body>

</html>
```

The code `GreetingController as greetingController` does the trick. Here, the `as` keyword sets the instance of `GreetingController` on the scope under the name `greetingController`. So, the `as` keyword exposes our controller instance to the view and, as a result, we can access its instance variables and methods through the reference `greetingController`.

Not all developers favor this approach. Let's see what's good and what's bad about the `as` keyword.

Cons:

■ Exposing the whole `controller` instance isn't a good idea in many cases. The `scope` object exists for clear separation of concern between `controller` and `view`.

■ The approach is not mainstream and also leads to more typing.

Pros:

■ When controllers are nested and both inner and outer controller scopes have models with the same names, the `as` keyword can really come in handy:

```
<div ng-controller='OuterController as outer'>
        <div ng-controller='InnerController as inner'<

        Outer={{outer.someModel}} and inner={{inner.someModel}}
```

 Nesting Controllers

Controllers can be nested and in such cases the inner controller scope inherits the outer controller scope (prototypal inheritance in effect). We'll discuss this in more detail in the next chapter.

Dependency Injection in Controllers With Minification

We have seen how to inject dependencies into controllers. AngularJS infers the controller's dependencies from the names of the arguments to its constructor function. But if you minify the JavaScript while deploying, the argument names will be shortened and as a result AngularJS will no longer be able to identify the dependencies. In that case you have two options to declare dependencies while still allowing for minification. Let's examine each of them.

Firstly, you can set a property called `$inject` on the controller, which is an array of dependencies:

```
function DemoController($rootScope,$scope,$http){

}

DemoController.$inject=['$rootScope','$scope','$http'];

angular.module('myApp',[]).controller('DemoController',
➥DemoController);
```

The `$inject` property declares dependencies of the controller in the order of arguments to the constructor function.

This second option is more popular among developers. Instead of passing the constructor function as the second argument to the `angular.controller()` you can pass an array. The array holds the names of dependencies, and the last item in the array is the controller's constructor function. Here is how we do it:

```
angular.module('myApp',[]).controller('DemoController',['$rootScope'
➥,'$scope','$http',function($rootScope,$scope,$http){

}]);
```

As you'll appreciate, the above code is pretty straightforward. The dependencies are injected into the constructor function in the order they are declared in the array.

Both these methods achieve same thing. The first approach is a little longer while the second is inline and shorter. Also in case of the second approach, the parameters lists are close to each other. As a result, if you need to change something, you have a single place to edit. You can even align both of the parameter lists into two subsequent lines so that you can see whether they match each other or not.

Overview of Two-Way Data Binding

Now that you are aware of modules and controllers, it's time to move forward a bit and explore one of the most important and fundamental features of AngularJS—the two-way data binding. Although this section just gives an overview of data binding, it's vital you nail this in order to understand the more advanced stuff coming in Chapter 3.

What Is Data Binding?

Data binding is the automatic synchronization of data between view and the model. When we say two-way, we mean the synchronization process works both ways. In AngularJS, we create models and set them on the `scope` object. Then we tie our UI components with these models. This establishes a two-way binding between our view (HTML) components and the model data. Whenever the model data changes, the view updates itself to reflect the change. On the other hand, when the value of the view component changes the model is also updated.

If you are from a Flex/ActionScript background you have probably used this kind of data binding almost every day. But this kind of feature is new in HTML. It lets you treat the model data as the single source of truth, which, in turn, frees you from programmatically manipulating the DOM. AngularJS guarantees that your view is always stays updated with the latest model data. So, you just change the data and your view is updated automatically without any extra effort. In other words, there's no need for `innerHTML`. But you can also certainly update the DOM manually in AngularJS if you wish to.

Two-Way Binding in AngularJS

The following example shows basic two-way data binding in action. For the sake of simplicity, I am bypassing the controller. Let's just focus on the data binding.

```
<!doctype html>
<html lang="en" ng-app>
<head>
```

```
    <meta charset="utf-8">
    <title>Two way data binding</title>
</head>
<body ng-init="name='AngularJS'">

    <input type="text" ng-model="name"/>

    <div><h2>Hello, {{name}}</div>

    <script src="lib/angular/angular.js"></script>
</body>
</html>
```

 What's the ng- Prefix?

The ng- prefixed attributes carry special meaning in AngularJS apps. Technically we call them **directives**. For the time being just treat them as attributes (and elements) that trick HTML into doing amazing stuff.

If you run the above code, you'll see that whenever the value in the input field changes the <div> is updated automatically. Well, let's see what happens step by step:

1. First the ng-app directive bootstraps the application. We don't have a module, so we just write ng-app without specifying any values. One thing to note is that whenever AngularJS encounters ng-app it creates a **root scope** for your HTML page. Again, the scope is a place where we store our model data so that they are accessible by the view.

2. Next, ng-init directive creates a model called name and keeps it in the root scope. The model is initialized with the value AngularJS.

3. We have attached the ng-model directive to our input element. This is the basis of two-way binding. Whenever you type something into the input field, the scope model name gets updated automatically. So, you don't have to manually write a keyup handler for the input field and update the model.

4. {{name}} is known as an expression which binds model data to view unidirectionally. This is the second part of two-way data binding. Expressions watch for the scope model value and update the DOM whenever the value changes.

5. So, whenever we type into input field the scope model name changes. As we also have an expression {{name}} in our view, it updates itself whenever the name property changes.

 Be Careful Where You Put Your Models

The above example code is placing the name model in the root scope, which would certainly not be desirable in most real world apps. Ideally you would want to put these models in a controller scope.

Doing Something Cool

The power of data binding becomes obvious when things get a little complex. So, let's do something cool! Let's say you have been given the following task:

1. Provide an input field for the users to type their Facebook ID.

2. As soon as the user is done typing, display the corresponding Facebook profile picture.

The only constraint is wanting to minimize the number of lines of code. The first option is to use plain JavaScript (or you could use jQuery for this). So, fire up your editor, write down some JavaScript for this functionality and then get back here. But let me give you a clue — the following URL returns the profile picture for a particular Facebook ID: https://graph.facebook.com/[id here]/picture?type=normal.

The plain JavaScript way:

```
<!doctype html>
<html lang="en">
<head>
  <meta charset="utf-8">
  <title>The Plain JS Way</title>
  <script type="text/javascript">
    document.addEventListener('DOMContentLoaded', function(e) {
      document.getElementById('fbID').addEventListener('keyup',
➥function(event) {
        var fbID = document.getElementById('fbID').value;
        var pictureURL = 'https://graph.facebook.com/' + fbID
➥+ '/picture?type=normal';
```

```
            document.getElementById('profilePic').src = pictureURL;
        });
    });
    </script>
</head>

<body>
    <input type="text" id="fbID" />
    <br/>
    <span><img src="" title="fb image" id="profilePic"/></span>
</body>
</html>
```

With two-way data binding in AngularJS:

```
<!doctype html>
<html lang="en" ng-app>

<head>
    <meta charset="utf-8">
    <title>Two way data binding</title>
</head>

<body ng-init="fbID='sandeep.panda92'">
    <input type="text" ng-model="fbID" />
    <br/>
    <span><img ng-src="https://graph.facebook.com/{{fbID}}
➥/picture?type=normal"/></span>
    <script src="lib/angular/angular.js"></script>
</body>
</html>
```

As you can see the Angular version is quite a lot more compact. So how did that happen? The two-way data binding has just started showing its power. Let's understand what's happening behind the scenes:

1. When we type into the input field, the model fbID gets updated, thanks to ng-model.

2. As we are using expression {{fbID}} in our view, whenever the model fbID is updated the expression updates itself, which results in a new image.

The most important thing about the AngularJS approach is that our code size decreased drastically. We even coded the feature with no JavaScript. This is the power of **Declarative Binding**. You can describe a particular scenario in your view by binding different UI components with different `scope` models. If some part of your view needs to be updated you just need to change the model. Also it enables you to express **what** data is loaded for a particular component and not **how**. If other developers just look at your code they can easily infer the flow of the application. So, rather than relying on JavaScript to control the program flow we are utilizing HTML's great declarative nature to express our app.

Using ng-src

You may have noticed that we used a directive called `ng-src` instead of `src`. We're doing that because if we just use `src`, the browser will start fetching the URL in raw format before AngularJS replaces the expression `{{fbID}}` with its actual value. This is obviously going to result in a 404. `ng-src` is used to prevent this.

UI Updates

Two-way data binding is definitely a big deal in AngularJS. We have seen just basic two-way data binding so far. But beware—there are pitfalls. Sometimes just changing a model's value doesn't update the UI. We need to use some special tricks in those cases which will be explored in next chapter.

To summarize, here is what the two-way data binding feature has to offer:

1. Keeps the view and model data in sync in both directions.

2. Provides a great declarative binding syntax to express what our app does.

3. Frees us from the tedious DOM manipulation, which is hard to test and debug.

4. Saves time by reducing the code size significantly.

Introducing Our Demo Application

Learning a technology without practice is not the ninja way! I want to make sure whatever you learn in each chapter you implement right away. Practice will give you confidence to work with large scale AngularJS apps in real world. So, we'll start building a demo app and keep adding features to it as we progress. Let's take a look at our sample app.

The Single Page Blogger

We are going to develop a simple blogging solution for all Single Page App (SPA) lovers. Imagine you have a powerful blogging system where a single page is in charge of loading various types of content into it. Here is an overview of the app:

- The home page displays all the blog posts. This includes the post title, author name and publication date.

- When a single blog entry is clicked the actual post content is loaded into the page asynchronously. This won't trigger a full page reload.

- There is an Admin Panel where the admin can perform CRUD operations.

So, these are the absolute basic features of the app. As we move forward in the book we will add more exciting features to it such as a comment system, authentication and authorization, Facebook/Twitter login etc.

Getting Ready

To start, let's modularize our code in terms of features—something we discussed earlier in this chapter. We have already seen how to tweak the Angular Seed project to introduce this pattern. So, what we need to do is separate this new project from Angular Seed and create a slightly different project structure. Only the directory structure under **app** needs to change. Everything else is untouched. I have shared the new directory structure, which you can download and get started on right away. Have a look at the screenshot shown in Figure 2.1 to see what's changed.

Figure 2.1. The file structure of our app

I have added a single module called posts to this app, which is empty right now. After you download the zip, you can explore the directory structure and check out the module. We'll resume developing this app in Chapter 05.

Conclusion

Every ninja developer loves super powers. Now you've got not just one but three: Modules, Controllers and Data Binding. I'm sure they'll help you tremendously throughout your AngularJS journey. The next chapter will take you a little further towards something new and exciting. But in the meantime you can try out some really cool tricks with data binding and impress your friends!

AngularJS Scope & Events

Scope Demystified

You have been listening me talk about scopes from the beginning of the book. But now (drum roll, please!) we're going to demystify the AngularJS scope.

Essentially, a scope is nothing but a plain old JavaScript object, and *that* is just a container for key/value pairs, as follows:

```
var myObject={name:'AngularJS', creator:'Misko'}
```

A scope—like other objects—can have properties and functions attached to it. The only difference is that we don't usually construct a scope object manually. Rather, AngularJS automatically creates and injects one for us.

In the Angular world, a scope object is useful for holding model values, which are presented by the view. In our previous example, we attached properties to the scope inside the controller: (`$scope.greeting='Hello'`). We did that so that the attached properties could be presented in the view through an expression: (`{{greeting}}`).

Every AngularJS application has at least one scope called $rootScope. This is created as a result of attaching the ng-app directive to any HTML element. In other words, when your AngularJS app bootstraps your app it creates a $rootScope for you. Next, when you attach ng-controller to any element, it creates a new child scope, which prototypally inherits from the $rootScope. Further, you can nest scopes by using an ng-controller directive inside another ng-controller. Have a look at the following snippet:

```
<div ng-app> <!-- creates a $rootScope -->
    <div ng-controller="OuterController"> <!--creates a scope
➡(call it scope 1) that inherits from $rootScope-->
        <div ng-controller="InnerController"> <!-- Creates a child
➡scope (call it scope 2) that inherits from scope 1
        </div>
    </div>
</div>
```

$rootScope is the parent of all scopes (except for **isolated scopes**, which we'll see later on). As a result, all the properties attached to $rootScope are implicitly available to scope 1. Similarly, scope 2 has access to all the properties attached to scope 1.

If you examine the above code closely, you'll find that scopes are nested in a manner that resembles the nesting of the DOM elements with which these scopes are associated. The most important thing about AngularJS scope inheritance is that scopes inherit each other prototypally. JavaScript, unlike many other programming languages such as Java, C++, C# etc., does not support traditional inheritance. It takes a different approach to keep things simple and make it easy to use. Every JavaScript constructor function has a property called prototype which points to an object. When you access a property on an object (someObject.someProperty) JavaScript searches for the property in that object. If it's found, it is returned. If not, then JavaScript starts searching for the property in the object's prototype. The prototype property is nothing but another object. Again, if the searched property is found in the prototype it's returned. If it's not found, then the search continues upwards in the prototype chain until the property is found or Object.prototype is reached. The following example will give an idea about prototypal inheritance.

```
function Car(color,steering){
  this.color=color;
  this.steering=steering;
}

Car.prototype.year=2012; // Car is a functional object, so it has
➥the `prototype` property

var car=new Car('red','left');

console.log(car.color); // prints color from car

console.log(car.year); //prints year from Car.prototype

console.log(car.hasOwnProperty('year')); //returns false
```

As you can see, the property `color` was found on the `car` object and thus it was returned. But there is no property called `year` in `car`. So, JavaScript searches for the property in `Car.prototype`, which is found and returned. So, whatever property you set to the constructor's prototype will be shared across all the instances of it.

The __proto__ Internal Property

The `prototype` property is only present in constructor functions. For example, `Car` has a `prototype` property while the object constructed from `Car` (that is to say, `car`) has an internal property called `__proto__` which holds its prototype.

```
var car=new Car('red','left'); //
➥sets car.__proto__=Car.prototype
```

But beware, IE doesn't use `__proto__` as the name of this internal property. ECMA5cript introduced a function `Object.getPrototypeOf(objectName)`, which can be treated as a standard way to retrieve the internal `__proto__`.

Writing Access with Prototypes

Things get a little bit more interesting when we discuss writing values to objects. Let's take a look at two example cases.

Writing a Primitive to an Object

Our object car does not have a property year, but Car.prototype does. When you try to read car.year you get the value from Car.prototype. But you can also attach the property year to car, like this:

```
car.year=2000 //sets property 'year' on car
console.log(car.year); // returns 'year' property from car and NOT
➥from Car.prototype
console.log(car.hasOwnProperty('year')); //returns true as car has
➥'year' propery
```

When you attach a new property to an object the property is attached to it and not the prototype. Subsequently when you access the property, JavaScript no longer consults the prototype because the property is found right there in the object itself.

Writing a Reference Type to an Object

Let's attach an object called data to Car.prototype:

```
Car.prototype.data={}; //set it to empty object
```

Now have a look at the following code:

```
car.data.engine='rear'; //This does not create a new property
➥called 'data' on car object
console.log(car.data.engine); //returns 'rear' and it comes from
➥Car.prototype
console.log(car.hasOwnProperty('data')); // false, as car
➥doesn't have own property 'data'
Car.prototype.hasOwnProperty('data'); // 'data' property is
➥created in prototype.
```

So, when you write a reference type to an object such as data.engine, JavaScript goes to the prototype, which is Car.prototype in this case, and checks if there's a property called data. If so, then it creates a new property in Car.prototype.data.

Objects Can Extend Objects

Objects can extend other objects in JavaScript, and this is the key to understanding AngularJS scope inheritance. Have a look at the following snippet:

```
var ferrari=Object.create(car);
console.log(Object.getPrototypeOf(ferrari)); //Car {}
```

`Object.create()` creates a new object whose internal __proto__ property points
to the object specified as the first argument to the function. As a result the `ferrari`
object's __proto__ now points to `car` object. So, `ferrari` has all the properties
defined in the `car` instance.

That was just a quick overview of prototypal inheritance. Now let's see how AngularJS utilizes this in scope inheritance.

Prototypal Inheritance in AngularJS Scopes

The `$rootScope` object has a function called `$new()` that's used to create child
scopes. Let's consider the previous example where we nested two controllers and
had one `$rootScope`. The code is repeated below:

```
<div ng-app> <!-- creates a $rootScope -->
        <div ng-controller="OuterController"> <!--creates a scope
➥(call it scope 1) that inherits from $rootScope-->
            <div ng-controller="InnerController"> <!-- Creates a
➥child scope (call it scope 2) that inherits from scope 1
            </div>
        </div>
</div>
```

Here is how AngularJS handles scope hierarchies:

1. AngularJS finds `ng-app` and therefore creates a `$rootScope` object.

2. It encounters `ng-controller` and finds that it points to `OuterController`. So, it
   calls `$rootScope.$new()`, which creates a child scope(let's call it `$scope1`) that
   prototypally inherits from `$rootScope`. At this point the prototype (__proto__)
   of child scope `$scope1` points to `$rootScope`. So anything attached to `$rootScope`
   is available in `$child1`. If the `OuterController` declares a dependency by adding
   a parameter `$scope` to the declaration of the constructor function, AngularJS calls
   it with the newly created scope `$child1` as an argument.

3. Next, while traversing the DOM, AngularJS encounters another `ng-controller`
   directive which points to `InnerController`. Now, it creates another child scope

that prototypally inherits from $scope2. As before, calling $new() on $scope1 creates this child scope $scope2. The result of this inheritance is that $scope2 has access to all the properties defined by $scope1.

The figure in Figure 3.1, taken from the AngularJS GitHub page, depicts how scopes inherit each other.

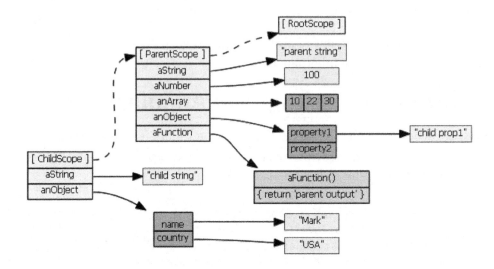

Figure 3.1. Inheritance in scopes

The inner scope always has access to the properties defined by the outer example. Apart from controllers, directives may also create child scopes. Some directives simply use the parent scope without creating a child. And some other directives create isolated scopes that don't inherit from any parent scope and exist on their own. We will discuss isolated scopes in the directives chapter.

To reinforce the above concepts let's create a sample app. We'll create an app that lists three books published by SitePoint. Using the Angular Seed project, follow these steps to create the app:

1. Create the module myApp. This will go into **app/js/app.js.**

```
'use strict';


angular.module('myApp', [
```

```
    'myApp.controllers'
]);

angular.module('myApp').run(function($rootScope){
    $rootScope.title='Famous Books';
    $rootScope.name="Root Scope";
});
```

2. Create the required controllers in **app/js/controllers.js**.

```
angular.module('myApp.controllers',[]).controller('SiteController'
➥, function($scope){
  $scope.publisher='SitePoint';
  $scope.type="Web Development";
  $scope.name="Scope for SiteController";
});

angular.module('myApp.controllers').controller('BookController'
➥, function($scope){
  $scope.books = ['Jump Start HTML5','Jump Start CSS','Jump Start
➥Responsive Web Design'];
  $scope.name="Scope for BookController";
});
```

3. Create the view. Name it **scopes.html** and this will be directly under **app**.

```
<!DOCTYPE html>
<html ng-app="myApp">
<head>
  <meta charset="utf-8" />
  <title ng-bind="title"></title>
</head>

<body ng-controller="SiteController">
  <span>{{publisher}} excels in {{type}} books</span>
  <div ng-controller="BookController">
    <h3>Some of the popular books from {{publisher}}</h3>
    <ul>
      <li ng-repeat="book in books">
        {{book}}
      </li>
    </ul>
```

```
      </div>
    </body>
      <script src="lib/angular/angular.js"></script>
      <script src="js/app.js"></script>
      <script src="js/controllers.js"></script>
    </html>
```

In the above code, the callback passed to `angular.module('myApp').run()` gets called when all the modules are loaded. Inside this we are setting a model `title` on $rootScope. This is our page's title. The second one `name` is just used to identify the scope. We also have two controllers: `SiteController` and `BookController` and the latter is nested inside the former within the HTML.

Now let's visualize the scope hierarchy. Have you installed Angular Batarang yet? You'll need it to visualize the scope hierarchy, so if you've yet to install it, now's the time.

Now run the server by the command: `node scripts/web-server.js`. Once the server is up open the browser and go to `http://localhost:8000/app/scopes.html`. Bring up the **Developer Tools** and in the last tab you'll find AngularJS. Just enable it and refresh the page. Now you should see something like Figure 3.2, which depicts the scope hierarchies!

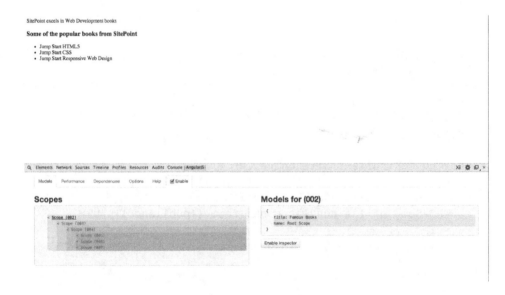

Figure 3.2. A depiction of scope hierarchies

As you can see `Scope (002)` is the root scope (`$rootScope`). `Scope (003)` is the scope for controller `SiteController` which prototypally inherits the `$rootScope`. `Scope (004)` is the scope for `BookController` which prototypally inherits from its parent `Scope (003)`.

`ng-repeat` is a directive and, as the name suggests, it repeats an element multiple times. Here, for each `book` in model `books` the `<li>` is repeated and each `<li>` is linked with a different scope. Here, we have three such scopes named `Scope (005)`, `Scope (006)`, `Scope (007)`. All these are siblings and prototypally inherit from `Scope (004)` Although the scopes are different the model name remains same i.e. `book`. The expression `{{book}}` in the HTML is repeated three times and, each time it's evaluated against three different scopes. That's why the result is different. So, an AngularJS `scope` is a context against which expressions are evaluated.

A model without an execution context is useless. Have a look at the view. We simply write model names in expressions like `{{book}}` and `{{publisher}}`. But AngularJS evaluates them against the correct context. When AngularJS sees `{{publisher}}` it evaluates this against the scope created for `SiteController`. You can also see that there's one more `{{publisher}}` expression in the markup under `BookController` scope. Still, we can see the value because this scope inherits from the `SiteController` scope and the models set on this scope are available in the child scopes.

 Using ng-blind

> What's the `ng-bind` directive doing here? Writing `<title ng-bind="title"></title>` is same as writing `<title>{{title}}</title>` with one small difference. If you use the later one, by the time AngularJS replaces the expression `{{title}}` with the actual model value, the browser will have displayed the raw text `{{title}}` for a fraction of second already. To prevent that we can use `ng-bind`. In this case you pass a model name and the value is 'innerHTMLed' into the element on which the `ng-bind` directive is attached (in this case `<title>`). There's also another AngularJS directive called ngCloak[1], which can be used to prevent the browser from temporarily displaying the raw non-compiled HTML. Let's save its details for our directives chapter.

---

[1] https://docs.angularjs.org/api/ng/directive/ngCloak

Advanced Scope Concepts

While we've discussed the basics of scopes, there are several advanced concepts that'll give you superhero powers in the world of AngularJS. Let's explore those one by one.

The Watchers in AngularJS

A **watcher** monitors model changes and takes action in response.

The $scope object has a function $watch() that's used to register a watcher. Let's modify our previous snippet. We want to give users the ability to add a book to their wish list. But once they add two books to their wish list we want to show a congratulatory message. So, we can keep a counter and, each time the user clicks on Add to wishlist link, we will increment this counter by one. But how do we know when the counter reaches two? This is where watchers help us. We can set up a watcher on the counter model to notify us when the value changes. So, if its value is two then we fire an alert. The modified HTML for this is shown below:

```
<body ng-controller="SiteController">
  <span>{{publisher}} excels in {{type}} books</span>
  <div ng-controller="BookController">
    <h3>Some of the popular books from {{publisher}}</h3>
    My Wish List Count: {{wishListCount}}
    <ul>
      <li ng-repeat="book in books">
        {{book}}. <a href="#" ng-click="addToWishList(book)">Add to
➥Wish List</a>
      </li>
    </ul>
  </div>
</body>
```

Note that I'm only showing <body> for the sake of brevity. Then our controller BookController can be modified as following:

```
angular.module('myApp.controllers').controller('BookController'
➥, function($scope) {
  $scope.books = ['Jump Start HTML5','Jump Start CSS','Jump Start
➥Responsive Web Design'];
  $scope.name="Scope for BookController";
```

```
$scope.addToWishList=function(book){
    $scope.wishListCount++;
};
$scope.wishListCount=0;
$scope.$watch('wishListCount',function(newValue,oldValue){
    console.log('called '+newValue+' times');
    if(newValue==2){
        alert('Great! You have 2 items in your wish list. Time to
➥buy what you love. ');
    }
});
});
```

We added a new model `wishListCounter` to the `BookController` scope. Each time user clicks `Add to wishlist` link `$scope.hide()` gets called, incrementing the model by one. Now let's get to the interesting part—setting up a watcher.

`$scope.watcher()` is what you need to do this. The first parameter is `watchExpression`. This can be the model under watch or a function. The second parameter is a callback function that's called whenever AngularJS detects a change in the model value or the return value of the passed function. This callback takes two parameters. The first is the new value of the model, while the second is the old value. If you're interested only in the new value you can skip the second parameter.

Now inside the watch callback (also called listener function) we check to see if the `newValue` is two. If it is we show an `alert`. We also have a `console.log()` so we can see how many times the listener function gets called.

 ### The Listener is Called Immediately

When you load the page you'll find that the listener function is called immediately. This may seem a little odd, but AngularJS executes the listener function as soon as the watcher is registered. If you don't want this to happen, you can insert an additional check to see if the `newValue` and `oldValue` are same. If that's the case, then this will be the first time the listener is called as a part of initialization. You can write something like this:

```
$scope.$watch('someModel',function(newValue,oldValue){
    if(newValue!=oldValue){
        //do something
    }
});
```

However, the second parameter to $watch() is optional. But, why would anyone want to have a watcher without a listener? We'll discuss that in the next section. The $watch() function also accepts an optional third parameter objectEquality. In this case we're watching a simple String. But sometimes you may need to watch an object for change. We want to be notified whenever any of the object's properties changes. In that case the above code won't work because AngularJS will compare the objects by reference. To make this work we can pass true as the third argument to $watch() function. This will compare individual properties of the object under watch and call our listener in case of mutation.

Unbinding a Watcher

The return value of $scope.$watch() is a function which can be used to unbind the watcher when needed. This is important because it clears the memory alloted to the watcher. So, after showing the alert if you want to unbind the watcher you can utilize this return value. The corresponding code is:

```
var unbindWatcher=$scope.$watch('wishListCount',function
➡(newValue,oldValue){
        console.log('called '+newValue+' times');
        if(newValue==2){
            alert('Great! You have 2 items in your
➡wish list. Time to buy what you love. ');
            unbindWatcher();
        }
});
```

The $watchCollection() Function

In many cases, instead of watching a simple value you may want to watch a collection of items, such as an array or an object. For that you need to use $watchCollection(). In case you are watching an array, your listener function will be called whenever a new item is added to the array or an existing one is removed, updated, or reordered. In case of objects, the listener will be triggered if a new property is added or an existing one is removed, updated, or reordered. Here is how you can watch a collection:

```
$scope.$watchCollection('myCollection',function(newCollection,
↪oldCollection){
    //handle the change
    console.log(newCollection); //print new collection
});
```

This is not the end of watchers. To understand watchers fully you need to understand two key AngularJS concepts: $digest() and $apply(). This is because these things are interrelated, and to understand one fully you need to know about the others.

The $apply() Function and the $digest Loop

Let's take a look at a very simple AngularJS snippet where you start typing your name into an input field. There is also a div that shows what you typed, in real time:

```
<input id="input" type="text" ng-model="name"/>
<div id="output">{{name}}</div>
```

You already know what expressions like {{name}} do—they provide a unidirectional binding from model to view. Whenever the name model changes the expression automatically updates itself. Is some kind of magic behind this? No. It's done just by setting up a watcher on the name model. The expressions are a special type of directive that set up a watcher on models or functions—something we did in the last section. But their purpose is to get notified when the value of the model changes and update the DOM accordingly.

This is only half of the story, however. How does Angular know when a model changes and calls its corresponding watcher? Does it run a function in an interval to check if the model value has changed? If I make an AJAX call and update my model with the response will Angular know about it?

An AngularJS $scope has a function called $apply() which takes a function as an argument. AngularJS says that it'll know about model mutations only if that mutation is done inside `$apply()`. So, you simply need to put the code that changes models inside a function and call `$scope.$apply()`, passing that function as an argument. After the `$apply()` function call ends, AngularJS knows that some model changes might have occurred. It then starts a digest cycle by calling another function—`$root-Scope.$digest()`—which propagates to all child scopes. In the digest cycle all the watchers are called to check if the model value has changed. If a value has changed, the corresponding listener function then gets called. Now it's up to the listener how it handles the model changes. The watcher set up by an expression (`{{}}`) updates the DOM with the new value of the model. In our previous example, we showed an `alert` when the model reached a value of 2.

But what if the listener function of the watcher itself changes any model? How does AngularJS account for that change? Actually, the digest cycle doesn't run only once after the `$apply()` call. After calling the listener functions, the digest cycle starts all over again and fires each watcher to check if any of the models have been mutated in the last loop. If any change is found, the corresponding listener is called as usual and, if none of the models have changed, the digest cycle ends. Otherwise, the digest cycle continues to loop until no model changes have been detected or it hits the maximum loop count of 10 (whichever comes first). The digest cycle will not run more than 10 times. So, it's good to refrain from making model mutations in the listener functions.

 The $digest() cycle Always Runs at Least Twice

At a minimum the `$digest()` cycle runs twice even if there are no model mutation in the listener functions. The cycle runs once more to make sure the models are stable and no change has been made in last loop. This is called **dirty checking**.

If you want to get notified whenever `$digest()` is called, you can set up a watcher without any listener function. The first and only argument to `$scope.$watch()` should be the function whose return value you want to monitor. This function gets called in every digest cycle. That is why the second argument to `$watch()` is optional.What you need to do is pass a simple function as the first argument to `$scope.$watch()`, as shown below:

```
$scope.$watch(function(){
  //do something here
  console.log('called in a digest cycle');
  return;
});
```

The function passed to $watch() gets called in each digest cycle. As you know digest cycle continues to run (a maximum of 10 times, of course) until the scope models stabilize. So, your function might get called multiple times in a digest cycle.

If the $apply() call is required to fire a digest cycle, how do directives like ng-model and ng-click tell Angular about the model mutations? The answer is that, internally, ng-click and ng-model wrap the code that changes the models inside an $apply() call. As a result digest cycle runs and watchers are called as usual. So, here's what happens when you write <input type="text" ng-model="name"/>:

1. The directive ng-model registers a keydown listener with the input field. When the input field text changes a keydown event is fired and the corresponding listener is called to handle it.

2. Inside the keydown listener the directive assigns the new value of input field to the scope model specified in ng-model. In our case the model name is updated with the new value. This code is wrapped inside $apply() call.

3. After $apply() ends the digest cycle starts in which the watchers are called. If you have an expression {{name}} in the view it has already set up a watcher on scope model name. So, in digest cycle this watcher gets called and the listener function executes with the newValue and oldValue as arguments. The job of this listener is to update the DOM with the newValue probably using innerHTML.

4. The overall result is that you see the {{name}} updated with whatever you type into the input field instantly.

 Using $apply()

Use $apply() when you want to make the transition from the non-AngularJS world to the Angular world and need a way to say **"Hey, Angular, I am mutating some models, and now it's your job to fire the watchers!"**

What about an AJAX call? If you make XHRs through Angular's built-in service $http (which you will do 99% of the time) the model mutation code is implicitly wrapped within the $apply() call, so you don't need any additional steps. But if, for some reason, you're writing XHRs manually with plain JavaScript, you need to mutate the models inside $apply().

$digest Gets Triggered Automatically

In most scenarios you don't need to call $digest() yourself. Calling $apply() will automatically trigger a $digest on $rootScope which subsequently visits all the child scopes calling the watchers.

It's Preferable to Call $apply with a Function as an Argument

You can call $scope.$apply() either with no arguments or a function as an argument. If a function (which changes models) is passed as an argument to $apply() it is evaluated and then $rootScope.$digest() is fired.

You can also change the models as usual and in the end just call $apply() to trigger a $digest cycle. But the former method ($apply() with argument) is the preferred approach and should always be used. This is because when you pass a function to $apply() the code will be wrapped in try/catch and any exceptions that occur will be passed to $exceptionHandler service.

You should also note that if you skip $apply() after changing some models, the changes won't reflect in the view. The changes will be reflected only if $apply() is called and $digest() runs.

$apply and $digest in Action

To see how $apply() is used in real world, let's create a very simple app that schedules a function to run after three seconds. This function simply updates a scope model and the view updates itself with the new model value. To do this we'll make use of setTimeout(). Here's the code:

View

```
<body ng-controller="TimeoutController">
  <button ng-click="scheduleTask()">Get Message after 3 seconds
➥</button>
  <br/>Message fetched: {{message}}
</body>
```

Controller

```
angular.module('myApp',[]).controller('TimeoutController',
➥function($scope) {

  $scope.scheduleTask = function() {
    setTimeout(function() {
      $scope.message = 'Fetched after 3 seconds';
      console.log('message='+$scope.message); //log this to console
    }, 3000);
  }

});
```

So, when you click on the button in the view, $scope.scheduleTask() runs which, in turn, uses setTimeout to run a function after a three-second delay. This function, when executed, updates our $scope.messgae model.

But if you run the above snippet and click on the button you won't see the view update itself after three seconds. However, in the console you can find the logged message. So, we're sure that the function was called and updated our model. But the view didn't update itself. The reason is that—and here's the 'aha moment'— we didn't wrap our code inside $apply(). So, you need to make the following modification in the code to get it working:

```
$scope.scheduleTask = function() {
  setTimeout(function() {
    $scope.$apply(function() { // wrapped the code in $apply()
      $scope.message = 'Fetched after 3 seconds';
➥//will reflect in view
      console.log('message=' + $scope.message);
```

```
    });
  }, 3000);
}
```

As you can see we have wrapped our code inside `$apply()` so that a `$digest()` cycle starts, the watchers are fired and our view is updated. Now if you click the `button` the delayed function runs and view displays the message as expected.

Introducing the `$timeout` Service

It's interesting to note that AngularJS supplies a built-in service called `$timeout` which delays the execution of a function by a given interval and automatically wraps your code inside `$apply()` so that you don't have to do it manually. Here's the example modified to take advantage of `$timeout`:

```
angular.module('myApp',[]).controller('TimeoutController'
➥, function($scope, $timeout){

  $scope.fetchMessage = function() {
    $timeout(function() {
      $scope.message = 'Fetched after 3 seconds'; //just update.
➥No need for $apply
      console.log('message=' + $scope.message);
    }, 3000);
  }

});
```

A few points to notice here:

■ Your controller should declare a dependency on `$timeout` service.

■ `$timeout()` takes a function as argument and delays its execution by specified interval.

■ The function call is automatically wrapped inside `$apply()`.

Now if you see this in browser and click the `button`, you will get the expected result.

$scope.$$phase

There is an internal variable called **$$phase** set on the **scope** object whenever a digest cycle is going on. It's worth you knowing that there is such a flag available in the **scope** object. While it's good to know, however, in real-world apps and following AngularJS best practices (and doing things the right way) you won't need this variable. Don't use it in your code as it's an internal implementation and isn't future safe. **$$** prefixed variables are regarded as internal variables and shouldn't be used in code.

Broadcasting & Emitting Events

One of the beautiful aspects of AngularJS scopes is the ability to broadcast events and its handling of them. Some of your controllers might be waiting for some event to occur such as waiting for particular data to be available from an AJAX request. So, the controller that's responsible for obtaining the data can notify other controllers that it's arrived and send the actual data, too. This is done by **emitting** or **broadcasting** events. By doing this controllers up in the scope hierarchy or down in the scope hierarchy can handle the event and do something meaningful.

AngularJS supports two types of event propagation:

1. Emitting the event upwards in the scope hierarchy.

2. Broadcasting the event downwards in the scope hierarchy.

Figure 3.3 depicts the propagation of events.

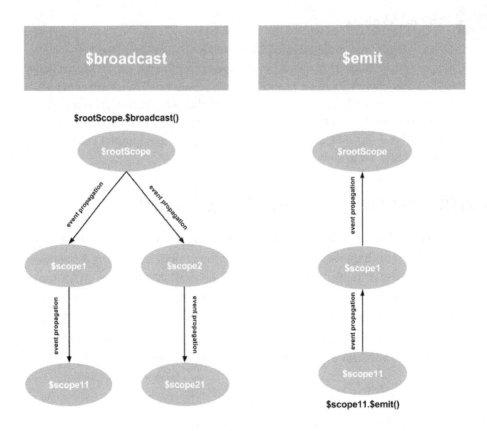

Figure 3.3. Propagation of events

Let's understand each of these.

`$scope.$emit(name,args)` For Emitting Events

The `$scope` has a function called `$emit()` that's used to emit an event upwards in the scope hierarchy. The event life cycle starts with the `scope` on which `$emit()` was called and is dispatched upwards in the scope hierarchy to all the registered listeners. Also it's interesting that the `$scope` which emits the event receives a notification (via `$on`) when it's emitted.

The first parameter to the `$emit()` function is the name of the event that is being emitted. The scopes that want to get notified when the event occurs should register listeners for this event name. After the first parameter you can pass multiple parameters to `$emit()`, which will be passed to the event listeners. Typically you pass the data which should be shared with the listeners here.

`$scope.$broadcast(name,args)` For Broadcasting Events

The `$broadcast()` function is the same as `$emit()` except the event propagates downwards in the scope hierarchy to all the child scopes. The parameters list is also same as that of `$emit()`. Like `$emit`, the `$scope` which broadcasts the event also receives a notification (via `$on`) when it's broadcast.

`$scope.$on(name,handlerFunction)` For Registering Listeners

The `$on` function registers event listeners that should be called when the event occurs. The first parameter is the name of the event you are interested in. The second parameter is a callback function which gets called when the event occurs. The callback takes two parameters:

1. `event`: This is an event object which has several useful properties and functions that give more information about the event. These are as follows:

   ▨ `name`: The name of the event that's broadcasted or emitted.

   ▨ `targetScope`: The `scope` that emitted/broadcasted the event.

   ▨ `currentScope`: The `scope` that's handling the event.

   ▨ `stopPropagation`: This is a function, which when called, stops further propagation of the event. But keep in mind this is available only in the events that were **emitted**. After an event is emitted, if a particular `scope` calls this function the event propagation stops. However, once an event is broadcast it can't be stopped. It's like this because the broadcast events can span across multiple branches as a parent `scope` may have multiple child `scopes`. So, if a `scope` in a particular branch stops the event it will still keep propagating in other branches. But in case of `$emit` the event propagates from child to parent and if it's stopped somewhere in between, it stops propagating further right there.

2. `args`: One or more arguments that represent the data that was emitted/broadcast as a part of the event.

Events in Action

Let's create a small app to demonstrate the usage of events. Suppose we have an app that generates a random message every three seconds. The app is divided into two sections: **Messages** and **Stats**. The messages section shows all the retrieved messages while the stats section shows the number of messages retrieved and connection status. If for some reason our app is unable to fetch a message we should notify the stats section about this. The stats section will then update the status to **Not Connected**. Let's create two controllers: `MessageController` and `StatsController`. The two controllers are nested in HTML so that the `MessageController` scope is the parent of `StatsController` scope. Note that I'm using the Angular Seed structure here, so be sure to put each file in its proper place.

app.js (app/js/app.js):

```
angular.module('myApp', [
  'myApp.controllers'
]);
```

controllers.js (app/js/controllers.js):

```
angular.module('myApp.controllers', []);

angular.module('myApp.controllers').controller('MessageController'
➥, function($scope, $timeout) {
  $scope.messages = [{
    sender: 'user1',
    text: 'Message1'
  }];
  var timer;
  var count=0;
  $scope.loadMessages = function() {
    count++;
    $scope.messages.push({
      sender: 'user1',
      text: 'Random message'+count
    });
    timer=$timeout($scope.loadMessages, 2000);
```

```
    if(count==3){
        $scope.$broadcast('EVENT_NO_DATA', 'Not Connected');
        $timeout.cancel(timer);
    }
  };
  timer=$timeout($scope.loadMessages, 2000);
  $scope.$on('EVENT_RECEIVED',function(){
    console.log('Received emitted event');
  });
});

angular.module('myApp.controllers').controller('StatsController'
➡, function($scope) {
  $scope.name = 'World';
  $scope.status = 'Connected';
  $scope.statusColor='green';
  $scope.$on('EVENT_NO_DATA', function(event, data) {
    console.log('received broadcasted event');
    $scope.status = data;
    $scope.statusColor='red';
    $scope.$emit('EVENT_RECEIVED');
  });
});
```

events.html (put it under **app**):

```
<!DOCTYPE html>
<html ng-app="myApp">

<head>
  <meta charset="utf-8" />
  <title>AngularJS Events</title>
</head>

<body>
  <div ng-controller="MessageController">
    <h4>Messages:</h4>
    <ul>
      <li ng-repeat="message in messages">
        {{message.text}}
      </li>
    </ul>
    <div ng-controller="StatsController">
      <h4>Stats:</h4>
```

```
     <div>{{messages.length}} Message(s)</div>
     <div>Status: <span style="color:{{statusColor}}">{{status}}
➥</span>
     </div>
   </div>
 </div>
</body>
<script src="lib/angular/angular.js"></script>
<script src="js/app.js"></script>
<script src="js/controllers.js"></script>
</html>
```

Now if you start the server and run `http://localhost:8000/app/events.html` you can see that a message is generated every three seconds. Just after the third message is fetched we simulate a connection failure.

Here's how we designed it:

1. First we create `MessageController` which sets an array of messages on its scope. It declares a dependency on Angular's built in `$timeout` service. This service delays the execution of code. So, to simulate message fetching every three seconds we use `$timeout` here.

2. The `var count` is used to track how many times we have fetched messages. After the third message, we simulate a connection failure and need to signal this to `StatsController`.

3. The `StatsController` scope is the child of `MessageController` scope. So, we need to broadcast an event from the parent `MessageController` (broadcast=parent-to-child). We use `$scope.$broadcast()` for this.

4. In `StatsController` we handle the event by registering a listener through `$scope.$on()`. In the handler we update the connection status from `connected` to `Not Connected` and the color from `green` to `red`.

5. Also in the event handler we emit an event to signify that we received the connection failure event. We do this by calling `$scope.$emit()` (emit=child-to-parent). In the `MessageController` we are listening for this event by calling `$scope.$on()`.

Check your browser's console to see the log messages.

Using $rootScope

What if `StatsController` scope were not the child of `MessageController` scope? What if both of the controllers were siblings? How would you design this app? In this case, we'd need to use the help of `$rootScope`. Inject `$rootScope` in both the controllers and when you want to send an event use `$root-Scope.$broadcast()`. Since both the controller scopes are the children of `$rootScope`, if you broadcast an event from `$rootScope` both of the child scopes can listen to it by registering listeners (employing the usual `$scope.$on()` way)

$rootScope Can Be Treated As a Central Message Bus

The `$rootScope` can be treated as a central message bus that can be used to notify all the child **scopes**. So, if there is an event that affects all the child **scopes**, you can broadcast the event on `$rootScope` and then let the children handle the event.

The $destroy event

When a `scope` is being destroyed a `$destroy` event is broadcast on the scope. You can listen for this event and perform any necessary cleanups. For example, if you have a timer (just as in above example) from the `$timeout` service you can cancel it so that it won't consume CPU cycles unnecessarily. You can also use this to cancel the watchers and any custom event listeners you set up earlier. When a scope is getting destroyed it also means that any digest cycle won't touch this and its child scopes anymore. As a result, the scope becomes eligible for garbage collection and the memory can be reclaimed.

The following snippet shows how to do this:

```
$scope.$on('$destroy',function(){
    //clean up code
});
```

Conclusion

So, we've reached the end of AngularJS scope and events. This was an important chapter and covered some of the core concepts of AngularJS. Here are some bullet points that summarize what we've learned so far.

- AngularJS scopes are plain old JavaScript objects where you can attach properties and functions.

- Scopes can be nested and prototypally inherit each other.

- Every app has one $rootScope which is at the root of scope hierarchy.

- You can get notified when a scope model changes by setting up a watcher on it.

- All the watchers that have been setup will be fired in each digest cycle.

- A digest cycle will continue to run until there are no model changes or it hits max loop count of 10.

- A call to $apply() automatically triggers a $digest cycle.

- When you change a model outside AngularJS context and want that change to reflect in your views wrap your code inside $apply().

- Events can be used to notify different parts of your app when something happens.

- $scope.$emit() is used to propagate an event from child scope to parent scope upwards in the scope hierarchy.

- $scope.$broadcast() is used to propagate an event from parent scope to child scope downwards in the scope hierarchy.

- $scope.$on() is used to register an event listener that will be notified when the event occurs.

- $destroy event is fired when a scope is being destroyed and allows you to perform any final clean ups like clearing timeouts, de-registering watchers and event listeners etc.

Multiple Views and Routing

By now you're about a quarter of the way to becoming an AngularJS ninja! You've mastered the basic AngularJS concepts (you probably see data binding in your dreams). But now is the time to take your skills to a whole new level with AngularJS routing. Every web app you'll build in future will have different views associated with it. For example, our blogging app has a view to display all the blog posts, and another view to display individual blog posts. Similarly, there can be separate views for different CRUD operations. As we're developing Single Page Apps, it's important to map each route to a particular view. This logically divides your app into manageable parts and keeps it maintainable. Fortunately, AngularJS provides excellent support for multiple views and routing via its routing API. Let's dive into it!

AngularJS's routing API enables us to map URLs within our application with specific functionalities. This is typically done by associating a template and controller with a particular URL. So, we can say that each AngularJS route is composed of a URL, a template, and a controller. When someone first lands on our web page, it's a full-page load. Subsequently, when the user clicks a link and navigates to a different URL, the route changes and content of the route are dynamically loaded into the page via an AJAX call.

The benefit of this approach is that it results in much less network traffic. In a typical web app, we'd load each page fully with each request, serving loads of repetitive content such as headers and footers multiple times in the process. But when you use multiple views and routing there's no repetitive content since the headers, footers, sidebars etc. are only served as a part of the first request. All subsequent requests simply update specific elements of your page. As you might expect, this leads to faster rendering of the views.

Creating Multiple Views

Views in your app are regular HTML files. As a result, we need to create a separate HTML file for each view. The next step is to tell AngularJS which view to use for which route. Assuming we have two views: **partials/view1.html** and **partials/view2.html**, the syntax to configure the routes is as follows:

```
angular.module('myApp').config(function($routeProvider) {
  $routeProvider.when('/view1', {
    controller: 'Controller1',
    templateUrl: 'partials/view1.html',
  }).when('/view2', {
    controller: 'Controller2',
    templateUrl: 'partials/view2.html',
  });
});
```

These Views are Just Partials

Please note that the views **view1.html** and **view2.html** are not complete HTML files—they're just partials.

angular.module() has a function config(), which lets us configure a module. We inject $routeProvider as an argument to the function. This is, in fact, a built-in AngularJS object. When you declare a function with the parameter $routeProvider, AngularJS automatically injects a $routeProvider object while calling it—this is another example of Dependency Injection in action.

Now, the when() function of $routeProvider can be used to configure your routes. This particular function takes two parameters: The first parameter is the **route name**, and is a string representing the route; the second parameter is the **route definition**

object. This is an object representing various details for a route. As a beginner you'll most commonly use the following two properties:

- `controller`: The controller which will be associated with the view. After all, we need a scope against which the template will be compiled.

- `templateUrl`: The HTML template to be used.

Here, you should note that the `controller` parameter is actually optional. You can either define the controller at route level as we are already doing or just use it in the template through `ng-controller`.

Also you should note that `$routeProvider.when()` adds a new mapping and returns the same `$routeProvider` instance. So, you can chain these function calls to add multiple mappings just as we did above.

ngRoute is Not Included by Default

The `$routeProvider` is defined in a module called `ngRoute` which is not present in the `angular.js` script you have included in your page. To use the `ngRoute` module you need to include **angular-route.js** as a script, which is present in the **angular-seed-master/app/lib/angular** directory.

In versions prior to AngularJS 1.1.6, the `ngRoute` module was used to be shipped out of the box. But all the subsequent versions don't include `ngRoute` by default. That's why we need to include additional **angular-route.js** which defines `ngRoute` module.

Let's get practical and create a simple app using two views: One for showing a "Hello. World!" message and another for showing current date. For this simple test, I recommend you use the Angular Seed project. You should use `sp-blogger`, which you have downloaded, only for developing the demo app.

The main app module (**app/js/app.js**):

```
'use strict';

angular.module('myApp', [
  'myApp.controllers',
  'ngRoute'
]);
```

```
angular.module('myApp').config(function($routeProvider){
    $routeProvider.when('/view1',{
        controller:'Controller1',
        templateUrl:'partials/view1.html'
    }).when('/view2',{
        controller: 'Controller2',
        templateUrl: 'partials/view2.html'
    });
});
```

Here, we've declared our main app module, which depends on myApp.controllers and ngRoute. We also used the $routeProvider to map view1 to **partials/view1.html** and view2 to partials/**view2**.html.

The controllers (**app/js/controllers.js**):

```
'use strict';

angular.module('myApp.controllers', []).controller('Controller1'
➥,function($scope){
    $scope.message="Hello, world";
}).controller('Controller2',function($scope){
    $scope.now=new Date();
});
```

We have two controllers: Controller1 associated with route /view1 and Controller2 associated with route /view2. The first controller should show a Hello World message. So, we have set a scope model message for this. The second controller sets a scope model now which stores the current date/time. Both of the controllers obtain their respective scopes by declaring dependency on $scope.

Main view (**app/index.html**):

```
<!doctype html>
<html lang="en" ng-app="myApp">
<head>
  <meta charset="utf-8">
  <title>AngularJS Routing</title>
  <link rel="stylesheet" href="css/app.css"/>
</head>
<body>
```

```
<ul class="menu">
  <li><a href="#/view1">view1</a></li>
  <li><a href="#/view2">view2</a></li>
</ul>

<ng-view></ng-view>

<script src="lib/angular/angular.js"></script>
<script src="lib/angular/angular-route.js"></script>
<script src="js/app.js"></script>
<script src="js/controllers.js"></script>
</body>
</html>
```

The most important point to note here is that our main view, index.html, has an element <ng-view>. This acts as a container for the different views (in our case **view1.html** and **view2.html**). When the user clicks on a link (for example #/view1), the route changes to index.html#/view1 and AngularJS searches for the template mapped with the current route. Once the template is found the content is fetched and included in <ng-view> and compiled against the $scope so that the expressions ({{}}) are evaluated. The same $scope is passed as an argument to the controller associated with the particular route. So, you can set required models on the $scope and access those in the template. Note that there should be only one <ng-view> in your page, which will be used to show content for different routes.

You can also use ng-view as an attribute or class. So, the above code can use ng-view as:

```
<div class="ng-view"></div>
```

and:

```
<div ng-view></div>
```

Don't Use the Element Version of ng-view if You Want to Support IE

Do not use the element version if you really want to be compatible with Internet Explorer. Instead, use the attribute version.

Also note that ng-view creates a new scope that prototypally inherits from the parent scope. This $scope is passed as an argument to the controller's constructor function associated with a particular route.

Template1 (**app/partials/view1.html**):

```
<p>From View 1: {{message}}</p>
```

Template2 (**app/partials/view2.html**):

```
<p>From View 2: {{now | date:'medium'}}</p>
```

 The app Directory Should Be the Root Directory

The **app** directory of Angular Seed should be the root directory of our server. So, instead of starting the server from angular-seed-master go to angular-seed-master/app and start the server from there.

```
node ../scripts/web-server.js
```

This will make the directory **app** the root of our web server. Now you can access **index.html** by typing http://localhost:8000/index.html in the browser.

Once you access **index.html** you'll find two links: view1 and view2. If you click on the links you can see the URL in the browser change and the content from the appropriate view template will be shown accordingly.

You might have already noticed the route name is prefixed with # in the URL. For example, when you click on hyperlink view1, the URL in the address bar changes to index.html#/view1. This is called **hashbang** mode, which is the default in AngularJS. The other option is to ask AngularJS to use HTML5 history API. This mode is called **html5Mode**. In this case, the URLs in address bar for the two routes will be changed to:

- /view1 from index.html#/view1

- /view2 from index.html#/view2

The html5Mode, when activated, removes # from your URLs and takes advantage of HTML5's pushState API.

The html5Mode can be introduced by injecting another built-in AngularJS object called $locationProvider into the callback passed to config(). Here's the modified code:

```
angular.module('myApp').config(function($routeProvider,
➥$locationProvider){
        $routeProvider.when('/view1',{
            controller:'Controller1',
            templateUrl:'partials/view1.html'
        }).when('/view2',{
            controller: 'Controller2',
            templateUrl: 'partials/view2.html'
        });
        $locationProvider.html5Mode(true); //activate HTML5 Mode
});
```

You also need to change the hyperlinks in the main page (index.html) to remove the # prefixes. Here's the modified code that should be placed in **index.html**:

```
<ul class="menu">
    <li><a href="/view1">view1</a></li>
    <li><a href="/view2">view2</a></li>
</ul>
```

Now if you refresh index.html and click any of the two links you can see the URL change to either http://localhost:8000/view1 or http://localhost:8000/view2 depending on the link clicked.

 What if the Browser Does Not Support the History API?

If you set html5Mode to true, AngularJS first checks for history API support in the browser. If it's available then the html5Mode is used, otherwise AngularJS falls back to the **hashbang** mode. In other words, it uses the best option transparently so that you don't have to worry about browser compatibility issues.

But there is a gotcha! When navigating inside of the app, everything works as expected. But if you try to open a URL like http://localhost:8080/view1 directly in the browser it will result in a 404. The reason for this is that there's no

AngularJS when you directly ask the server for `http://localhost:8080/view1`. But in the case of the hashbang version, the browser always loads the **index.html** first, and AngularJS then steps in to resolve the hashbang URL. Hence this is the limitation of html5Mode. If you want to stick to html5Mode, you'll need some kind of server-side configuration to resolve this issue.

If you're really interested in learning about the HTML5 history API you should go through the following link: http://diveintohtml5.info/history.html [1]

 ### The otherwise() Function

There is also an `otherwise()` function in `$routeProvider`, which can be used to redirect users to a particular route when no route match is found. It can be done in this way:

```
$routeProvider.otherwise({redirectTo:'/view1'});
```

Every AngularJS app will have a fixed set of routes. So, if somebody tries to mess around and tries loading a route that doesn't exist (like `http://local-host:8000/index.html#/view3`) your app won't break. You can safely redirect the user to a default route with the help of `otherwise()`.

Using $routeParams in the Controller

Sometimes it's necessary to pass some parameters to the controller associated with your view. For example, in a blogging app, you may want to pass a post ID in the URL, which the controller can grab and then fetch the related content via an Ajax call. These parameters passed in the route are called route parameters and are exposed by a integrated AngularJS service called `$routeParams`. To demonstrate this concept let's adjust our previous demo app to use `$routeParams`.

Let's modify the two routes as follows:

- `/view1`: This allows users to enter their first and last names. On the click of a button, we load route `/view2`, passing the first name and last name as route parameters.

---

[1] http://diveintohtml5.info/history.html

▓ /view2: It retrieves the passed first name and last name from the route and displays them.

Here are the updated files:

app.js:

```
'use strict';

angular.module('myApp', [
  'myApp.controllers',
  'ngRoute'
]);

angular.module('myApp').config(function($routeProvider,
➥$locationProvider){
    $routeProvider.when('/view1',{
        controller:'Controller1',
        templateUrl:'/partials/view1.html'
    }).when('/view2/:firstname/:lastname',{
        controller: 'Controller2',
        templateUrl: '/partials/view2.html'
    }).otherwise({redirectTo:'/view1'});
    $locationProvider.html5Mode(true);
});
```

While configuring route details for /view2 we passed '/view2/:firstname/:lastname' as the first parameter to when(). This specifies that firstname and lastname are two route parameters here. Furthermore, inside the controller associated with this view (Controller2) we can refer to these route params via the keys $routeParams.firstname and $routeParams.lastname.

Did you notice the templateUrl is prefixed with a /? This is because when /view2 is loaded, the URL will be something like /view2/myfirstname/mylastname. So, if you don't prefix the template path (such as partials/view2.html) with a / AngularJS will look for the template inside /view2/myfirstname/lastname/partials/view2.html due to the changed URL, and this will result in a 404 error. So, a / tells AngularJS that the template partials/view2.html is in the root directory.

partials/view1.html:

```
<p>
    First name: <input type="text" ng-model="firstname"/> <br/>
    Last name: <input type="text" ng-model="lastname"/> <br/>
    <button ng-click="loadView2()">Load View2</button>
</p>
```

As you can see, we have two input fields that are bound to two models: `firstname` and `lastname`. There's also a button which, when clicked, triggers the scope function `loadView2()`. This function is responsible for handling `firstname`, `lastname` and loading `/view2`, with these model values as route parameters.

partials/view2.html:

```
<p>
    From View2.
    <ul>
        <li>First name: {{firstname}}</li>
        <li>Last name: {{lastname}}</li>
    </ul>
</p>
```

This template is very simple—it simply uses expressions to display scope models.

controllers.js:

```
use strict';

angular.module('myApp.controllers', []).controller('Controller1'
➥,function($scope,$location){
    $scope.loadView2=function(){
        $location.path('/view2/'+$scope.firstname+'/'
➥+$scope.lastname);
    }
}).controller('Controller2',function($scope,$routeParams){
    $scope.firstname=$routeParams.firstname;
    $scope.lastname=$routeParams.lastname;
});
```

`Controller1` declares a dependency on something new: the `$location` service. This is a built-in service that parses the URL in the browser address bar and exposes it to our app via several functions. We'll discuss `$location` in detail later on in this chapter. For now, just note that `$location.path()` is used to load a new route.

Controller2 declares a dependency on `$routeParams`, which is an AngularJS service that exposes the route parameters to our controller.

Now, if you run the app and access `http://localhost:8080/index.html` you'll end up in the `/view1` route. If you fill out the first name and last name input fields and hit `Load View2` you will be redirected to `/view2`, which looks something like Figure 4.1.

From View2.

- First name: Sandeep
- Last name: Panda

Figure 4.1. Using route parameters

$routeParams Also Parses the Query String

Apart from named parameters, `$routeParams` also parses the query string, if present. So, if your URL contains a query string like `?key1=value1`, the key/value pair is added to `$routeParams`.

Using ng-template

We've seen how to put views for different routes into different HTML files. For example, the templates for `/view1` and `/view2` go into `partials/view1.html` and `partials/view2.html`, respectively. But we also have an option to define templates inline, which is done through the `ng-template` directive. Let's modify our code to use `ng-template`. The changes will be made to **app.js** and **index.html**.

index.html

```
<!doctype html>
<html lang="en" ng-app="myApp">
<head>
  <meta charset="utf-8">
  <title>AngularJS Routing</title>
  <link rel="stylesheet" href="css/app.css"/>
  <script type="text/ng-template" id="/view1.tpl">
      <p>
        First name: <input type="text" ng-model="firstname"/> <br/>
        Last name: <input type="text" ng-model="lastname"/> <br/>
```

```
            <button ng-click="loadView2()">Load View2</button>
        </p>
    </script>
    <script type="text/ng-template" id="/view2.tpl">
        <p>
          From View2.
          <ul>
              <li>First name: {{firstname}}</li>
              <li>Last name: {{lastname}}</li>
          </ul>
        </p>
    </script>
</head>
<body>
  <ul class="menu">
    <li><a href="/view1">view1</a></li>
    <li><a href="/view2">view2</a></li>
  </ul>

  <div ng-view></div>


  <script src="lib/angular/angular.js"></script>
  <script src="lib/angular/angular-route.js"></script>
  <script src="js/app.js"></script>
  <script src="js/controllers.js"></script>
</body>
</html>
```

You can define templates using <script type="text/ng-template">. This loads
the content of the <script> into the $templateCache service so that ng-view (and
other directives) can use it. You also need to give it an id through which it can be
referenced in other places. In our case we'll use this id in app.js while configuring
modules.

Here is the modified **app.js**:

app.js

```
$routeProvider.when('/view1',{
      controller:'Controller1',
      templateUrl:'/view1.tpl' // The ng-template id
   }).when('/view2/:firstname/:lastname',{
```

```
          controller: 'Controller2',
          templateUrl: '/view2.tpl' // The ng-template id
});
```

You should note that the extension .tpl in the id is optional. You can give it any extension you want or leave it. All you need to do is specify a name that you can use afterwards to refer to the template.

Now if you refresh the browser the app will work as expected.

Use Separate HTML Files for Templates

If your template is really tiny you might benefit from declaring it inside ng-template. But in a real-world app, you won't probably ever need this. Rather it's best to create different HTML files for different templates as it keeps your app maintainable in the long run and does not clutter your main view with <script> tags.

The resolve Property in the Route Config Object

There is a resolve property in the Route Config object we pass as the second argument to the $routeProvider.when() function. This can be used to pass additional dependencies to the controller. For example, for a controller to work we might need to retrieve all the users in our system, typically by doing an AJAX call. This is what resolve does. We provide an object as the value to the resolve property. This object has keys, which can be used as the names for the controller's dependencies. In other words you'll declare your controller's constructor function with these names as parameters. The value to the key can be a string or a function. If it's a string, AngularJS will try to find a service with that name. If it's a function its return value is used.

Now, the function's return value can be of two types. The first consists of simple values (string, array, object etc.) in which case the dependency in resolve takes that value.

The second value is a special case. Most of the times the value you return from the function is a **deferred type** (also known as a **promise**), which means the returned value is just a placeholder for an actual value that'll be available in the near future (by the time your controller is instantiated). Consider an AJAX call that retrieves a blog post from its `id`. You can use `resolve` here to get the `post` object. In your function you simply return a deferred/promise and the `resolve` property will automatically be updated when the actual `post` arrives. Don't worry, we'll get into the details of deferred types later on.

So, before the route change ends, all these dependencies listed in `resolve` should be resolved, or at least one should be rejected. Again let's consider our AJAX call to obtain a `post` object. While fetching a post the network may fail and, with it, the dependency may fail to get its actual value (which means the dependency—the deferred value—was rejected). On the other hand, if everything goes well, the dependency listed in `resolve` gets its value successfully. In this case we say that the dependency was resolved. If all the dependencies are resolved a `$routeChangeSuccess` event is broadcast. If one of the dependencies fails to resolve a `$routeChangeError` event is broadcast. If you're interested in these events you can subscribe to them using `$rootScope.$on()` and do something meaningful. Again, don't worry too much about this for now as we'll be returning to dependencies later on.

Let's modify our previous code to introduce an additional dependency to our controller `Controller2`. In `/view2`, apart from showing the first name and last name, we also need to display all our users. Typically, you'll get this list from an Ajax call to the server. But as we don't know how to do that yet in AngularJS, let's hard code the array of names.

The first change is carried out in **app.js**, and adds this dependency to the `resolve` property:

```
'use strict';

angular.module('myApp', [
  'myApp.controllers',
  'ngRoute'
]);

angular.module('myApp').config(function($routeProvider,
➡$locationProvider) {
  $routeProvider.when('/view1', {
    controller: 'Controller1',
    templateUrl: '/partials/view1.html'
  }).when('/view2/:firstname/:lastname', {
```

```
    controller: 'Controller2',
    templateUrl: '/partials/view2.html',
    resolve: {
      names: function() {
        //typically you will use a service to retrieve values from
➥the server here
        return ['Misko', 'Vojta', 'Brad']; //this is used as
➥dependency value
      }
    }
  }).otherwise({
    redirectTo: '/view1'
  });
  $locationProvider.html5Mode(true);
});
```

You should also note here that we can add other dependencies besides names.

Now our controller can be modified as follows:

```
'use strict';

angular.module('myApp.controllers', []).controller('Controller1'
➥,function($scope,$location){
    $scope.loadView2=function(){
        $location.path('/view2/'+$scope.firstname+'/'
➥+$scope.lastname);
    }
}).controller('Controller2',function($scope,$routeParams,names){
➥//names is now a dependency
    $scope.firstname=$routeParams.firstname;
    $scope.lastname=$routeParams.lastname;
    $scope.names=names;
});
```

So, before instantiating Controller2 AngularJS executes the function provided to the names property in resolve. The return value of this function is used as the value of the names dependency declared by the controller.

The final change is made to our partial view2.html. I assume we're using the partials as regular HTML files, and not as ng-template.

partials/view2.html:

```
<p>
  From View2.
  <ul>
    <li>First name: {{firstname}}</li>
    <li>Last name: {{lastname}}</li>
  </ul>
  Our additional users are:
  <ul>
    <li ng-repeat="name in names">
      {{name}}
    </li>
  </ul>
</p>
```

Now, if you refresh the browser, fill out the first name/last name fields and hit the button, you'll see something like Figure 4.2.

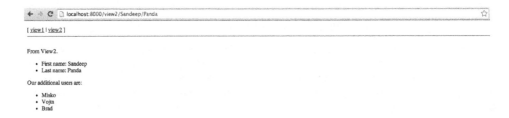

Figure 4.2. Using the resolve property

As we've seen, the `resolve` property is about pre-loading your controller's dependencies. You'll see this more often when we learn about services and use it in the demo app.

Exploring the $location Service

`$location` is an AngularJS service that exposes the current browser URL (obtained from `window.location`) through a well-defined API. Besides that, it keeps itself and the URL in sync. Any change you make to `$location` is propagated to the URL, and whenever the URL changes (such as when a new route is loaded) the `$location` service updates itself.

You can use this service to update the browser's URL to navigate to a different route, or to watch for changes in `$location` and take appropriate actions in your app.

Updating $location Does Not Cause a Full Page Refresh

When you use $location to update browser URL, this just loads a new route and does *not* cause a full page refresh. If you want to trigger a full page refresh, or redirect the user to a different website or URL, you can do that using $window.location.href.

The API

$location service offers several getters and setters to read and update different parts of a URL. Some parts of the URL like host, protocol, port etc are not writable and therefore $location service offers only getters for them. For writable parts like path, search, hash you receive both read and write options.

Have a look at Figure 4.3 taken from the AngularJS website. It describes the different parts of a URL.

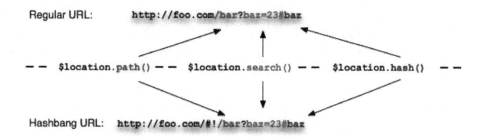

Figure 4.3. The different parts of a URL

Writable Parts

path:

Path is the part of URL that comes after the hostname and protocol. For a URL like http://localhost:8000/view1, the path is /view1.

```
$location.path(); // gets the current path

$location.path('/view2'); // sets the current path and updates URL
```

The above also holds true for hash-based URLs.

When you change the path inside AngularJS' handlers, such as ng-click, ng-model etc., the path is updated and the change is reflected in the URL. This is because these function calls are wrapped inside $apply() and a $digest cycle begins, which in turn fires watchers set up by $location to update the browser URL. If you're updating the path outside of AngularJS world (in a custom event handler, for example) you need to call $scope.$apply() after calling $location.path().

 $location is Aware of the AngularJS Scope Life Cycle

$location, being a built-in service, is aware of the AngularJS scope life cycle. So it integrates with the scope life cycle by updating itself and calling $apply() whenever the browser URL changes. This is necessary because you might want to set up watchers on $location.path() and receive notifications when it changes.

Also, when you call a setter method such as path() on $location, it doesn't immediately push the change to the URL. They're actually committed and pushed to the URL in the digest cycle.

A path name always starts with a /. If you don't prefix the path name with a / while passing it to $location.path() AngularJS automatically adds a /.

search:

search() lets you provide key/value pairs as search parameters to the URL. So, instead of using $routeParams you can also use the search() function to pass params to the route and read them in the controller. The key/value you pass will be appended to the path with ? as the prefix and & as a separator.

For example: http://localhost:8000/view2?firstname=fname&lastname=lname

```
$location.search(); //get an object that has key/values as search
➥parameters

$location.search({key1:value1,key2:value2}); //set the search
➥parameter
```

hash:

hash() function lets you get or set the hash part of the URL.

```
$location.hash(); //get the hash part. e.g. #div1, #div2 etc

$location.hash('div1'); //changes URL to /view1#div1
```

 #div1 is a Real Anchor

Here, #div1 is a real anchor and has nothing to do with routes. As you can see in the snippet above, the hash() function simply appends #div1 at the end of current URL.

These function calls return the same $location instance. So, you can chain the calls to update various parts in a single go.

For example:

```
$location.path('/view2').search({key1:value1}).hash('div1');
```

Non-Writable Parts

The following functions of $location can be used to read the non-writable parts of the URL.

▨ host(): Returns the host name, such as localhost

▨ port(): Returns the port the server is listening on, such as 8000

▨ protocol(): Returns the protocol used, such as http

▨ url(): Returns the part of the URL after hostname and protocol (i.e. only path+search+hash). e.g. /view1?key1=value1#div1

- absUrl(): Returns the whole URL, such as http://local-host:800/view1?key1=value1#div1

Adding a New History Entry Versus Replacing One

Whenever you update the $location service and changes are pushed to the browser URL it creates a new history entry. A new history entry essentially means, when you hit the browser's back button, it'll behave as expected and go to the previous route. But in case you want to replace the last history entry instead of creating a new entry, you should use the $location.replace() function after modifying one or more parts. An example of this might be:

```
$location.path('/view2').search({key1:value1}).hash('div1');
//change the parts

$location.replace(); // changes the URL, but does not create
a new history entry.
```

Do this and, next time, when the $location syncs itself with the URL (in a digest cycle, of course!) it'll change the URL and update the last history entry instead of creating a new one. This works well for both HTML5 and Hashbang modes.

Events in Routing

There are couple of events in routing that you should be aware of. These are:

$location related events

- $locationChangeStart: This event is broadcast on the $rootScope just before the URL in the browser changes as result of the mutations done to $location via setters—such as calling path().

- $locationChangeSuccess: This event is broadcast just after URL in the browser changes. But, if some part of your code listens to the $locationChangeStart event and calls preventDefault on it, this event won't be fired.

$route related events

- $routeChangeStart: This event is broadcast just before AngularJS starts changing the route. At this point, the $route service starts resolving all the dependencies needed to effect this change. This typically involves fetching the view template and resolving all the dependencies listed in `resolve` property in the route definition. You can, for example, listen for this event and display some kind of loading image or progress bar in the listener function.

```
angular.module('myApp').run(function($rootScope){
    $rootScope.$on('$routeChangeStart',function(){
        //do something magical here
    });
});
```

The `run()` function gets called when all the modules are successfully loaded. In this case we're simply registering a listener which will be notified every time the route change starts.

- `$routeChangeSuccess`: This event is broadcast after the `$route` service is able to successfully resolve all the dependencies needed to load the new route. The `ng-view` directive listens to this event so that it can instantiate the related controller, and the view can be rendered.

```
angular.module('myApp').run(function($rootScope){
    $rootScope.$on('$routeChangeSuccess',function(){
        //do something magical here. maybe stop the animation
➥you started in
        $routeChangeStart listener.
    });
});
```

- `$rootChangeError`: If the `$route` service is unable to resolve at least one of the dependencies needed to change the route,the `$routeChangeError` event is broadcast.

All These Events Are Broadcast on the `$rootScope`

All these events are broadcast on the `$rootScope`. In other words, the `$route` service calls `$rootScope.$broadcast()` to broadcast the event. And you already know that if a `$scope` broadcasts an event it can also listen to the same event.

The ng-include Directive

Sometimes, it's desirable to divide your HTML template into reusable parts so that they can be included in the main view. The `ng-include` directive can be used to fetch, compile and include an external HTML fragment in your main page. For example, your main HTML file can have different sections like a header, a footer, a sidebar etc. You can put the template for these components in separate HTML files, and include them into your main HTML.

So, let's modify our `/view2` to divide the template into two different HTML fragments. Create a new directory `fragments` inside `partials` and create two files inside it:

selected-user.html:

```
From View2.
<ul>
    <li>First name: {{firstname}}</li>
    <li>Last name: {{lastname}}</li>
</ul>
```

The above template is used to list the first name and last name passed from `/view1`.

all-users.html:

```
Our additional users are:
<ul>
    <li ng-repeat="name in names">
        {{name}}
    </li>
</ul>

This is used to list all the available users.
```

Now let's modify the template for `/view2`. The modified template will be:

```
<p>
    <div ng-include="'/partials/fragments/selected-user.html'">
➥</div>
    <div ng-include="'/partials/fragments/all-users.html'"/></div>
</p>
```

Or, you may use `ng-include` as a standalone element and use it, like so:

```
<p>
    <ng-include src="'/partials/fragments/selected-user.html'">
➥</ng-include>
    <ng-include src="'/partials/fragments/all-users.html'"/>
➥</ng-include>
</p>
```

Now, if you refresh **index.html** and proceed as usual you'll see that the app works with this modification. AngularJS fetches the content from the file specified in `src`, and compiles it, so that expressions like `{{firstname}}` are evaluated, and includes the content in our view.

You'll also notice that `ng-include` creates a new `scope` that prototypally inherits from the parent scope (the controller's scope, associated with the route).

This was just a small example to show the usage of `ng-include`, but hopefully it gives you an idea about how to use it in our apps. We'll be using it often while developing the demo app.

Using ng-include

`ng-include` expects an expression to be passed as the value to `src` attribute. For example, if you have a scope model, which points to a template, you can pass that model name directly to `src`. But, if you want to pass a string like `/partials/fragments/selected-user.html` to `src`, make sure to wrap it inside single quotes just as we did above.

Introducing the Angular UI Router

When you are starting with AngularJS routing, it's a good idea to begin with `ngRoute`. That said, it has one serious limitation in that you can't have nested views in your app—just the one `ng-view`. But when your app grows in complexity, you may wish to have views within views. For example, your app's admin panel will be loaded inside an `ng-view`. Furthermore, this admin panel could have several sub views, which should ideally be loaded inside the admin panel's own `ng-view`. But we know this isn't possible with AngularJS' default routing system.

The solution to this problem is to use the Angular UI Router—a third-party routing module that has many awesome features, including nested views support. If you're working on a serious real-world app, consider using UI Router instead of the default routing system.

We'll be using UI Router for developing our demo app. So, let's take a quick overview and learn how to make the transition from ngRoute to UI Router.

Getting Started With UI Routter

Instead of working with URLs, UI Router takes a state-based approach. A state describes how your UI looks at a particular time. To put it simply, the state can be composed of a URL, controller and template. Let's modify our previous snippet to use UI Router.

Requirements

1. Download the UI Router script from http://angular-ui.github.io/ui-router/release/angular-ui-router.min.js and include it in your **index.html**.

2. To use UI Router you need to add a dependency on ui.router module to your main app module.

Defining States

We can modify our **app.js** as follows to introduce states:

```
'use strict';

    angular.module('myApp', [
      'myApp.controllers',
      'ui.router' //this is the dependency on ui.router module
    ]);

    angular.module('myApp').config(function($stateProvider,
➡$urlRouterProvider,$locationProvider){ //$stateProvider and
➡ $urlRouterProvider are from ui.router module
        $stateProvider.state('view1',{
            url: '/view1',
            controller:'Controller1',
            templateUrl:'/partials/view1.html'
        }).state('view2',{
```

```
        url: '/view2/:firstname/:lastname',
        controller:'Controller2',
        resolve:{
            names: function(){
                return ['Misko','Vojta','Brad'];
            }
        },
        templateUrl: '/partials/view2.html'
    });
    $urlRouterProvider.otherwise('/view1'); // when no route
➥match found redirect to /view1
    $locationProvider.html5Mode(true);
});
```

When you use UI Router you need to think in terms of states rather than URLs. As you can see we have two states : view1 and view2. A state is registered with the method state() and the first argument to it represents the state name. Each of the states consist of three components: url,templateUrl, and controller. Also note that the second state uses the resolve property, which is written as usual.

Now, when a state is activated the browser's address bar is updated with the url associated with the state. So, you should always focus on changing states rather than URLs. I'll show you how shortly!

The following changes should be made to **index**.html:

```
<ul class="menu">
    <li><a ui-sref="view1">view1</a></li>
    <li><a ui-sref="view2">view2</a></li>
</ul>
```

Also, the UI Router script should be present in the page:

```
<script src="lib/angular-ui-router/angular-ui-router.min.js">
➥</script>
```

As you can see, the hyperlinks now use a special attribute ui-sref instead of just href. This is because we are concerned with changing the state. The ui-sref means that when the link is clicked the corresponding state activates.

Now, we need to make a small change in $scope.loadView2() inside Controller1. This is done so that, when users click on the button in view1, they're taken to state view2.

```
angular.module('myApp.controllers', []).controller('Controller1',
➥function($scope, $location, $state) {
  $scope.loadView2 = function() {
    // the following activates state view2
    $state.go('view2', {
      firstname: $scope.firstname,
      lastname: $scope.lastname
    });
  }
});
```

As you see, our controller declares a dependency on $state which comes from ui.router module. We don't use $location.path() anymore to change route. Instead $state.go() is used to activate a new state and make the transition. The first argument to this function is the new state name. The second argument can be an object that is used to pass $stateParams to the new state (As opposed to $routeParams).

Our last change will be in Controller2 to use $stateParams instead of $routeParams to obtain the named parameters passed to the state.

```
angular.module('myApp.controllers').controller('Controller2',
➥function($scope,$stateParams,names){
        $scope.firstname=$stateParams.firstname;
        $scope.lastname=$stateParams.lastname;
        $scope.names=names;
});
```

Now if you access http://localhost:8000/index.html the app should work as expected. But the difference is that we're now using a more powerful routing system. As we develop our demo app using UI Router you'll get to know more about it.

You can also check out their GitHub[2] repository to explore more about UI Router.

---

[2] https://github.com/angular-ui/ui-router

Conclusion

So far we have covered the basics of AngularJS routing. But before implementing this in our app it's important to be aware of service and factories because we'll be using these to store/retrieve the posts. The next chapter is all about services, factories and providers. Once you have a clear idea about these we can start generating views and related services for our Single Page Blogger.

Chapter 5

AngularJS Services, Factories, and Providers

We've already mentioned **services** several times in the last few chapters. You have already used several built-in AngularJS services like $location, $timeout, $root-Scope etc. But, in a real world application, the built-in services are not always going to be sufficient so you'll need to create custom services. This chapter will give you a comprehensive guide to three critical components of AngularJS: **services**, **factories**, and **providers**.

The main purpose of these components is that they hold some logic that's required at multiple points within your app. Although services, factories and providers are all used to accomplish the same task (encapsulating repetitive logic), there are subtle differences between them.

Services, factories, and providers are all **injectable types**. As you've seen in previous chapters, this means that they can be injected into controllers and other services through Dependency Injection. Apart from these there are also two more injectable types: **value** and **constant**. Let's explore each of these types in detail, starting with the simplest—services.

Service

An AngularJS service encapsulates some specific business logic and exposes an API, to be used by other components, to invoke this logic. For example, the built-in $timeout service executes a function after a specified interval. The $http service encapsulates the logic required to interact with REST back-ends. We ask AngularJS to inject these services into our controllers so that we can utilize them. service is an injectable type, and this means it can be inserted into different AngularJS components through dependency injection.

 AngularJS Services are Always Singletons

> It's important to note that AngularJS services are always singletons. This means that, once AngularJS constructs a service object, the same instance is reused throughout your app. There are never ever two service instances. This makes them great candidates to share application data across multiple components. For example, after a successful login, you'll need to store the login status where the status can be retrieved in all other components. In this scenario, you can store the status in a service and then, whenever you need to read the value, you can just inject it into your controller/service and check it.

Take a look at the following snippet:

```
angular.module('myApp').controller('TestController',
➥function($http,$timeout){
  //use $http, $timeout here
});
```

In the above snippet our controller TestController declares dependency on two services: $http and $timeout. So, when the controller is instantiated, AngularJS passes the two services to it.

Similarly, you can create your own services that encapsulate the business logic specific to your apps. Here is how you register a service in a module:

```
angular.module('myApp').service('helloService',function(){
  this.sayHello=function(){ // define an instance method
    alert('Hello!! Welcome to services.');
  }
});
```

As you see, `angular.module()` provides a function `service()` that's used to register a service. The first argument to this function is the `service` name. The second argument is a constructor function. It can have usual instance variables and functions. Now, in a controller, if you ask for this service AngularJS constructs an object by invoking the constructor function with the `new` keyword. This object is then injected into your controller. If you want to use our `helloService` in a controller you can do this:

```
angular.module('myApp').controller('TestController',
➥function(helloService){
  helloService.sayHello(); // helloService is the service object.
➥It has sayHello function.
});
```

 ### Why Use CamelCase?

You might think 'why choose camelCase to name a service if we're passing a constructor function to the `service()` method?' The reason is that, when you ask for the service in a different component—a controller, say—all you get is an instance of that constructor function. That's why I prefer camelCase and not PascalCase.

It's also worth looking at how we're attaching functions to our service. If you define functions for instances using **this** keyword it's usually bad practice. The reason for this is that the same function is copied across all the instances. Indeed, certain JavaScript gurus might even feel offended if they see you doing this. However, in AngularJS we have a get out. Since Angular services are singletons it's guaranteed that there'll be only one instance of your service. As a result, it doesn't matter if you define functions using **this** or use the `prototype` property.

In the controller we declare a dependency on `helloService`. When AngularJS resolves this dependency it'll take the constructor function associated with the service name `helloService` and instantiate it. The result is an object that's finally injected into our controller. Just note that this is done only once. Afterwards, the service returned is the cached version of the first call to the service constructor function.

In the above case, the service just displayed a simple `Hello` message. But our service can also have dependencies on other services. For example, it can depend on the `$timeout` service and defer the `alert` by an interval you specify. The service can be rewritten as follows:

```
angular.module('myApp').service('helloService',function($timeout){
  this.sayHello=function(name){
    $timeout(function(){
      alert('Hello '+name);
    },2000);
  }
});
```

Our service, here, is dependent on the built-in `$timeout` service. When AngularJS invokes this constructor function it'll pass the dependency i.e. `$timeout`. Now the instance method has been modified to take a name and show a customized `Hello` message. With the help of `$timeout` we display the message after a two-second delay. Finally, we can inject this into our controller and use it, as follows:

```
angular.module('myApp').controller('TestController',
➥function(helloService){
  helloService.sayHello('AngularJS'); // Alerts Hello AngularJS
});
```

These basic examples show how to create and use services. In real life, you should use them to encapsulate the repeatable logic and share data among different components of your app. For example, you might need to perform REST interactions at various places in your app. To do this, you can build a service that internally uses `$http` to communicate with the server and inject this into controllers. Also, if you have data that may be needed in multiple locations you can encapsulate it in the service and use it wherever required.

Here are the most important points to remember about services:

1. A service is registered using the `service()` function of `angular.module()`.

2. The second argument to `service()` is a constructor function. When we ask for the service as a dependency, AngularJS creates an object from this constructor function and injects it.

3. A service is a singleton. AngularJS instantiates the service object only once and all other components share the same instance.

4. Services are **lazily instantiated**. This means AngularJS instantiates the service only when it encounters a component that declares dependency on the service.

Eager Loading of a Service

Services are always lazily instantiated. But what if we have a heavy service that consumes resources and takes a while to get created? In this case, we certainly don't want a bad user experience, so we'd want to load our services eagerly just after the module loads. The good news is that this is easy to do with the `module.run()` function. As the name suggests, once a module is loaded, its `run()` function executes. You can pass a callback to it with your service names as arguments, so that when the `run()` runs, the passed callback also executes. As a result, the listed dependencies are resolved and get instantiated, and your service will be ready before someone asks for it in your app. A logging service would be a good example of a service that should be eagerly loaded. For now, here is how we can **eagerly load** our `helloService`:

```
angular.module('myApp').service('helloService',function($timeout){
  this.sayHello=function(name){
    $timeout(function(){
      alert('Hello '+name);
    },2000);
  }
});

angular.module('myApp').run(function(helloService){
    //helloService can be used here. It has been instantiated.
});
```

Factory

A factory is another injectable type. Effectively it's the same as a service. However, it's more verbose and configurable, by which I mean it gives you the freedom to determine what to instantiate and return from the factory. As its name suggests, it's a factory for a service.

You register a factory by calling the `factory()` function on `angular.module()`. For example, we can implement `helloService` as a factory as follows:

```
angular.module('myApp').factory('helloService',function(){
  return {
    sayHello: function(name){
      alert('Hello '+name);
    },
    echo: function(message){
      alert(message);
    }
  }
});
```

The first argument to `factory()` is obviously the name you want to use for the factory. The second argument is a normal function (*not* a constructor function), which can return an object or a function. When we ask for the factory as a dependency in a controller/service, AngularJS invokes the factory function (the second argument to `factory()`) and injects the value it returns. The value, as I said above, can be a function, object, or value. In our case, we are just returning an object with two instance methods. So, this object is assigned to the variable `helloService` while instantiating the controller. In simpler terms, your service is nothing but the return value obtained from calling the factory function.

The above factory can be used in a controller in exactly the same way as services:

```
angular.module('myApp').controller('TestController',
➦function(helloService) {
  helloService.sayHello('AngularJS'); //alerts Hello AngularJS
  helloService.echo('I Love AngularJS'); //alerts I Love AngularJS
});
```

Usually, the object you return from the factory function, has several functions that perform different tasks. For instance, in a note-taking app you can have a `noteFactory`. The instance returned by the factory function may have functions such as:

```
angular.module('myApp').factory('noteFactory',function($http){
➥//declare dependency on $http
  return {
    addNote: function(note){
      // save the note. may be use $http to persist on server
    },
    updateNote: function(note){
     //update note
    },
    getNotes: function(){
      //get all notes
    },
    getNote: function(noteId){
      //get a single note
    }
  }
});
```

This factory can be injected into a controller or some other service whenever required.

Remember that factories, like services, are singletons. A factory can also depend on other services or factories. The above example demonstrates this by declaring a dependency on $http. Both services and factories are used to accomplish the same task: sharing data and encapsulating business logic. Note that you return an object from the factory function, so you have the freedom to determine which object to return based on certain parameters. This is not the case with services where you simply pass a constructor function to service(). That said, in many instances, you can use either a service or factory.

Provider

A provider is the most configurable and verbose version of services because it's based on prior settings or logic. For example, the built-in $route service may behave differently based on the mode (html5Mode or hashbang) you configured in $route-Provider. In short, a provider, as its name suggests, acts as a provider of some sort of service.

Every Service Has a Provider

Every service you create has an associated provider (AngularJS does this automatically for you). But don't worry about this for now as we'll explore these details in our chapter on Dependency Injection.

As you might have guessed, a provider can be injected into our module's `config()` block, where a user can configure it before the app starts. Now let's modify our previous snippets to use a provider. We don't want to greet our users with just `Hello!`. We want to be able to configure the greeting text first. This configured text should be used subsequently to greet users.

You register a provider by writing:

```
angular.module('myApp').provider('greet', function() {

  this.greeting = 'Hello'; //we can configure this.
➥The default is Hello.

  this.$get = function() { //this will be called to obtain greet
➥service
    var greeting = this.greeting;
    return function(name) {
      alert(greeting + ', ' + name);
    }
  }

  this.setGreeting = function(greeting) { //setter for greeting text
    this.greeting = greeting;
  }

});
```

The `provider()` function of `angular.module()` is used to register a provider. The second argument to `provider()` is a constructor function. This must have an instance method called `$get()` in order for the provider to work. In the above snippet, we have created a provider called `greetProvider`. Note its name. When we create a provider, the first argument to the `provider()` function is the name of the service that's being provided. In this case, we're exposing a service called `greet`. But the actual provider name is `greetProvider`. So, we'll use the name `greet` to get a reference to the service and `greetProvider` to get a reference to the provider (in `module.config()`).

Using Providers and Services

Although we've passed the name `greet` as the first argument to `provider()` AngularJS understands that the actual provider's name is `greetProvider`. So, in our module's `config` block, when you declare a dependency on `greetProvider`, AngularJS knows that it needs to instantiate the constructor function passed to `provider()` using `new`, and inject it. Similarly, when another component declares a dependency on the `greet` service, AngularJS knows that it needs to call `$get()` on the `greetProvider` instance and inject whatever it returns.

Now we can configure and use the provider as following:

```
angular.module('myApp').config(function(greetProvider) { //get the
➡provider injected
  greetProvider.setGreeting('Hola'); //configure our provider
});

angular.module('myApp').controller('TestController',
➡function(greet) {
  greet('Sandeep'); // use the greet service
});
```

When the module `myApp` loads, the `config()` function runs. The function passed to `config()` declares a dependency on `greetProvider`. By this time AngularJS has already instantiated `greetProvider` by invoking `new` on the function passed to `angular.module().provider()`. So, this provider instance is injected and then configured inside `config` block. Then, in a different component, `TestController`, we declare a dependency on `greet` service. Hence AngularJS will call the `$get()` function on the `greetProvider` instance and return whatever it returns. As a result, the value returned from `greetProvider.$get()` will be assigned to the argument of `greet` in the `TestController`. In this way we get a reference to the `greet` service, which is a simple function. When invoked, it shows an `alert`. In this case we have configured the provider to use `"Hola"` as greeting text. So, if you run the app it will alert **Hola, Sandeep**. Try changing the greeting text in `config()` and see the result.

Providers are Instantiated Only Once

Providers are instantiated only once and you can inject them only inside the `config()` block. This is because you get a chance to configure your provider when the module loads. Later, your other app components just need to ask for the service provided by the provider.

When you define a provider you don't necessarily need to refer to it in a `config()` block. AngularJS automatically instantiates your provider when the module loads. You can directly ask for the service in an app component and, at that time, the service instance will be created out of the provider. You need to refer to the provider in `config()` block only when you want to configure it.

 What's Returned?

In the above example, the following rules hold true for the two dependencies:

- `greetProvider` = Result of invoking the constructor function passed to `provider()` with `new`. This returns an object.

- `greet` = Result of calling `greetProvider.$get()`. In this case it returns a function which displays an alert. But the return type can be anything in general.

We just outlined the three most commonly used injectable types in AngularJS: services, factories, and providers. We also discussed the basic differences between the three and saw how they can be used in our apps.

But there are two more injectable types we can use: **value** and **constant**, and we'll briefly cover them here. The great news is that they're much simpler than the previous injectable types.

Value

A value is an injectable type that is used to register a simple service, which can be a string, number, array, function, or an object. Suppose you want to provide a version number for your website; you can just use a value service. A value service is registered using the `value()` function of `angular.module()`. The following example registers a value that represents the version number:

```
angular.module('myApp').value('appVersion','1.0');
```

The above snippet registers a value service `appVersion` whose value set to 1.0. A controller or some service in our app can declare a dependency on this value and use it. Note that the second argument to the `value()` function can be anything. Whatever you pass here will be passed to you when you declare a dependency on it somewhere in the code. You should also note that `value` can't be injected in `module.config()`; this is one of the important differences between values and constants. This is done to prevent accidental instantiation of services during the configuration phase.

Constant

A constant is an injectable type that is the same as a value except that it *can* be injected into `module.config()`. You register a constant by calling `constant()` function of `angular.module()`:

```
angular.module('myApp').constant('DATA_SOURCE','a string here');
```

Using Decorators

Sometimes, you'll need to extend the default functionality of certain third-party services, but won't have permission to alter their source code. Aside from which, it's not a good idea to modify third-party libraries to suit your needs. No problem: This is where **decorators** come in! A decorator intercepts the creation of a service and modifies its default behavior on the fly. It may return an object which wraps the original service and delegate tasks to it, or simply attach new functions/properties to the original service.

Let's look at an example. There is a built-in `$log` service in AngularJS which is used to log messages to the console by default. However, say we need a different functionality: Our app should be able to send some log data to the server apart from logging to the console.

The `$log` service has five simple methods for logging:

- `log()`

- info()

- debug()

- warn()

- error()

We need a different method in the $log service, which logs to console and also sends the data to a server. Let's implement this using a simple decorator that'll add a new function to the $log service dynamically.

You register a decorator as follows:

```
angular.module('myApp').config(function($provide) {
  $provide.decorator('$log', function($delegate) { //$delegate is
➥the original $log service.
    $delegate.postInfoToURI = function(message) {
      //send data to server. Maybe inject a service here which
➥interacts with the server
      $delegate.log('Data to post:' + message);
      $delegate.log('Sending data to server');
    }
    return $delegate; //this is the modified $log service
  });
});
```

We create the decorator in config(), which runs when our module loads. Don't worry about $provide. This is an built-in service and we're using it here simply to register a decorator. The first argument to decorator() should be the name of the service we want to decorate. In this case we want to decorate $log, so we pass $log as the first argument. The second argument is a simple function which can declare multiple dependencies. The argument $delegate represents the service to be decorated which is, in this case, the $log service. Apart from $delegate you can declare dependencies on other built-in and custom services.

 Check for the Existence of Functions/Properties Before Attaching Them

Before attaching a new function or property to a service inside a decorator you should always check for the existence of the function or property. This is because, in a future release, AngularJS might itself define a new function that happens to have the same name your decorator uses. Doing some extra checking doesn't hurt. This can be done easily with the `Object.hasOwnProperty()` function and, in case the service already has the function, you can throw an exception.

In this scenario we need a separate method for sending data to our server. So, we call this method `postInfoToURI()` and attach it to `$delegate`, which is nothing but the `$log` service. Finally, we return this updated `$delegate` object. As a result, if you ask for a `$log` service in a different component (such as a controller), you will get `$log` service with one extra function: `postInfoToURI()`.

The following snippet shows how to use this modified `$log` service in a controller:

```
angular.module('myApp').controller('TestController', function($scope,
➥ $log) {
  $scope.data='sample data';
  $log.postInfoToURI('Added some data to scope'); //call the newly
➥added function
});
```

In the above example, the decorator simply adds a new behavior to an existing service. You can also do pretty complex things with decorators. For example, it's possible to wrap the service in a new object and delegate the function calls to the original service. This is useful in cases where you want to perform additional logics before or after delegating to actual function. For instance, if you want to log the current timestamp before a log message is written you can use this pattern to decorate `$log` service.

Now that we've seen decorators, this gives us another difference between a `value` and a `constant`. While values can be decorated and thereby extended, the same can't be done with constants.

 What About $provide?

We've only really touched on the `$provide` service, so far, but it's definitely a big deal. Indeed, `$provide` is what actually makes registering different components possible. All the functions you called on `angular.module()`—such as. `service()`,`factory()`,`provider()`,`value()` and`constant()`—also exist in the `$provide` service. These are exposed on `angular.module()` for convenience and, internally, they all delegate to the corresponding functions defined in `$provide`. But you don't have to worry about it now as we have a dedicated chapter on dependency injection which explores `$provide` in detail.

Conclusion

In this chapter we've looked at the various injectable types in AngularJS—in particular services, factories and providers. We also took a look at decorators. By now you're probably itching to get your hands dirty and write some real AngularJS code. Don't worry, in the next chapter, you'll get to do just that as we'll start developing our demo app, Single Page Blogger.

Developing Single Page Blogger

Developing Our App

Now the fun really begins! In Chapter 2 you downloaded a zip containing the source code for our app. At present it doesn't do very much: It has the starter source code, a good directory structure and includes some modules to make a start. Like every other blogging system, our app also has a posts module. And everything related to the posts module goes into the directory **posts**. Let's start with the routing first.

Defining Routes

After extracting the zip you downloaded in Chapter 2 you'll have a directory called sp-blogger. This is our working directory.

We'll use Angular UI-router, discussed in Chapter 4, to define states. To do this, simply add the following code to **sp-blogger/modules/posts/postModule.js**:

```
angular.module('spBlogger.posts').config(['$stateProvider',
➡'$locationProvider',function($stateProvider,$locationProvider){
    $stateProvider.state('allPosts',{
        url:'/posts',
```

```
            templateUrl: 'modules/posts/views/posts.html',
            controller: 'PostController'
    });
    $stateProvider.state('singlePost',{
        url:'/posts/:id/:permalink',
        templateUrl: 'modules/posts/views/singlePost.html',
        controller: 'PostDetailsController'
    });
}]);
```

Here's what we just did, step-by-step:

1. First, we need to configure our module to define different states. For this we inject `$stateProvider` from the `ui.router` module.

2. There are currently two states. The first one is `allPosts`, which deals with showing all the blog posts. This state consists of three properties: `url`, `templateUrl`, and `controller`. As we've set the `url` to `/posts`, when the state `all-Posts` is activated, the user is taken to the URL: `/posts`. The `templateUrl` points to the appropriate HTML template, which loops through all the posts and displays them. The `controller` points to `PostController`, which we're going to create shortly.

3. The second state deals with displaying details about a single blog post. When the app is in the first state, the users see all the posts. So, once they click on any single post the second state is activated displaying more details about the selected post. In the `url` you can see two named parameters: `id` and `permalink`. We will use `id` to fetch a single post. The `permalink` property is there for creating search engine friendly URLs. It represents the hyphen-separated title of a post. We'll see that while storing posts. The `templateUrl` and `controller` for this state are : `singlePost.html` and `PostDetailsController`.

4. Note we're not using `html5Mode` here and that's why the URLs will be prefixed with #. It's a great idea to turn off `html5Mode` during development so that you can directly access routes without any server-side configuration. Later on, we'll see how to take advantage of `html5Mode`.

5. Finally, when all the modules finish loading we make a transition to the state `allPosts` by calling `$state.go('allposts')`. As a result, when someone visits

`http://localhost:8000` the state `allPosts` is activated and they see all the blog posts. The code for this goes into `/sp-blogger/app/js/app.js`:

```
angular.module('spBlogger').run(['state ,function(state)
➥{ $state.go('allPosts'); }]);
```

Now that we have the routing in place, let's get our service ready; it exposes a method to retrieve the blog posts. The service will then be injected into our controllers so that we can fetch the posts and stick them in the `$scope`.

Creating Our Service

Our service will typically interact with a REST back-end to fetch the blog posts. But, as we haven't yet developed that back-end yet, let's just hard code a few post objects and provide some functions that expose them. Later on, we can change the internal implementation of our service regarding how we fetch posts, but the client code that uses our service will remain the same. Here is our service, which should go into **sp-blogger/app/modules/posts/js/services.js** as this is a part of the `posts` module:

```
angular.module('spBlogger.posts.services', []).factory('postService'
➥, function() {
  return {
    posts: [{
      id: 1,
      title: 'Simple title1',
      content: 'Sample content...',
      permalink: 'simple-title1',
      author: 'Sandeep',
      datePublished: '2012-04-04'
    }, {
      id: 2,
      title: 'Simple title2',
      content: 'Sample content...',
      permalink: 'simple-title2',
      author: 'Sandeep',
      datePublished: '2012-05-04'
    }, {
      id: 3,
      title: 'Simple title3',
      content: 'Sample content...',
      permalink: 'simple-title3',
```

```
      author: 'Sandeep',
      datePublished: '2012-06-04'
    }, {
      id: 4,
      title: 'Simple title4',
      content: 'Sample content...',
      permalink: 'simple-title4',
      author: 'Sandeep',
      datePublished: '2012-07-04'
    }],
    getAll: function() {
      return this.posts;
    },
    getPostById: function(id) {
      for (var i in this.posts) {
        if (this.posts[i].id == id) {
          return this.posts[i];
        }
      }
    },
  }
});
```

1. As you can see we've taken the factory approach and hard-coded four post objects in the instance returned by the factory. Each post has six properties—id, title, content, permalink, author, datePublished—which are self-explanatory. The permalink property represents a search engine-friendly URL, which is created by rendering the title in lowercase, and converting the spaces into hyphens.

2. We expose two methods: getAll() and getPostById(). The former returns all the posts and the latter one finds a single post specified by an id.

Now that we have our service ready let's create the controller and utilize the service.

Creating the Controller

The controllers: PostController and PostDetailsController are part of the posts module. The following code will go into **sp-blogger/app/modules/posts/js/controllers.js**:

```
angular.module('spBlogger.posts.controllers',[]).controller
➥('PostController',['$scope','postService',
➥function($scope,postService){
```

```
    $scope.getAllPosts=function(){
        return postService.getAll();
    };

    $scope.posts=$scope.getAllPosts();

}]).controller('PostDetailsController',['$stateParams','$state',
➥'$scope','postService',function($stateParams,$state,$scope,
➥postService){

    $scope.getPostById=function(id){
        return postService.getPostById(id);
    };

    $scope.closePost=function(){
        $state.go('allPosts');
    };

    $scope.singlePost=$scope.getPostById($stateParams.id);

}]);
```

1. The controller `PostController` gets a reference to `postService` through dependency injection. It attaches a function `getAllPosts()` to the $scope which, under the hood, calls the function `getAll()` on `postService`.

2. Similarly, the controller `PostDetailsController` attaches a function `getPostById()` to the $scope, which retrieves a single post based on the post id. The id is passed in the URL and was declared as a named parameter while configuring the states. So, it's available in $stateParams. The controller also attaches another function `closePost()` to the $scope, which takes users from a single post page to home (back to all blog posts). This function is called when they click on the close button.

3. After fetching the post(s) we attach them to our $scope so that the templates can access them.

Now that we have the controllers ready let's move towards the templates.

Creating the Templates

We need two templates, which are as follows:

1. Template for showing all posts (state allPosts). This template loops through all the posts ($scope.posts model) and lists them. This should go into **sp-blogger/modules/posts/views/posts.html**.

```html
<div class="row">
  <div class="col-xs-3" ng-repeat="post in posts track by $index">
    <div class="well">
    <h3 class="postTitle"><a ui-sref="singlePost({id:post.id,
➥permalink:post.permalink})">{{post.title}}</a></h3>
      <h5>By: {{post.author}} | {{post.datePublished}}</h5>
    </div>
  </div>
</div>
```

As you can see, we loop through the posts and show title, author and the published date of each. We also use ui-sref directive from ui.router module to take users to the state singlePost from allPosts. We also pass id and permalink to the state which appear in the URL. So, when somebody clicks on the title they're taken to something like this: http://local-host:8000/#/posts/1/simple-title1 and the state singlePost is activated.

2. Template for showing details about the selected post (state singlePost). This template uses $scope.singlePost model to show the details. This should go into **sp-blogger/modules/posts/views/singlePost.html**.

```html
<div class"row">
  <div class="col-xs-8 col-xs-offset-2">
  <span class="pull-right cross-btn" ng-click="closePost()">×
➥</span>
  <h1>{{singlePost.title}}</h1>
  <h5>By: {{singlePost.author}} | {{singlePost.datePublished}}</h5>
  <div class="postContent">

  {{singlePost.content}}

  </div>
  </div>
</div>
```

This page utilizes expressions {{}} to display the model properties. We have an × button which, when clicked, calls $scope.closePost() and takes users back to state allPosts.

App Entry Point (index.html)

When the user accesses localhost:8000 the **index.html** loads where AngularJS kicks in. Here we'll use some Bootstrap CSS to quickly create a layout for us. We also use the directive ui-view from ui.router module where our templates will load. Here is what **index.html** looks like:

```html
<!doctype html>
<html lang="en" ng-app="spBlogger">
<head>
  <meta charset="utf-8">
  <base href="/">
  <title>The Single Page Blogger</title>
  <link rel="stylesheet" href="css/bootstrap.min.css">
  <link rel="stylesheet" href="css/app.css">
  <link rel="stylesheet" href="modules/posts/css/posts.css">
</head>
<body>
  <div class="container">
    <br/>
    <div class="jumbotron text-center">
        <h1>The Single Page Blogger</h1>
        <p>One stop blogging solution</p>
    </div>
    <div ui-view></div>
    <div class="row footer">
        <div class="col-xs-12 text-center">
            <p>The Single Page Blogger <app-version/></p>
        </div>
    </div>
  </div>
</body>
</html>
    <script src="lib/angular/angular.min.js"></script>
    <script src="lib/angular-ui-router/angular-ui-router.min.js">
➥</script>
    <script src="js/app.js"></script>
    <script src="js/controllers.js"></script>
    <script src="js/directives.js"></script>
    <script src="js/filters.js"></script>
    <script src="js/services.js"></script>
```

```
    <script src="modules/posts/postModule.js"></script>
    <script src="modules/posts/js/controllers.js"></script>
    <script src="modules/posts/js/filters.js"></script>
    <script src="modules/posts/js/directives.js"></script>
    <script src="modules/posts/js/services.js"></script>
</html>
```

Be sure to download the updated **web-server.js** from the code archive and replace **scripts/web-server.js** with the new one. I have tweaked some code so that you just type `http://localhost:8000` and Node serves **index.html** automatically. If you open up the browser and go to `http://localhost:8000` you'll see the result, shown in Figure 6.1 and Figure 6.2.

Figure 6.1. Our blogging app, showing all of the posts

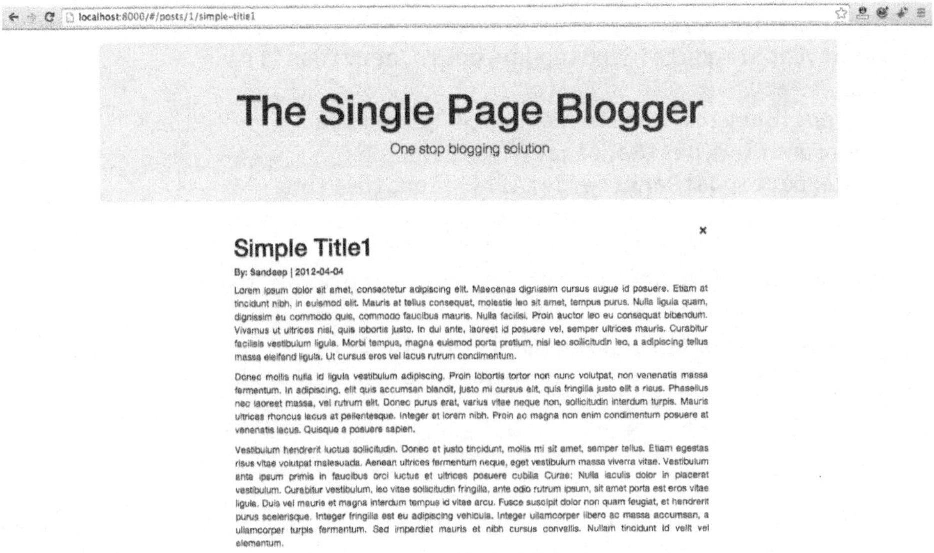

Figure 6.2. Our blogging app, showing a single post (lorem ipsum text added for testing purposes)

How About Some Unit Tests?

If you recall, in Chapter 1 we set up our test environment, but now it's actually time for us to embrace best practices and unit test our code. Having already seen why we unit test our code let's move towards the 'how' part and start with our service.

Before anything else, be sure to download **karma.conf.js** and **protractor-conf.js** from Chapter 6's codebase. The files should be (re)placed in the **/sp-blogger/config** directory.

Unit Testing `postService`

Let's unit test our `postService` to ascertain two things:

1. When `postService.getAll()` is called it returns four post objects. Here, I assume that we have four hard-coded posts in `postService` instance.

2. When we call `postService.getPostById(id)` passing two as the argument, we get only one post object.

Here is the test written in Jasmine syntax. Paste this into **sp-blogger/test/unit/servicesSpec.js**.

```
describe('postService test\n',function(){
    beforeEach(module('spBlogger.posts.services'));

    it('postService should return 4 post objects',
➥inject(function(postService){
        expect(postService.getAll().length).toBe(4);
    }));

    it('postService should return one object for id 2',
➥inject(function(postService){
        var post=postService.getPostById(2);
        expect(post).not.toBe(undefined);
    }));
});
```

We also need to tell Karma, the test runner, where to look for our modules. So, go to **karma-conf.js** present inside **sp-blogger/config** and make sure the following two lines are present in the `files` array:

```
'app/lib/angular-ui-router/angular-*.js', //for ui.router module
'app/modules/**/*.js' //for our app modules
```

Now run the script **scripts/test.sh** or **scripts/test.bat** as explained previously. On Mac you simply need to go to **sp-blogger/scripts** in the terminal and run `sh test.sh`. If you're on Windows just double-click on **test.bat**. If everything goes well, the Karma server will start. Click on the debug button and you'll be taken to the debug screen. If you open up the browser console you can see the test succeed with a message as shown in Figure 6.3.

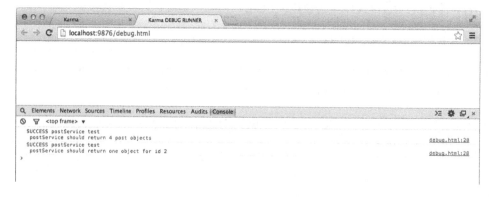

Figure 6.3. Successful Karma test of our app

Now let's understand what really happens in the above unit test.

1. The unit test you see above is written with Jasmine syntax. The `describe()` function is known as a test suite and groups a set of related tests. Inside this we can have multiple test specs. The `it()` function creates one such test spec.

2. The `beforeEach()` function runs before each `it()`. We want our module to be loaded before the `it()` function runs. So, we call the `module()` function with our module name `spBlogger.posts.services` and pass it to `beforeEach()`.

3. The `it()` function does the actual task. The first argument is a string indicating the result you expect from the test. You may pass `inject()` function as the second argument. The `inject()` function takes a callback where you can write your test spec and also declare your dependencies. In this case we ask for `postService` instance so that we can call the functions on it.

4. The first argument to `expect()` is the value you want to check and `toBe()` function takes the expected value. In case the value of the first argument does not match the expected value the test fails. You can play around with these values and tweak the tests to see them fail.

5. In the above cases, if you change value in `toBe()` or add or remove some hard-coded posts in the `postService` the tests will fail.

Now, if you change anything in your `postService` implementation, you ensure that you didn't break any of the previous code just by refreshing the browser.

Similarly, we can also unit test our controllers `PostController` and `PostDetailsController`.

Unit Testing Controllers

The following unit test validates that when the controller `PostController` is instantiated, the `$scope.posts` model is initialized with four posts. When the controller `PostDetailsController` is instantiated, we ensure that the model `$scope.singlePost` is initialized with a single post object. Make sure to put the test inside **sp-blogger/test/unit/controllersSpec.js**.

```
describe('PostController Test\n', function(){
  beforeEach(module('spBlogger.posts.controllers'));
  beforeEach(module('spBlogger.posts.services'));

  it('Should initialize controller with 4 posts',
➥inject(function($rootScope,$controller,postService) {
      var $scope=$rootScope.$new();
      $controller('PostController',{$scope:$scope,
➥postService:postService});
      expect($scope.posts.length).toBe(4);
  }));


});

describe('PostDetailsController Test\n', function(){
    beforeEach(module('spBlogger.posts.controllers'));
    beforeEach(module('ui.router'));
    beforeEach(module('spBlogger.posts.services'));

    it('Should initialize controller with 1 post',
➥inject(function($state,$stateParams,$rootScope,$controller,
➥postService) {
        var $scope=$rootScope.$new();
        $stateParams.id=2;
        $controller('PostDetailsController',{$scope:$scope,
➥$stateParams:$stateParams,$state:$state,postService:postService});
        expect($scope.singlePost).not.toBe(undefined);
    }));

});
```

Now if you refresh the browser you can see the result of this new test. Figure 6.4 is how it looks on my machine.

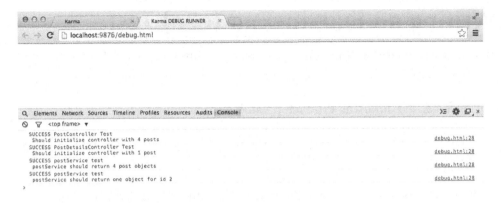

Figure 6.4. Testing the controllers

The unit test for our controllers is similar to the one created previously, with only a few differences:

1. We load the required modules using `beforeEach()` so that our components can be discovered.

2. We pass three and five dependencies to the callback passed to `inject()` for `PostController` and `PostDetailsController` respectively .

3. The `$controller` is a built in AngularJS service which instantiates a controller. While instantiating we pass the required dependencies to it.

4. The `$rootScope.$new()` creates a new child `$scope` needed by our controller.

5. The first test spec is pretty simple. But in the second test spec we assume that the app is in state `singlePost`. So, we grab the `$stateParams` service and set `$stateParams.id` to two explicitly. Finally, `$state` along with `$stateParams` and `postService` are passed to `$controller`.

6. Once the controller is instantiated, in the first test spec we validate that `$scope.posts` model has four objects. In the second one we validate that `$scope.singlePost` is an object and not undefined.

We have just two unit tests for now. As we develop more features, we'll create more such tests.

Writing an End-to-End (e2e) Test

Now that we've written some unit tests, let's wrap up with a simple e2e test. Note that the protractor configurations are present in **sp-blogger/config/protractor-conf.js**.

This test, carried out using Protractor, validates two things:

1. When the users navigate to `http://localhost:8000` the state `allPosts` loads and they see four posts.

2. When the first post is clicked, the new route with URL `http://local-host:8000/#/posts/1/simple-title1` loads.

So, here is the e2e test that should go into **sp-blogger/test/e2e/scenarios.js**.

```
describe('The Single Page Blogger E2E Test', function() {

  browser.get('/'); //go to http://localhost:8000

  protractor = protractor.getInstance();

  it('Should have 4 posts', function() {
    var posts = element.all(by.repeater('post in posts'));
    expect(posts.count()).toBe(4); // we have 4 hard coded posts
  });

  it('Should redirect to #/posts/1/sample-title1', function() {
    var posts = element.all(by.repeater('post in posts'));
    posts.first().then(function(postElem) {
        postElem.findElement(by.tagName('a')).then(function(a) {
            a.click(); //click the title link of 1st post
            expect(protractor.getCurrentUrl()).toMatch
➥('/posts/1/simple-title1');
        });
    });
  });

});
```

Now if you run **scripts/e2e-test.sh** or **scripts/e2e-test.bat** (depending on your OS) you can see the test succeed! Let's have a closer look at the above test scenario to understand more about e2e tests:

1. With the help of Protractor we programmatically open the HTML page, click links just like a real user would, and finally check the outcome.

2. `browser.get()` function accepts the HTML file name where we want to conduct the tests.

3. `element.all(by.repeater('post in posts'));` accepts the repeater expression present in the view and returns the number of elements present. Since we have four hard-coded posts in the service, the value obtained here must exactly be four.

4. Next, we want to validate that when someone clicks on the first post, he is taken to the URL `http://localhost:8000/posts/1/simple-title1`.

5. `posts.first()` let's grab the first post element in the repeater. We pass a callback to `posts.first().then()`, which is subsequently called by Protractor with the first element as an argument.

6. `findElement()` and `by.tagName()` together help us select the `<a>` tag (hyperlink on post title) present on the view for the first post. When we say `a.click()`, this link is clicked and in the next step we make sure the newly loaded URL matches the expected URL.

This was our first taste of End-to-End tests with Protractor. We'll see more variations as we progress.

Conclusion

In this chapter, we finally started making significant progress with our demo app! We developed some components for it and also unit tested them to make sure everything works as expected. In the end we also saw how to run End-to-End tests. At this point we are confident about creating routes, controllers and services for our app. The next chapter will show how you can accept user inputs and take the app one step further with AngularJS forms.

Understanding AngularJS Forms

A form is one of the basic requirements for any CRUD app. You'll likely have different forms for different kind of operations. The good news is that AngularJS offers a nice form API that, not only lets you bind form controls to scope models, but also allows you to validate each control easily. This chapter will focus on form handling and validation in AngularJS.

AngularJS Forms

What's a form? Well, it's just a container that groups several related input controls together. A control is an HTML element (such as `input`, `select`, `textarea`) that lets users enter data. You already know AngularJS provides us with the very useful `ng-model` directive that keeps the input control value and `scope` model in sync. So, to begin with, let's see how you can use `ng-model` with different input controls.

 The `<form>` Element

Please note that in the following examples, the `<form>` element isn't doing anything extra. All the data bindings will still work without `<form>`. Later on, we will see how the `<form>` element is useful.

`<input>` and `<textarea>` controls

As you've already seen, to tie the input control value to a `scope` model, you need to attach the `ng-model` directive to it:

```
<form name="myform">
    <input type="text" name="firstname" ng-model="user.firstname" />
</form>
```

By doing this you bind the `input` field's value to the `scope` model `user.firstname`. A `textarea` can also be bound to a `scope` model in exactly the same way:

```
<form name="myform">
    <textarea name="bio" ng-model="user.bio"></textarea>
</form>
```

Now, let's see some more controls we haven't used so far.

`<select>` control

To bind the selected option of a `<select>` element to the `scope` model you need to use the `ng-model` directive as follows.

```
<form name="myform">
  <select name="country" ng-model="user.country">
    <option value="US">United States</option>
    <option value="GB">United Kingdom</option>
    <option value="AU">Australia</option>
  </select>
</form>
```

In this case whatever value you select is passed to the `$scope.user.country` model. There is nothing extra you need to do. AngularJS automatically detects the currently selected option and sets it to the `scope` model.

Handling Empty Options

One of the common problems encountered while dealing with `<select>` is that, initially, AngularJS automatically inserts an empty `<option>` to the `<select>`. This is because, to begin with, `$scope.user.country` doesn't match any option values. So, in the above example, you'll see an empty option in addition to the three

country options. To ensure this doesn't happen you can insert something like this
to the `<select>`:

```html
<select name="country" ng-model="user.country">
    <option value="">Please select an option</option>
    <option value="US">United States</option>
    <option value="GB">United Kingdom</option>
    <option value="AU">Australia</option>
</select>
```

If you do this, the first option in the select drop down will be `Please select an
option` rather than an empty value.

Getting Options From the Scope Model

In a real world app you would most likely fetch the different options for the select
menu via a web service and store them in a scope model. The next task for you is
to loop through the array of options and generate the select menu dynamically. This
can be achieved easily with the `ng-options` directive. So, let's modify our previous
snippet to do this.

Script:

```html
<script type="text/javascript">
  angular.module('myApp', []).controller('UserController',
➡function($scope) {
    $scope.user = {};
    $scope.countries = [{
      id: 'US',
      desc: 'United States'
    }, {
      id: 'GB',
      desc: 'United Kingdom'
    }, {
      id: 'AU',
      desc: 'Australia'
    }];
  });
</script>
```

HTML Markup:

```
<body ng-controller="UserController">
  <form name="myform">
    <select name="country" ng-model="user.country" ng-options=
➡"country.id as country.desc for country in countries">
    </select>
  </form>
  <div>Selected Country: {{user.country}}</div>
</body>
```

As you can see, we have a scope model $scope.countries, which holds an array of country objects. Right now it's hard coded. Each object has two properties : id and desc. Now take a look at the ng-options directive attached to <select>. Its value is as follows:

```
ng-options="country.id as country.desc for country in countries"
```

We can break the above expression into two smaller chunks.

1. Loop through the countries array present in $scope and in each loop assign the current object to the variable country.

2. Create an <option> element. The value attribute of the element should be country.id. The actual label that the users will see should be country.desc.

As we have three objects in the array AngularJS will create three <option> elements for our select menu. After that, the value you select will go into the scope model $scope.user.country. As usual there will also be an empty value in the select initially. This can be resolved by writing something like this:

```
<select name="country" ng-model="user.country" ng-options=
➡"country.id as country.desc for country in countries">
  <option value="">Please select an option</option>
</select>
```

 ### Adjusting the Code to Return the Country Object

When you select an option in the drop-down the scope model $scope.user.country is set to the value of country.id (country represents the selected country in drop-down) and *not* the country object. So, if you want to have the actual country object you can tweak ng-options as follows:

```
ng-options="country as country.desc for country in countries"
```

Note we're not using `country.id as country.desc`. Rather we use `country as country.desc`. So, when an option is selected in the drop-down, your scope model `user.country` is assigned to the selected `country` object.

Handling Multi Select

If you attach an attribute `multiple` to a `<select>` then it becomes a multi select. This means users are allowed to select multiple options rather than just one. In that case if you have `ng-model` attached to the `<select>`, the scope model will hold an array of choices rather than just a string. Try adding a `multiple` attribute to the select element in above snippet to see the change.

Radio Button Control

Assume that you have a set of radio buttons, out of which only a single button can be selected. In this case you can use `ng-model` as follows:

Script:

```
<script type="text/javascript">
  angular.module('myApp', []).controller('UserController',
➡function($scope) {
    $scope.user = {};
  });
</script>
```

HTML Markup:

```
<body ng-controller="UserController">
  Hey, what do you love?
  <form name="myform">
    <input type="radio" ng-model="user.choice" value="Coffee" />
➡Coffee
    <input type="radio" ng-model="user.choice" value="Beer" />
➡Beer
```

```
  </form>
  <div>I love: {{user.choice}}</div>
</body>
```

Basically, you need to bind multiple radio buttons to the same `ng-model` and the `scope` model will be updated with the currently selected value.

Checkbox Control

Binding checkboxes to a scope model is very simple and can be done like this:

```
<body ng-controller="UserController">
  Hey, do you love coffee?
  <form name="myform">
    <input type="checkbox" ng-model="user.choice" />Coffee
  </form>
  <div>{{user.choice}}</div>
</body>
```

For the sake of brevity I'm only showing the markup that's been altered. In this case, if the checkbox is checked the `scope` model `user.choice` will be set to `true`. Similarly, when it's left unchecked the value of scope model will be `false`. If a true/false combo doesn't suit, you can use the `ng-true-value` and `ng-false-value` to set a custom value. Here is how you do it:

```
<input type="checkbox" ng-model="user.choice" ng-true-value="yes"
➥ ng-false-value="no"/>Coffee
```

Now, the scope model `user.choice` will be set to yes or no, depending on whether the checkbox is checked or unchecked.

Okay, we've discussed using different controls. Now let's see how we can easily validate our forms while providing instant feedback to our users.

AngularJS Form Validation

Validating form controls and providing feedback to users is very important. To provide the best experience, users should be immediately notified about any errors and allowed to correct them. As discussed above, AngularJS is pretty good at this;

it offers a well-defined API to validate forms and notify the users about errors intuitively. Let's see how to use it.

Don't Forget Server-Side Validation

Although doing client-side validation is good, it can be easily bypassed. So, in addition to client-side validation, you should always have validation on the server side. That way, even if somebody bypasses your AngularJS validation you're still protected.

When you write a `<form>` element in AngularJS, it has a special meaning. A `form` is an AngularJS directive. When we reach the directives chapter, you'll discover that directives can also have controllers associated with them. An AngularJS `form` directive instantiates a `FormController`, which keeps track of its child controls and their states (such as valid, invalid, etc.). If you attach a `name` attribute to `<form>` (thereby giving it a name) then the `FormController` instance is published to the enclosing scope under that name. Similarly, an `ng-model` directive instantiates `NgModelController` and, if you attach a `name` attribute to the field, the instance is published to the enclosing scope. `NgModelController` exposes an API to validate the field, format or parse the values, track the field state, etc.

Having these things in mind, let's modify our previous examples, add some more fields to the `<form>`, and validate them as follows:

1. The **First Name** and **Last Name** fields should be mandatory and should contain a minimum of two characters.

2. The phone number field is optional and should contain exactly 10 digits, if filled.

AngularJS offers a set of built-in directives to validate form controls:

1. `ng-maxlength`: Validates the maximum allowable characters in a field.

2. `ng-minlength`: Validates the minimum allowable characters in a field.

3. `ng-required`: Marks the fields that are mandatory.

4. `ng-pattern`: Validates a field against a given **regex** (regular expression).

Let's create a simple form with **First Name**, **Last Name** and **Phone Number** fields, and validate them with the built-in AngularJS directives:

```html
<html ng-app="myApp">

<head>
  <title>AngularJS Form Validation</title>
  <script src="https://code.angularjs.org/1.2.16/angular.js">
➥</script>
  <script type="text/javascript">
    angular.module('myApp', []).controller('UserController',
➥function($scope) {
      $scope.user = {};
    });
  </script>
  <style>
    .error-message {
      color: red;
    }
    input.ng-dirty.ng-invalid {
      border-color: red;
    }
  </style>
</head>

<body ng-controller="UserController">
  <form name="myform" novalidate>
    First Name:
    <input type="text" name="firstname" ng-model="user.firstname"
➥ ng-required="true" ng-minlength="2" />
    <span class="error-message" ng-show="myform.firstname.$dirty
➥&& myform.firstname.$error.required">The First Name is Mandatory
➥</span>
    <span class="error-message" ng-show="myform.firstname.$dirty
➥&& myform.firstname.$error.minlength">The First Name should be
➥minimum 2 characters</span>


    <br/>Last Name :
    <input type="text" name="lastname" ng-model="user.lastname"
➥ng-required="true" ng-minlength="2" />
    <span class="error-message" ng-show="myform.lastname.$dirty
➥&& myform.lastname.$error.required">The Last Name is Mandatory
➥</span>
    <span class="error-message" ng-show="myform.lastname.$dirty
```

```
➥&& myform.lastname.$error.minlength">The Last Name should be
➥minimum 2 characters</span>

    <br/>Phone No. :
    <input type="text" name="phoneNumber" ng-model="user.phoneNumber"
➥ng-maxlength="10" ng-minlength="10" ng-pattern="/^\d{10}$/" />
    <span class="error-message" ng-show="myform.phoneNumber.$dirty
➥&& myform.phoneNumber.$invalid">The phone number field should be
➥of 10 digits</span>
    <br/>
  </form>
</body>

</html>
```

If you type into the fields (first name and last name) and erase them you'll see an error message. Also, you'll see validation errors until the fields contain a minimum of two characters. Similarly, as you type into the phone number field you'll see an error message until the value is 10 characters long and consists of numbers only.

Let's take a look at what's happening behind the scenes.

Applying Validation

You can attach the built-in validation directives listed above to kick-start the validation process. AngularJS will apply the validation automatically once you attach a validation directive. The next step for you is to detect when the fields become invalid and show corresponding error messages.

Tracking Validity of a Form

As I mentioned earlier, the `form` directive publishes an instance of `FormController` into the scope. In this case, the name of our form is `myform`. So, we automatically get a model `myform` in the `$scope` passed to `UserController` and, as you know, we can use this model in our view. This scope model has various properties that let us track the status of our form. These are as follows

1. `$pristine`: If true then the user has not started interacting with our form. Once the user interacts with the form, the `$pristine` property is set to false. So, in our case you can use `myform.$pristine` to track whether a user has interacted with the form or not.

2. $dirty: This is the reverse of $pristine. Initially, the property $dirty is set to false. Once the user starts interacting with any of the form controls, the form becomes dirty and $dirty property is set to true. Ideally, we don't want to show any validation messages until the user starts interacting with the form. In that case you can use $dirty property to check whether the form is dirty or not.

3. $valid: The $valid property of the form is set to true when all the individual fields of a form become valid. So, in our case we can just check myform.$valid to make sure we are displaying error messages only after the user starts interacting with our form.

4. $invalid: The $invalid property of the form is set to true if at least one field in the form is invalid.

You should also note that all the above properties are also available at the individual field level. As you know, the ng-model directive publishes an instance of NgModel-Controller to the scope. This model also exposes the four properties discussed above to track the status of the particular field. For example, when you say my-form.firstname.$valid you are checking the validity of the individual field (firstname) rather than the form. When all these individual fields become valid, the enclosing form becomes valid. Similarly, you can check other properties like $pristine, $dirty and $invalid at the field level.

In the previous snippet, we first added novalidate to our form so that the default HTML5 validation is turned off. We do this because we don't want the browser to apply its own validation. Our AngularJS code will take care of validation here, and prevent the form from getting submitted in case of validation errors. We attach the ng-required directive to the firstname and lastname fields so that they are always filled before the form is submitted. We also use ng-minlength to make sure firstname and lastname are at least two characters long.

Now we need to show different error messages for these fields depending on the type of error present. This is because we have multiple validators attached to the first name and last name fields and they can go into $invalid state due to any of the validations. So, you can use $error property which contains all the validation errors associated with the field as keys. We can use different keys for showing different validation messages. Take a look at the following list to know the key names in form.fieldName.$error for different validators:

1. ng-required: form.fieldName.$error.required

2. ng-maxlength: form.fieldName.$error.maxlength

3. ng-minlength: form.fieldName.$error.minlength

4. ng-pattern: form.fieldName.$error.pattern

In our form above we are using ng-show="myform.firstname.$error.required" to show a particular error message for required validation errors. When the error is related to minlength we use ng-show="myform.firstname.$error.minlength" to show a different error message.

We also need to ensure that the error message is displayed only after the user interacts with the field (in other words, when the field is dirty). So, we write:

```
<span class="error-message" ng-show="myform.firstname.$dirty &&
➥myform.firstname.$error.required"></span>
```

This way our message is displayed only if the field is dirty and not valid.

Next, we need to validate that the phoneNumber should be of exactly 10 digits. Note that phoneNumber field is optional and should only be validated if it's filled. So, we use ng-pattern to validate that the field contains exactly 10 digits and omit the ng-required directive to make it optional. ng-pattern can take a regular expression (regex) and validate the field against it. So, I have used the regex /^\d{10}$/ to make sure non-digit characters are not allowed and exactly 10 digits are present. If you have some other constraints you can roll out your own regex and use it with ng-pattern. Since there is only one validator attached to phoneNumber field we can simply do the following to display a message in case of validation error:

```
<span class="error-message" ng-show="myform.phoneNumber.$dirty &&
➥myform.phoneNumber.$invalid">The phone number field should be
➥of 10 digits</span>
```

Applying Color to Invalid Input controls and Messages

When an input control becomes invalid due to some validation errors AngularJS automatically adds the ng-invalid class to it. So, you can easily write CSS rules against this class so that, for example, the field becomes red (or any color you wish) when a user types some incorrect value and the field becomes invalid. Also when the field becomes valid again, AngularJS remembers to take out that `ng-invalid` class and add `ng-valid` to the field, and so the input field looks normal again..

In our form we're using the following CSS to trigger this:

```
input.ng-dirty.ng-invalid{
    border-color:red;
}
```

The following CSS is used to display the error message inside <span> in a red color:

```
.error-message {
    color: red;
}
```

Form Submission

So far so good. We've validated our fields. But how do you submit an AngularJS form? To do that, you simply attach `ng-submit` to the <form> and pass a function to it. Then you'll need an <input type="submit"/> button somewhere in the form to trigger the submission. Further inside the submission handler function you can check whether the form is valid or invalid and proceed accordingly.

Here's how to modify our form to trigger submission:

1. Add <input type="submit" value="Save"/> to the <form>

2. Add a function to scope that will handle the form submission. This is done in the controller.

```
$scope.saveUser = function() {
    if($scope.myform.$valid)
        console.log('saving user'); // save $scope.user object
    else
        console.log('Unable to save. Validation error!');
}
```

3. Attach `ng-submit` to our <form>:

```
ng-submit="saveUser()"
```

So, when the user clicks the submit button, `$scope.saveUser()` runs. Inside the function you can check `$scope.myform.$valid` to ensure that the form is valid and proceed with the submission. Remember that a form is valid when all the fields of the form are valid.

Using ng-form

There is also an `ng-form` directive which is useful if you want to nest forms. Actually, the browser won't allow you to nest forms by default. So, if you have a form and want to group together a set of elements inside it, you can use `ng-form`.

You should note that `ng-form` is *not* a replacement for the `form` directive. `ng-form` should only be used to group fields and check their validity. You might wonder why we need this extra `ng-form` directive. Why we can't just use a normal `div` to group several form controls inside the main form? Well, `ng-form` comes to the rescue when we dynamically output `input` controls and need to validate those. Take a look at the following code:

```
<body ng-controller="MainController">
  <form name="outer">
    <div ng-repeat="item in items" ng-form="inner">
      Name:
      <input ng-model="item.name" name="name" ng-required="true" />
➡<span ng-show="inner.name.$dirty && inner.name.$invalid">
➡Name is required</span>
      <br/>Price:
      <input ng-model="item.price" name="price" ng-required="true"
➡/><span ng-show="inner.price.$dirty && inner.price.$invalid">
➡Price is required</span>
      <hr/>
    </div>
  </form>
</body>
```

Here, based on the number of `items` present in the `scope`, we'll output input controls. If you didn't use `ng-form` as shown above and used a `div` to group the `input` controls, we won't, now, be able to validate them. Like `form`, `ng-form` accepts a name and publishes the `FormController` to the enclosing scope. In each iteration we can refer to this name and apply validations to the dynamically output fields.

Custom Validators

While built-in validators certainly come in handy, in real-world apps you'll often need to create custom validators to validate data. AngularJS has full support for creating custom validators through directives. But we're not going to cover directives for a while yet! So, let's save custom validators for our chapter on directives.

Updating Models With a Twist

Here, I'd like to mention something interesting. While accepting user inputs, sometimes, you'll want to trigger model updates in a different way. As you already know, `ng-model` attaches a `keydown` listener to the input field so that, each time someone types into it, the scope model gets updated. But you may want to trigger the view to model update on some other event, such as `mousedown` or `blur`. For example, you may like to update the model only when the input field loses focus. So, you can tell AngularJS to update the scope model on a `blur` event. This is done through the `ng-model-options` directive:

```
<input type="text" ng-model="firstname" ng-model-options="
➡{updateOn: 'blur'}" />
```

In this case, the model doesn't get updated while the user is typing. Instead it updates when the field loses focus—in other words, when you click somewhere outside of the field. If you want to update the model on multiple DOM events you can do so. For example, the following snippet updates the model on both `blur` and `mousedown` events:

```
<input type="text" ng-model="firstname" ng-model-options="
➡{updateOn: 'blur mousedown'}" />
```

You can also preserve the default behavior i.e. updating the model as the user types and add additional events. This is done like this:

```
<input type="text" ng-model="firstname" ng-model-options="
➥{updateOn: ' default blur mousedown'}" />
```

You also get another feature with `ng-model-options`: You can perform debounced model updates with the `debounce` property in `ng-model-options`. Debounced update means the model should not be updated immediately. By default when the DOM event fires, the `ng-model` updates the scope model immediately. But if you want to introduce some delay before the model update you can use `debounce`. The following snippet explains this:

```
<input type="text" ng-model="firstname" ng-model-options="
➥{updateOn: 'blur', debounce:100}" />
```

The above snippet introduces a100 millisecond delay while updating the model. If you want different delay periods for different events you can do so like this:

```
➥<input type="text" ng-model="firstname" ng-model-options="
➥{updateOn: 'blur', debounce:{default: 100, blur:200}}" />
```

In default case, the model update gets delayed by 100 ms and in case of `blur` the delay is 200 ms.

Forms in Action : Single Page Blogger v1.1

We've discussed many aspects of AngularJS forms. Now let's add a simple form to our example app that takes inputs from the admin to create a blog post. We won't create the post or store it somewhere. We'll just create a form and validate it to reinforce the concepts discussed in this chapter.

Post CRUD operations is the functionality of the admin panel. So, first we need to create an admin module and define the states. For now we won't implement any authentication or authorization. The aim is that, when we type the URL for the admin panel in the browser, our route should load. Later on, when we have the admin panel completely ready we'll implement authentication or authorization.

Creating the `admin` Module

The admin module is created in the same way as the `posts` module. Take a look at the screenshot shown in Figure 7.1 see the differences.

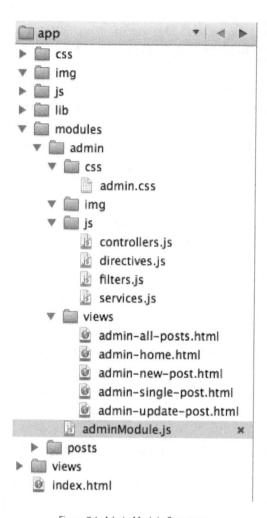

Figure 7.1. Admin Module Structure

Defining States

Now we need to define some states using the ui.router module. The content should go into **modules/admin/adminModule.js**:

```
angular.module('spBlogger.admin').config(['$stateProvider',
➡function($stateProvider){
    $stateProvider.state('admin',{
        url:'/admin',
        abstract:true,
        controller:'AdminController',
        templateUrl:'modules/admin/views/admin-home.html'
```

```
    }).state('admin.postNew',{
        url:'/posts/new',
        controller: 'PostCreationController',
        templateUrl:'modules/admin/views/admin-new-post.html'
    }).state('admin.postUpdate',{
        url:'/posts/:id/edit',
        controller: 'PostUpdateController',
        templateUrl:'modules/admin/views/admin-update-post.html'
    }).state('admin.postViewAll',{
        url:'',
        controller: 'PostListController',
        templateUrl:'modules/admin/views/admin-all-posts.html'
    });
}]);
```

As you see, `AdminPanelController` is the central control that'll be used for the admin panel. For CRUD operations, we have different states with different controllers.

In UI router, states can be nested. The `templateUrl` of state `admin` (**modules/admin/views/admin-home.html**) has a sidebar and also a `ui-view`. The sidebar contains all the admin operations like "Create Post", "Update Post", etc. The `ui-view` is used for loading the child states of `admin`. You should also note that in UI router if you use a period . in the name of a state, say, `admin.postViewAll`, then the part after the period (in this case `postViewAll`) becomes a child to the part before the period (in this case, `admin`). So here we have three child states of `admin`: `admin.postNew`, `admin.postUpdate`, `admin.postViewAll`. You can see that the state `admin` is marked as `abstract`. This means the state can't be activated directly. Rather it will be loaded when any of its child states is activated. As we have set the `url` of state `admin.postViewAll` to `''`, this becomes the default child state. This means when the state `admin` loads, its `ui-view` is automatically loaded with its child state `admin.postViewAll`.

Creating Controllers

Now the following controllers should go into **modules/admin/js/controllers.js**:

```
angular.module('spBlogger.admin.controllers',[]).
➥controller('AdminController',['$scope',function($scope){

}]).controller('PostCreationController',['$scope',function($scope){
```

```
}]).controller('PostUpdateController',['$scope',function($scope){

}]).controller('PostListController',['$scope',function($scope){

}]);
```

The controllers don't do anything yet, but we'll fill them later on.

Admin Panel Template

The template for Admin Panel is added to **modules/admin/views/admin-home.html**. The content is as follows:

```
<div class="row">
    <div class="col-xs-3">
        <ul class="nav nav-pills nav-stacked on-click-make-active">
            <!--Loads admin.viewAll state, doesn't contain
➥anything right now -->
            <li><a ui-sref="admin.viewAll">View All Posts</a></li>
            <!--Loads admin.postNew state -->
            <li class="active"><a ui-sref="admin.postNew">Add Post
➥</a></li>
        </ul>
    </div>

    <div class="col-xs-9 border-left">
        <div ui-view></div> <!--The nested views are loaded here -->
    </div>

</div>
```

We are using nested views here. When the admin state is activated the above template will be loaded into ui-view present in index.html. But when the state for adding a new post, i.e. newPost is activated, its template (**admin-new-post.html**) is loaded into ui-view present in the above template. If you look at the states you'll see that the states for CRUD operations are prefixed with admin. So, from this ui.router knows that the CRUD states are nested inside admin state.

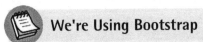

We're Using Bootstrap

We are using Bootstrap 3 to quickly create layouts.

Template For Adding a New Post

Here, we'll create a template that contains a simple form to get inputs from admin in order to create a new post. The file is named **admin-new-post.html** and goes into **modules/admin/views**. The validation rules are simple and as follows:

1. The Post Title and Content are mandatory.

2. The Keywords and Tags fields can't contain any special characters, except commas.

3. The Add Post button is enabled only when all the validation conditions are satisfied.

```
<div class="row">
    <div class="col-xs-8">
        <form name="newPostForm" class="form-horizontal" novalidate
►role="form">
            <div class="form-group" ng-class="{'has-error'
►:newPostForm.title.$dirty && newPostForm.title.$invalid}">
                <label for="title" class="col-sm-2 control-label">
►Post Title</label>
                <div class="col-sm-10">
                    <input type="text" name="title" ng-model=
►"post.title" ng-required="true" class="form-control" id="title"
►placeholder="Title">
                    <span class="error-message" ng-show="newPostForm.
►title.$dirty && newPostForm.title.$invalid">Title is mandatory
►</span>
                </div>
            </div>
            <div class="form-group" ng-class="{'has-error':
►newPostForm.content.$dirty && newPostForm.content.$invalid}">
                <label for="content" class="col-sm-2 control-label">
►Content</label>
                <div class="col-sm-10">
                    <textarea cols="8" rows="6" name="content"
►class="form-control" ng-model="post.content" ng-required="true"
►id="content" placeholder="Content"></textarea>
```

```
                       <span class="error-message" ng-show="newPostForm.
➡content.$dirty && newPostForm.content.$invalid">You need to have
➡some content!</span>
                   </div>
               </div>
               <div class="form-group" ng-class="{'has-error':
➡newPostForm.tags.$dirty && newPostForm.tags.$invalid}">
                   <label for="tags" class="col-sm-2 control-label">
➡Tags</label>
                   <div class="col-sm-10">
                       <input type="text" name="tags"
➡class="form-control" id="tags" ng-pattern="/^[\w,]+$/"
➡ ng-model="post.tags" placeholder="Comma separated tags"/>
                       <span class="error-message" ng-show="newPostForm
➡.tags.$dirty && newPostForm.tags.$invalid">Sorry! No special
➡characters allowed here.</span>
                   </div>
               </div>
               <div class="form-group" ng-class="{'has-error':
➡newPostForm.keywords.$dirty && newPostForm.keywords.$invalid}">
                   <label for="keywords" class="col-sm-2
➡control-label">Keywords</label>
                   <div class="col-sm-10">
                       <input type="text" name="keywords" class=
➡"form-control" id="keywords" ng-pattern="/^[\w,]+$/"
➡ng-model="post.keywords" placeholder="Comma separated keywords"/>
                       <span class="error-message" ng-show="newPostForm.
➡keywords.$dirty && newPostForm.keywords.$invalid">Sorry! No special
➡ characters allowed here</span>
                   </div>
               </div>
               <div class="form-group">
                   <div class="col-sm-offset-2 col-sm-10">
                       <button type="submit" class="btn btn-success"
➡ ng-disabled="newPostForm.$invalid">Add Post</button>
                   </div>
               </div>
           </form>
       </div>
</div>
```

Now we're all set. If you type http://localhost:8000/#/admin/posts/new in your browser you'll be taken to this form. Take a look at the screenshot in Figure 7.2 to check it out.

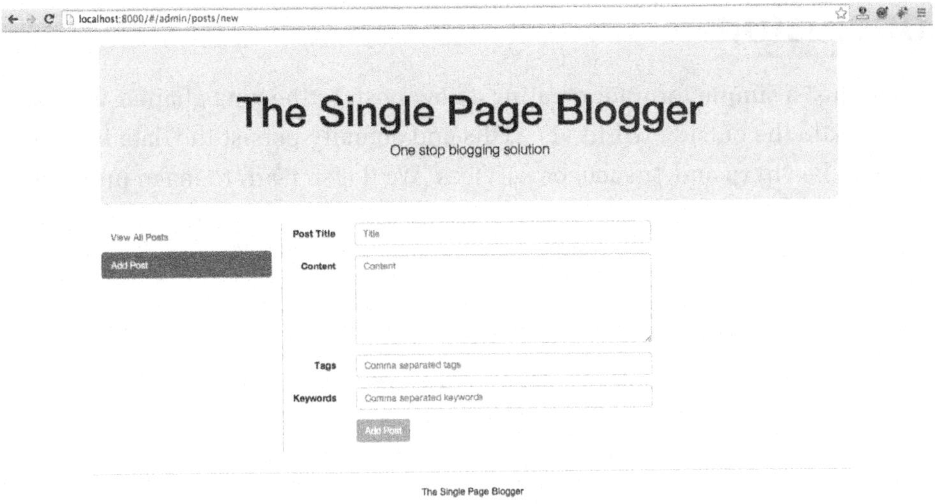

Figure 7.2. The New Post Form

Now, the form looks like Figure 7.3 if the validation fails:

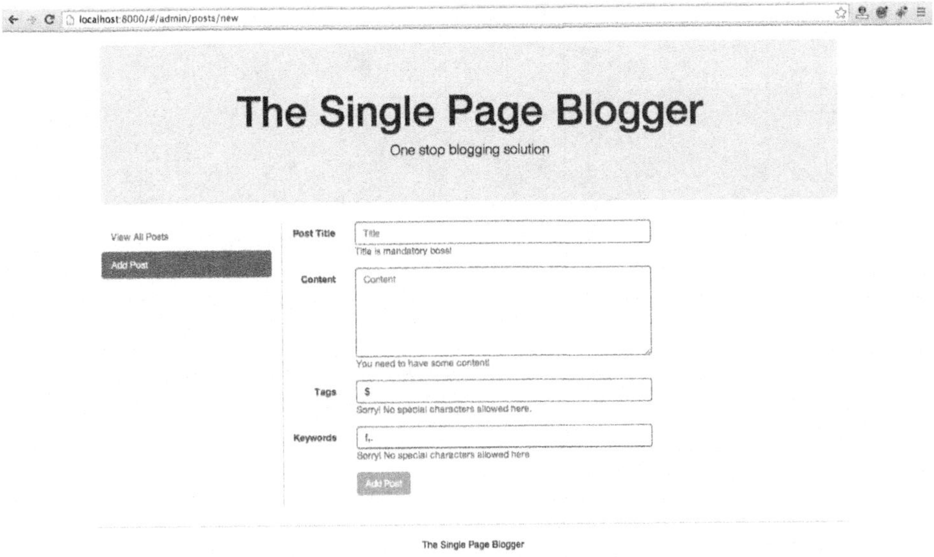

Figure 7.3. The New Post Form, with Failed Validations

We won't create any other forms for now. The other forms will be created as a part of CRUD operations when we'll learn to interact with REST APIs.

Conclusion

This was just a simple form for creating a new post. In the next chapter we'll see how to talk to the outside world via XHRs and actually persist the data in a back-end using the `$http` and `$resource` services. We'll also learn to make promises!

Interacting with REST APIs

Up to this point in our project, we've been storing all the blog posts in a custom service. But in a real-world app, you'll need to store your data in persistent storage: your server will normally expose a REST API, which will enable you to perform CRUD operations on your app. In AngularJS, we interact with these REST APIs using services such as $http and $resource. But before you do this, you need to be aware of a concept called **promises**. This chapter will first introduce the concept of promises and then explain how to work with REST APIs using $http and $resource.

In the next chapter we'll revamp our demo app to use a REST back-end to store our blog posts. We'll also see how to unit test controllers that involve REST interaction. Let's start with promises first. They're both fun and enjoyable (promise!)

A Primer on Promises

A promise object represents a value that may not be available yet, but will be at some point in future. It enables you to write asynchronous code in a more synchronous way. This means your asynchronous function will return immediately and you can treat this return value as a proxy to the actual value that'll be obtained in future.

A typical example of the use of a promise object is in an AJAX request to a remote server. If you use promises, your AJAX call should return a promise object immediately rather than waiting for a response. This won't hold any value yet; it just acts as a proxy to the actual value that will be received from the server later. When the AJAX request completes and an actual response arrives from the server, the `Promise` is resolved with that data. If the response can't be obtained due to some error, the promise is rejected with an error message. The promise object also exposes several methods that enable you to write callbacks, which will be called once the it's resolved or rejected.

The figure shown in Figure 8.1 depicts the basic idea behind Promises:

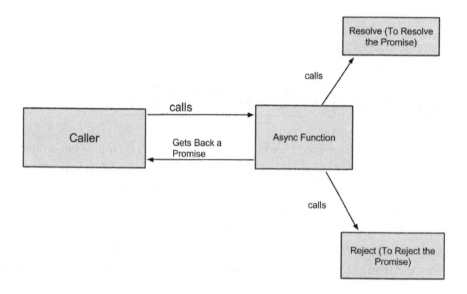

Figure 8.1. How promises work

Let's take a look at some pseudo code that logs in a user and (once the login is successful) performs some other task. In the first scenario we pass a callback to `login()` that's called after login is successful:

```
user.login(username,password,function(){
    //This callback is passed to login() so that it's called only
➥after login is successful.
});
```

Now, here's the `login()` function returning a promise, and we use it to perform some task once login is successful:

```
user.login(username,password).then(function(){
    //do something here
});
```

The following section discusses the Promise API in detail.

The Promise API

AngularJS enables you to create and use promises through a built-in service called $q. The following pseudo code shows how to use the API exposed by $q:

```
function getPromise(){

    var deferred=$q.defer(); // Line 1 : Creates a new deferred
➥object

    doAsyncTask(function(err,data){
        if(err)
            deferred.reject('Promise Rejected'); // Reject the
➥Promise associated with the deferred object
        else
            deferred.resolve('Promise Resolved'); // Resolve the
➥Promise associated with the deferred object
    });

    return deferred.promise;    //return the Promise associated with
➥the deferred object

}
```

Assuming $q is available in the scope, the method `$q.defer()` creates a new deferred object, which has an associated Promise instance. Within the code is an imaginary function `doAsyncTask()` that performs a task asynchronously . For instance, if you want to retrieve data from a remote server you'd make an AJAX call;

If you want to delay the execution of an expression you could use `$timeout/$interval` here. When the actual result of the operation is available you should resolve the associated promise by calling `deferred.resolve()`. In case of an error, you can reject the promise with an error message. This is done by calling `deferred.reject()`. The last thing to note is that the above function returns **immediately** with `deferred.promise` as the return value. So, whoever calls this function will get the promise instance in return.

$q Inspirations

The $q service was inspired by Kris Kowal's Q[1]. The difference is that $q is tightly integrated with the scope life cycle and contains all the features needed by common asynchronous tasks.

Let's see how we can deal with the promise:

```
function showResult(){

    var promise = getPromise(); // get the Promise instance

    promise.then(function(message) {
      console.log('Promise Resolved with Message: '+message);
    }, function(message) {
      console.log('Promise Rejected with Message: '+message);
    });
}
```

The function `getPromise()` returns a promise instance. This has a method `then()`, which takes three callbacks as follows:

```
promise.then(successCallback,failureCallback,notifyCallback);
```

The success callback is called when the promise is resolved (as a result of calling `deferred.resolve()`). The callback accepts one argument, which represents the resolution value (the value passed to `deferred.resolve()`). The second callback passed to `then()` is the error callback and is called when the `Promise` is rejected as a result of calling `deferred.reject()`. Again it accepts a single argument, which represents the rejection reason (the value passed to `deferred.reject()`). The third

---

[1] https://github.com/kriskowal/q

argument is the notify callback which may be called multiple times to indicate the operation progress (we'll see it shortly). Note that not every callback is mandatory. In the snippet above we only used the success callback. But if you don't provide an error callback you won't be able to know if your promise gets rejected. So, in most cases it's a good idea to pass both success and error callbacks.

Promise Resolution

A promise instance can be resolved or rejected only once in its lifetime. If a promise is not yet resolved/rejected it's said to be in a pending state. You should also note that in the world of promises we are not concerned about when a promise is resolved/rejected. Rather we're interested in the final outcome of the promise. So, if a promise has already been resolved and, later, you pass two callbacks to the `then()` function, the success callback will be correctly called. Since promises are resolved/rejected only once, if you try to resolve/reject a promise multiple times such operations will be ignored.

Promises Shorthand

You can also use `promise.catch(errorCallback)` for handling rejections. It's a shorthand for `promise.then(null,errorCallback)`

There is also a `promise.finally(callback)` method, which can be used to perform some tasks regardless of whether a promise is resolved or rejected. Use cases for this method include performing final cleanups, releasing resources etc. But beware! As `finally` is a reserved keyword in JavaScript you should write your method like `promise['finally'](callback)` to keep IE8 happy!

Example Usage

Keeping the above points in mind, let's simulate an asynchronous task using promises. First we need to create an empty controller as follows:

Controller:

```
angular.module('mainApp', []).controller('MainController',
➥['$scope','$q','$interval',function($scope, $q, $interval) {
```

```
    // we wil use $q here

}]);
```

Now, inside the controller, we'll attach a method to `$scope`, which will use the built-in `$interval` service to perform a simple task asynchronously:

getPromise():

```
$scope.getPromise = function() {
    var i = 0;
    var deferred = $q.defer(); //creates a new deferred object

    var timer = $interval(function() {

        if ( !! $scope.cancelRequested) { //if cancellation is
    ➥requested from UI, reject the Promise
            deferred.reject('Promise Rejected due to cancellation.');
            $interval.cancel(timer);
        }

        i = i + 1; //increment i each time

        if (i == 5) {
            deferred.resolve('Counter has reached 5'); //once the value
    ➥of i=5, resolve the promise
            $interval.cancel(timer); //make sure to cancel timer
        } else {
            deferred.notify('Counter has reached ' + i); //else notify
    ➥the client about the progress
        }
    }, 1000); //run the task every 1 second

    return deferred.promise; //finally, return the Promise instance
}
```

Our function is pretty simple. It runs a task every second and increments a variable i by 1. In each iteration we check if the value of i has reached 5. If so, we resolve the promise. Otherwise, we call `deferred.notify()` to notify the user about its progress. If the model $scope.cancelRequested is set to true, it means somebody has requested to cancel the task. In this case, we reject the promise and cancel the timer. Finally, the function returns `deferred.promise` to return the `Promise` instance to the caller.

Now, we need to add another function `getAsyncMessage()` to the `$scope` which calls the above function:

getAsyncMessage():

```
$scope.getAsyncMessage = function() {

    var promise = $scope.getPromise(); //get hold of the Promise
➥instance

    promise.then(function(message) {
      $scope.status = 'Resolved : ' + message;
    }, function(message) {
      $scope.status = 'Rejected : ' + message;
    }, function(message) {
      $scope.status = 'Notifying : ' + message;
    });
}
```

Here we get the promise instance by calling `$scope.getPromise()`. Next, we pass three callbacks to the function `promise.then()`. Notice the third callback. This is called whenever `deferred.notify()` is called while performing an asynchronous task. So, in our case, it'll execute multiple times while the first two callbacks will execute only once. Also note that, for a particular `Promise` instance, either the success callback or the error callback will be called, depending on whether the promise is resolved or rejected.

 Causing a $digest Cycle

When the different callbacks passed to `then()` execute, a `$digest()` cycle runs. So, if you change any **scope** models inside these callbacks (like we did above), the view will be updated.

Now, let's quickly create some markup that shows two buttons: One to start the asynchronous task and the other one to cancel it.

index.html:

```
<body ng-controller="MainController">

<input type="button" ng-click="getAsyncMessage()" value="Get me an
↪async message"/>
<input type="button" ng-click="cancelRequested=true" value="Cancel
↪Fetching Message"/><br/>
Promise Status - {{status}}
</body>
```

Now, if you hit the first button you'll see the task progress via the notify callback. Finally, when the promise is resolved, the `status` text will be updated with the resolution message. But if you cancel the task in the meantime, by clicking the second button,the promise will be rejected and the `status` text will be updated with the corresponding message.

Promise Chaining

Chaining is one of the most important aspects of promises. The basic idea is that promises can be composed through chaining. This means you can trigger a specified task *only* after previous promise has been resolved.

The function `promise.then()` returns another promise instance, which is resolved via the return value of a success callback. Take a look at the following example:

```
promise.then(function(message) {
  return "success";
}).then(function(message) {
  console.log(message); // prints "success"
});
```

Now we have two promises chained together. Note that the success callback passed to the first `then()` returns a simple value "success". So, the promise instance returned by `then()` is resolved immediately with the value `success`. As the second `then()` waits on this promise, the success callback passed to it gets called immediately.

But what if the success callback returns another promise instead of a simple value? How do we handle this? Let's modify our previous code:

```
promise.then(function(message) {
  //we have our message here
  return getAnotherPromise(); //return a promise here again
}).then(function(message) {
  //handle the final result
});
```

In this case the success callback to first `then()` returns another promise instance. So, the second `then()` waits on this promise until it's settled (resolved or rejected) and the appropriate callback is called with a resolution or rejection message as an argument. The figure shown in Figure 8.2 depicts what's happening here:

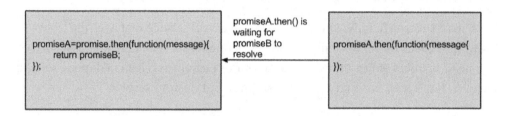

Figure 8.2. Promise chaining

Now that you have multiple promises chained you can attach a `catch()` to `promise` object (like `then()`) to handle any rejections.

Creating a Promise that Always Rejects

Sometimes it's useful to create and return a promise that is always rejected. This is useful if you want to tell a user about the occurrence of an error but in terms of a promise rather than a simple value.

For now let's see how to create such a promise:

```
function getPromise(){
    return $q.reject('Rejection Reason');
}
```

The above function creates a promise that's always rejected. So, if you attach a `then()` function to the returned promise instance and pass two callbacks the error callback will be correctly called.

```
getPromise().then(function(message) {
    // Doesn't get called
},function(message) {
    //This is called
});
```

The main focus of this chapter is to give you an idea about how to perform REST interaction with a back-end server. In AngularJS, you can talk to REST APIs through a service called $http, which heavily relies on promises. Now that you've seen promises, it's time for us to move on and learn about the $http service.

Understanding the $http Service

Let's meet $http officially. $http is a core AngularJS service that uses the browser's XMLHttpRequest object to communicate with remote servers. Like all other services you need to inject $http into your controller or custom service via dependency injection. Here's how you can inject $http into your custom service:

```
angular.module('mainModule',[]).service('customService',
➥function($http) {
  this.getData=function(){
    return $http({method:'GET',url:'/api'}); //use $http() here.
➥This function returns a Promise.
  }
});
```

The $http service is a function that accepts a single argument, called the config object.

This config object defines various parts of the HTTP request, such as method, url, data etc. As $http is based on the $q service, the return value of the function $http() is a promise instance. So, you can attach then() to it as usual and pass success/error callbacks that'll be called appropriately. So, here is how we can use the customService defined in the above snippet.

```
angular.module('mainModule').controller('TestController',
➥function($scope, customService) {
    $scope.getData=function(){
        customService.getData().then(function(data,status,config,
➥headers){
```

```
            console.log('Response from server: '+data); //called
➥when responses arrives from server
        },function(data,status,config,headers){
            console.log('Some error occurred!'); //called in case of
➥error
        });
    }
});
```

The success callback is called asynchronously when the request completes and the response arrives from the server. Similarly, in the case of any error the error callback is fired. These callbacks can even be rewritten as follows:

```
angular.module('mainModule').controller('TestController',
➥function($scope, customService) {
    $scope.getData=function(){
        customService.getData().success(function(data,status,config,
➥headers){
            console.log('Response from server: '+data); //called
➥when responses arrives from server
        }).error(function(data,status,config,headers){
            console.log('Some error occurred!'); //called in case of
➥error
        });
    }
});
```

Note the usage of success() and error() methods.

These callbacks accept the following parameters:

▓ data: This is the response obtained from server.

▓ status: The HTTP status code (e.g. 200, 401 etc) returned from server.

▓ config: The config object that was used to generate the request.

▓ headers: This is a map which contains the headers sent by the server.

▓ statusText: The HTTP status text (e.g. OK for 200) for the status code.

Now, you can either use $http() passing a config object to it or just use one of the following shorthand methods:

- `$http.get(url)`

- `$http.post(url,data)`

- `$http.put(url,data)`

- `$http.delete(url)`

- `$http.head(url)`

The above methods also accept an extra optional parameter, `config`, which is used to configure other parts of the request if any.

The `config` Object

The `config` object can be used to configure several options for generating the request. The most common properties that you're going to use are:

- `url`: The URL to which a request will be made. This may be relative or absolute. Just note that the URL should be from your own domain in order for `$http` to work. But if you want to work with remote URLs outside your domain the URLs must be CORS enabled. In other words, the remote server must specify that your domain is allowed to interact with it by setting a header called `Access-Control-Allow-Origin` in the response.

- `method`: This represents your request method i.e. GET, POST , PUT etc.

- `data`: If you're making a POST/PUT request you might need to send some data as request body. This is configured in the `data` property of `config` object and can either be a simple string or an object. In the case of an object, the `data` will be serialized to a JSON string before getting sent as request body.

- `headers`: This is a simple object for configuring the headers. The key corresponds to the header name and the value corresponds to the header value.

- `params`: If you're making a GET request and want to send query parameters (such as `?key1=value1&key2=value2`) you can configure that here via a simple object.

There are several other properties in the `config` object that we'll cover as we proceed.

Cross Origin Resource Sharing

When you provide a cross-domain URL to `$http`, the browser will first perform an OPTIONS request to the remote URL to check if `Access-Control-Allow-Origin` is present in the response. If it exists then it'll proceed with the actual request, or else, won't go any further.

You can learn more about CORS (Cross Origin Resource Sharing) at Wikipedia[2]. There is also a method called `$http.jsonp()`, which facilitates interaction with remote URLs, but it expects the server to return a response in a slightly different way. That said, in general, CORS is the modern way of doing things. If you want to support really old browsers (like IE 7 or earlier) you might want to use `jsonp`. If you want to have a CRUD API you're going to have a hard time with `jsonp`.

A Weather Search Service

Let's build something fun and practical to understand how `$http` works. In this section we'll build a simple AngularJS app that returns the current weather data for your favorite city.

The OpenWeatherMap[3] website exposes a nice API, which returns our required weather data. Let's see how to do it:

Assuming our main module has already been defined as `mainApp`, here is how we define our service:

```
angular.module('mainApp').factory('weatherService',
➥function($http) {
  return {
    getWeather: function(city, country) {
      var query = city + ',' + country;
      return $http.get('http://api.openweathermap.org/data/2.5/
➥weather', {
        params: {
          q: query
        }
      }).then(function(response) { //then() returns a promise which
➥is resolved with return value of success callback
        return response.data.weather[0].description; ///extract
```

---

[2] http://en.wikipedia.org/wiki/Cross-origin_resource_sharing
[3] http://openweathermap.org/

```
➥weather data
        });
    }
  }
});
```

Our API endpoint is : `http://api.openweathermap.org/data/2.5/weather`. It additionally expects a query parameter q, which should contain value in the following format:

```
?q=cityName,countryName
```

So, our custom service `weatherService` defines the `getWeather()` function, which accepts `city` and `country` and uses them to send a GET request to the API.

Now, we need to use this service in our controller as follows:

```
angular.module('mainApp').controller('WeatherController',
➥function($scope, weatherService) {
  $scope.getWeather = function() {
    $scope.weatherDescription = "Fetching . . .";
    weatherService.getWeather($scope.city, $scope.country).
➥then(function(data) {
      $scope.weatherDescription = data;
    }, function() {
      $scope.weatherDescription = "Could not obtain data";
    });
  }
});
```

As you can see we call `weatherService.getWeather()` and pass success and error callbacks to the promise returned by it. When the response comes from the remote server, the success callback is called, setting a scope model called `$scope.weather-Description`. The first parameter `data` to the success callback is the weather data returned by the server.

Also, just before making the request we change the `$scope` model `weatherDescription` to `Fetching . . .` so that the UI will be updated through data binding.

Finally, we create the view as follows:

```
<body ng-controller="WeatherController">
  City :
  <input type="text" ng-model="city" placeholder="Enter city name
➥here" />Country:
  <input type="text" ng-model="country" placeholder="Enter country
➥name here" />
  <button ng-click="getWeather()">Get Weather</button>
  <br/>
  <br/>
  <b>Weather Condition:</b>  <span>{{weatherDescription}}</span>
</body>
```

We simply ask the user for city and country names. When the button is clicked the controller method `getWeather()` is called to obtain the weather information.

If you open up the code archive and run this app, you will see the weather data as expected.

Setting Request Headers

If you want to configure headers for every HTTP request, you can do so in `config` block as follows:

```
angular.module('mainApp').configure(function($httpProvider){
    $httpProvider.defaults.headers.common.Accept="applcation/json";
});
```

Or in a run block, as a part of `$http.defaults`:

```
angular.module('mainApp').run(function($http){
    $http.defaults.headers.common.Accept="applcation/json";
});
```

If you need to configure headers only for PUT or POST requests you need to use the object `$httpProvider.defaults.headers.put` or `$httpProvider.defaults.headers.post`.

Apart from `post` and `put` if you want to configure headers for other requests (such as GET) you can do so as follows:

```
angular.module('mainApp').configure(function($httpProvider){
    $httpProvider.defaults.headers.get={'Content-Type':
➥'application/json'};
});
```

Please note the lowercase `get` in the above code!

The above was all about setting headers globally. But you might want to override the headers for a particular request. In that case you should set the `headers` property in the request `config` object. Take a look at the following code:

```
$http.({url:'/api',method:'GET',headers:{'Content-Type':
➥'text/plain'}});
```

In this example, we have safely overridden the headers for a particular request without changing global configurations.

Request and Response Transformers

Whenever we are using the `$http` service there are some transformations going on under the hood. These transformations are:

1. If you pass a JavaScript object as POST `data` in a POST/PUT request, it's serialized to JSON before getting sent.

2. Similarly, if the server responds with a JSON string it's parsed into a JavaScript object and passed to the success callback attached to the promise.

Apart from these, sometimes you might need to transform the request or response before sending the request or after receiving the response. You can do this by configuring `transformRequest` and `transformResponse` properties of `$httpProvider.defaults`.

transformRequest

The `transformRequest` property can be set to a function that accepts two parameters, *a and `getHeaders`, and returns a serialized version of `data`. Inside the function
n add or modify the headers, and also manipulate the `data` dynamically for
st. To put it another way, you get a chance to modify the request before
'ing it.

```
angular.module('mainApp',[]).config(function($httpProvider){
    $httpProvider.defaults.transformRequest=function(data,
➥getHeaders){
        var headers=getHeaders(); //obtain the headers
        headers['Content-Type']='text/plain'; // add a header
➥dynamically
        return JSON.stringify(data); //return serialized data
    }
});
```

You can also configure `transformRequest` property for a particular request in the config object.

```
$http.({url:'/api',method:'GET',
➥transformRequest:transformRequestFunc});
```

Using Multiple Request Transformers

If you directly assign a transformation function to `$httpProvider.defaults.transformRequest` it will be the only transformer and remove any other request transformers that were previously present. If you would rather like to have multiple request transformers you can push or unshift your function to `$httpProvider.defaults.transformRequest` property as follows:

```
$httpProvider.defaults.transformRequest.push
➥(yourTransformerFunction);
```

transformResponse

With the `transformResponse` property you get a chance to transform the response before handing it to your application code. You configure a response transformer as follows:

```
angular.module('mainApp',[]).config(function($httpProvider){
    $httpProvider.defaults.transformResponse=function(data,
➥getHeaders){
        data.someProperty='something else'; //change the response
```

```
        return JSON.stringify(data); //return serialized data
    }
});
```

Like `transformRequest`, this can also be set for a particular request through the `config` object. If you want to have multiple response transformers you can `push/unshift` your function, as we did in the case of `transformRequest`.

Caching

Once users are on your website you may not want to hit the server every time you need to obtain data. Chances are that the data might not have been changed at all; often it's a good idea to cache the response obtained from server.

There's a `cache` property in the request `config` object. If you set it to `true`, the first request made to the URL is actually sent to server. All the subsequent requests made to the same URL are served from `cache` without hitting the server. So, in our weather tracking app, we can use caching as follows:

```
return $http.get('http://api.openweathermap.org/data/2.5/weather?'
↩+ query,{cache:true});
```

Now try entering a particular city and country name and hit the button. Next time whenever you enter same city and country name into the fields the response will be served from `cache`.

You should note that cached response is stored locally in a service called `$cacheFactory`. As it uses the browser's memory to store the cached data, everything will be erased if you even refresh the page. So, if you want to persist the cached data across page reloads you may use `localStorage`.

Interceptors

Interceptors are useful for pre-processing the request before it's sent to the server, and for post-processing of the response before it's handed to your application code. A few examples of interceptors are authentication, logging, error handling etc.

As the name suggests, interceptors are used to intercept the request/response at different points, and to perform processing. There are two types of interceptors: request and response, and these can be written as factory methods:

```
angular.module('mainApp',[]).factory('customInterceptor',
➡function($q,dependency1,dependency2){
    return {
        request: function(config){

            //A request interceptor is called before the request is
➡sent to server and is passed a request config object.
            //You can either return a modified/new config object
➡here
            //You can also return a Promise which resolves with a
➡config object
            //In case of any error you can return a Promise that is
➡rejected or throw an exception

            return config;
        },
        requestError: function(rejectionReason){
            //If a previous request interceptor returned a rejected
➡Promise, this interceptor is called
            //You might try to recover from the error here and
➡return a new config.
            // If all else fails let it fail by returning a promise
➡that is always rejected

            if(ableToRecover(rejectionReason)){
                //constructs a config object
                return config;
            }
            else
                return $q.reject('Could not recover'); //return a
➡Promise which always rejects
        },

        response: function(response){
            // This interceptor is called when $http receives the
➡response from the backend.
            //but before the response is handed to the application
➡code the interceptor kicks in.
            // The response object contains: data,status,config,
➡headers and statusText.
            // You return a new/modified response or a Promise that
```

```
➥resolves with a response object.
           ///In case of error return a Promise that's always
➥rejected.

           return response;
       },
       responseError:function(rejectionReason){
           // Sometimes a backend call may fail
           // Or a previous response interceptor may return a
➥rejected Promise
           // In that case you might try to recover from that here

           if(ableToRecover(rejectionReason)){
               //create a response here
               return response; //You may also return a Promise
➥here
           }
           else
               return $q.reject('Could not recover'); //return a
➥Promise which always rejects
       }
   }
});
```

Now, you can push your interceptor to the list of interceptors as following:

```
angular.module('mainApp').config(function($httpProvider) {
    $httpProvider.interceptors.push('customInterceptor'); //factory
➥name here
});
```

Now, depending on the interceptors you've configured, the methods will be called at appropriate points.

Differences Between Transformers and Interceptors

An interceptor can be used to intercept the request/response at various points, as discussed above. But transformers can be applied just before sending a request or after receiving a response. Another important consideration is that, using transformers, you just get access to `data` and `headers` of request/response while interceptors have access to the `config` object.

The real advantage of `$http` is that it's very low level and therefore gives you great flexibility. But, should you need more abstractions it's important to use the `$re-source` service, as it's best suited for CRUD apps, and is, itself, based on `$http`. There are some situations in which you might want to switch to `$resource` as it gets you started quickly and offers useful out-of-the-box methods for dealing with classic RESTful APIs. Let's see how to use `$resource` in our AngularJS apps.

Understanding AngularJS $resource

Most AngularJS apps will involve some level of CRUD operation. As such, you can use `$resource` service to get started quickly. `$resource` is built on the top of `$http`, but provides a higher level of abstraction.

Prerequisites

The `$resource` service doesn't ship with the AngularJS script out of the box. This is because not every Angular app involves CRUD operations, and developers already have `$http` for interacting services. So, if you need the `$resource` service you must download `angular-resource.js` separately and include it in your page.

So, open up the directory `Angular-Seed-Master/app/lib/angular` and find `angu-lar-resource.js`. This is the script file you'll need. After including it in your page you need to declare a dependency on the module `ngResource` as follows:

```
angular.module('myApp',['ngResource']);
```

We're doing this because the `$resource` service is defined in the module `ngResource`.

How Does $resource Work?

`$resource` expects a classic RESTful API. This means your URLs should be in the following format:

URL	HTTP Verb	Request Body	Result
/api/entries	GET	empty	Returns all entries
/api/entries	POST	JSON String	Creates new entry
/api/entries/:id	GET	empty	Returns single entry

URL	HTTP Verb	Request Body	Result
/api/entries/:id	PUT	JSON String	Updates existing entry
/api/entries/:id	DELETE	empty	Deletes existing entry

To use $resource inside your controller or service you need to declare a dependency on $resource. The following snippet shows how to use $resource in your custom service:

```
angular.module('myApp').factory('Entry', function($resource) {
    return $resource('/api/entries/:id'); // Note the full endpoint
➥address
});
```

As you can see, you need to pass the full endpoint URL to the $resource() function. Its return point is a $resource class representation. This is nothing but a constructor function that may be instantiated to get a $resource instance. So, we have named our service as Entry (not entry) because this is going to be a $resource class representation.

Also note that Entry is just an example name here. In a real world app, this would represent the name of something you want to persist in a back-end. For example, in a movie store app, the service could be named Movie.

The $resource class has five methods by default:

1. get()

2. query()

3. save()

4. remove()

5. delete()

Now let us see how to use the methods through a simple example:

```
angular.module('myApp').controller('ResourceController',
➥function($scope, Entry) {

  var entry = Entry.get({ id: $scope.id }, function() {
    console.log(entry);
  }); // get() returns a single entry

  var entries = Entry.query(function() {
    console.log(entries);
  }); //query() returns all the entries

  $scope.entry = new Entry(); //You can instantiate resource class

  $scope.entry.data = 'some data'; //so $scope.entry=
➥{data:'some data'}

  Entry.save($scope.entry, function() {
        //saves serializes $scope.entry object as JSON and sends as
➥POST body
  });

  Entry.delete({ id: $scope.id }, function() {
    console.log('Deleted from server');
  });

});
```

The get() function issues a GET request to the URL /api/entries/:id. We replace
the named parameter :id in the URL with $scope.id before the request is sent. You
should also note that the function get() returns an empty object (rather than a
Promise). This is populated automatically when the actual data comes from server.
The second argument to get() is a callback which is executed when the data arrives
from server. This is a useful trick because you can set the empty object returned by
get() as a $scope model and refer to it in the view. When the actual data arrives
and the object is populated, the data binding kicks in and your view is also updated.

Why Show an Empty Object?

You might question the wisdom of showing an empty object initially. Actually
it's a good thing because you can omit the callback passed to get() function. If
all you want is to set the model to $scope and you are not interested in knowing
when response comes you can just do the following:

```
$scope.entry=Entry.get({ id: $scope.id });
```

And now you can refer it in the template as usual. If the `get()` function didn't return an empty object initially you would always need a callback, like this:

```
Entry.get({ id: $scope.id }, function(entry) {
    $scope.entry=entry;
});
```

The function `query()` issues a GET request to `/api/entries` (notice there is no `:id`) and returns an empty array (not a simple object). This array is populated when the data arrives from the server. Again you can set this array as a `$scope` model and refer to it in the view through `ng-repeat`. You can also pass a callback to `query()`, which is called once the data comes from the server.

The `save()` function issues a POST request to `/api/entries` using the first argument as the POST body. The second argument is a callback, which is called once the data is saved. You might recall that the return value of the `$resource()` function is a resource class. So, in our case, we can call `new Entry()` to create an actual resource instance, set various properties to it and finally save the object to the back end.

`delete()` and `remove()` work identically and issue a DELETE request to the URL `/api/entries/:id`.

 ## Use `remove()` to Ensure Compatibility with IE

The `delete()` method might not work in certain versions of IE, as `delete` is a reserved keyword. To ensure your code works everywhere, use `remove()` instead.

Ideally, you'll only use `get()` and `query()` on the resource class (`Entry` in our case). All the non GET methods, such as `save()` and `delete()` are also available in the instance obtained by calling `new Entry()` (let's call this a `$resource` instance). But the difference is that these methods are prefixed with a `$`. So, the methods available in the `$resource` instance (as opposed to `$resource` class) are:

```
$save()
$delete()
$remove()
```

For instance, the method `$save()` can be used as follows:

```
$scope.entry = new Entry(); //this object now has a `$save()` method
$scope.entry.$save(function() {
  console.log('data saved');
}); //$scope.entry is serialized to JSON and sent as the POST body.
```

We've explored the create, read and delete parts of CRUD. Now we're left with update. To support an update operation we need to modify our custom factory `Entry` as shown below.

```
angular.module('myApp').factory('Entry', function($resource) {
  return $resource('/api/entries/:id', { id: '@_id' }, {
    update: {
      method: 'PUT' // this method issues a PUT request
    }
  });
});
```

The second argument to `$resource()` is a map indicating what the value of the parameter `:id` in the URL should be. Setting it to `@_id` means that, whenever we call methods like `$update()` and `$delete()` on the resource instance, the value of `:id` will be set to the `_id` property of the instance. This is useful for PUT and DELETE requests. Also note the third argument. This is a map that allows us to add any custom methods to the resource class. If the method issues a non-GET request it's made available to the `$resource` instance with a $ prefix. So, let's see how to use our $update method. Assuming we are in a controller:

```
$scope.entry = Entry.get({ id: $scope.id }, function() {
  // $scope.entry is fetched from server and is an instance of Entry
  $scope.entry.data = 'something else';
  $scope.entry.$update(function() {
```

```
      //updated in the backend
  });
});
```

When the $update() function is called, it does the following:

1. AngularJS knows that $update() function will trigger a PUT request to the URL /api/entries/:id.

2. It reads the value of $scope.entry._id, assigns the value to named parameter :id and generates the URL.

3. It then sends a PUT request to the URL with $scope.entry as the post body.

Similarly, if you want to delete an entry it can be done like this:

```
$scope.entry = Movie.get({ id: $scope.id }, function() {
  // $scope.entry is fetched from server and is an instance of Entry

  $scope.entry.$delete(function() {
    //gone forever!
  });
});
```

It follows the same steps as above, except the request type is DELETE instead of PUT.

 Using MongoDB

If MongoDB is used in the server, the $scope.entry instance you obtain from the back-end will usually have a property called _id. It works as a unique identifier for the particular instance. So, by writing { id: '@_id' } we ensure that whenever $update() or $delete() is called on the resource instance, the named parameter :id in the URL gets the value of _id property of that instance.

We've covered all the operations in a CRUD. But the $resource function also has an optional fourth parameter. This is a map with custom settings. Currently, there is only one setting available which is stripTrailingSlashes. By default this is set to true, which means trailing slashes will be removed from the URLs you pass to $resource(). If you wish to turn this off you can do so like this:

```
angular.module('myApp').factory('Entry', function($resource) {
  return $resource('/api/entries/:id', { id: '@_id' }, {
    update: {
      method: 'PUT' // this method issues a PUT request
    }
  }, {
    stripTrailingSlashes: false
  });
});
```

No you know all about the $resource service. If you wish to learn more about the settings and configurations available in $resource I encourage you to go through the documentation: https://docs.angularjs.org/api/ngResource/service/$resource.

Now that you know how to talk to the outside world it's time to create different views for our Single Page Blogger and store all the data in a remote server. In the next chapter, we'll focus on implementing this new functionality.

Conclusion

So, we've ventured out into the world using AngularJS. Firstly, we learned about $q service and promise API. Next, we saw how to make AJAX calls with built in $http service. Finally, we explored $resource and revamped our app to store the posts in a remote server. We also wrote couple of unit tests to test our controllers using $httpBackend.

Next up, we'll walk you through the creation a CRUD app with $resource.

Using REST APIs in Single Page Blogger

Applying $resource to Our App

Let's return to our Single Page Blogger app and use AngularJS's $resource to store all our blog posts on a remote server. I've developed a RESTful back end to store blog posts using Node.js and MongoDB. The app has been deployed to OpenShift Cloud and can be accessed at http://spblogger-sitepointdemos.rhcloud.com.

Here is what the API looks like:

URL	HTTP Verb	Request Body	Result
/api/posts	GET	empty	Returns all posts
/api/posts	POST	JSON String	Create new post
/api/posts/:id	GET	empty	Returns single post
/api/posts/:id	PUT	JSON String	Updates existing post

URL	HTTP Verb	Request Body	Result
/api/posts/:id	DELETE	empty	Deletes existing post

 Making Cross-domain API Calls

Normally you won't be able to make cross-domain API calls from your AngularJS app. But since I have enabled CORS in my Node.js app you'll be able to make calls to the above URLs from your app, which is great for testing purposes. But, in the real world, be careful whitelisting different domains to access your API.

Let's start by creating three services:

1. A value service `API_ENDPOINT` that stores our end point URL.

2. A custom service `Post` that internally uses `$resource`.

3. A service called `popupService` which will show a prompt message to the users when required.

Here's how we define the services. These definitions should go into **modules/admin/js/services.js**.

```
angular.module('spBlogger.admin.services', []).factory('Post',
➥['$resource','API_ENDPOINT',function($resource,API_ENDPOINT){
    return $resource(API_ENDPOINT, { id: '@_id' }, {
        update: {
            method: 'PUT'
        }
    });
}]).service('popupService',['$window',function($window){
    this.showPopup=function(message){
        return $window.confirm(message); //Ask the users if they
➥really want to delete the post entry
    }
}]).value('API_ENDPOINT','http://spblogger-sitepointdemos.rhcloud.
➥com/api/posts/:id'); // This is our end point
```

As you can see, our custom service `Post` uses the `$resource` service exactly as we've discussed previously. The only difference is that it uses a real API. This URL is stored in a `value` service called `API_ENDPOINT`.

To keep things simple, let's assume that each blog post has four properties, which will be collected via our AngularJS forms. These are as follows:

1. `title`

2. `content`

3. `tags`

4. `keywords`

Additionally there are two properties that are set on the server-side and, as such, we don't provide them.

1. `author` – Defaults to `Admin`

2. `datePublished` – The current date.

In addition, there's a `permalink` property, which is derived from the `title` property by replacing all spaces with `dashes`. This is for showing the post title in the URL to end users.

Defining Templates

Here we'll define templates for CRUD operations. The first one is **_form.html**. This template only contains the form fields and is used by both the Create and Update templates. Here's the markup:

_form.html

```
<div class="form-group" ng-class="{'has-error':postForm.title.$dirty
➥&& postForm.title.$invalid}">
    <label for="title" class="col-sm-2 control-label">Post Title
➥</label>
    <div class="col-sm-10">
        <input type="text" name="title" ng-model="post.title"
➥ng-required="true" class="form-control" id="title"
➥placeholder="Title">
        <span class="error-message" ng-show="postForm.title.$dirty
➥&& postForm.title.$invalid">Title is mandatory</span>
    </div>
</div>
<div class="form-group" ng-class="{'has-error':postForm.content.
```

```
➥$dirty && postForm.content.$invalid}">
    <label for="content" class="col-sm-2 control-label">Content
➥</label>
    <div class="col-sm-10">
        <textarea cols="8" rows="6" name="content"
➥class="form-control" ng-model="post.content" ng-required="true"
➥ id="content" placeholder="Content"></textarea>
        <span class="error-message" ng-show="postForm.content.$dirty
➥&& postForm.content.$invalid">You need to have some content!</span>
    </div>
</div>
<div class="form-group" ng-class="{'has-error':postForm.tags.$dirty
➥&& postForm.tags.$invalid}">
    <label for="tags" class="col-sm-2 control-label">Tags</label>
    <div class="col-sm-10">
        <input type="text" name="tags" class="form-control"
➥id="tags"
➥ ng-pattern="/^[\w,]+$/" ng-model="post.tags"
➥placeholder="Comma separated tags"/>
        <span class="error-message" ng-show="postForm.tags.
➥$dirty && postForm.tags.$invalid">Sorry! No special
➥characters allowed here.</span>
    </div>
</div>
<div class="form-group" ng-class="{'has-error':postForm.keywords.
➥$dirty && postForm.keywords.$invalid}">
    <label for="keywords" class="col-sm-2 control-label">Keywords
➥</label>
    <div class="col-sm-10">
        <input type="text" name="keywords" class="form-control"
➥id="keywords" ng-pattern="/^[\w,]+$/"  ng-model="post.keywords"
➥placeholder="Comma separated keywords"/>
        <span class="error-message" ng-show="postForm.keywords.
➥$dirty && postForm.keywords.$invalid">Sorry! No special
➥characters allowed here</span>
    </div>
</div>
<div class="form-group">
    <div class="col-sm-offset-2 col-sm-10">
        <button type="submit" class="btn btn-success" ng-disabled=
➥"postForm.$invalid">{{buttonText}}</button>
    </div>
</div>
```

Now let's move on to the next template.

admin-new-post.html:

```
<div class="row">
    <div class="col-xs-8">
        <form name="postForm" ng-submit="savePost()"
➥class="form-horizontal" novalidate role="form">
            <div ng-include="'/modules/admin/views/_form.html'"
        </form>
    </div>
</div>
```

As you can see this template dynamically includes the **_form.html** template using `ng-include`.

admin-update-post:

```
<div class="row">
    <div class="col-xs-8">
        <form name="postForm" ng-submit="updatePost()"
➥class="form-horizontal" novalidate role="form">
            <div ng-include="'/modules/admin/views/_form.html'"
        </form>
    </div>
</div>
```

This template, like the above one, dynamically includes the `_form.html` template using `ng-include`.

admin-home.html:

```
<div class="row">
    <div class="col-xs-3">

        <ul class="nav nav-pills nav-stacked on-click-make-active">
            <li ui-sref-active="active"><a ui-sref=
➥"admin.postViewAll">View All Posts</a></li>
            <li ui-sref-active="active"><a ui-sref=
➥"admin.postNew">Add Post</a></li>
        </ul>

    </div>
```

```
        <div class="col-xs-9 border-left">
            <div ui-view></div>
        </div>

    </div>
```

This template is for the Admin Panel. In the left sidebar it contains two links: **View All Posts** and **Add Post**. It also includes a ui-view, which loads the templates for different CRUD operations.

admin-all-posts:

```
<div class="row">
    <div class="col-xs-8">
        <table class="table">
            <tr>
                <td><h3>View All Posts</h3></td>
                <td></td>
            </tr>
            <tr ng-repeat="post in posts | orderBy:'-_id'">
                <td>{{post.title}}</td>
                <td>
                    <a class="btn btn-primary"
➥ui-sref="admin.postUpdate({id:post._id})">Edit</a>
                    <a class="btn btn-danger"
➥ng-click="deletePost(post)">Delete</a>
                </td>
            </tr>
        </table>
    </div>
</div>
```

This template lists all the posts and provides options for editing and deleting them.

Defining Controllers

Now we need to create three controllers in total. Let's see what each of them does. These controllers go into modules/admin/js/controllers.js:.

PostCreationController:

This controller helps to create a new post. Upon instantiation, the following controller creates a new $resource instance and sets it to scope model post. The function

`$scope.savePost()` uses the `$save()` method of `$resource` instance to save the post. Once saved we navigate to `admin.postViewAll` state to see all the posts.

```
angular.module('spBlogger.admin.controllers',[]).controller
➥('PostCreationController',['$scope','$state','Post',
➥function($scope,$state,Post){

    $scope.post=new Post(); // Create an empty Post instance

    $scope.buttonText="Create"; // Set initial label for button

    $scope.savePost=function(){
        $scope.buttonText="Saving. . ."; //Once clicked change
➥button text
        $scope.post.permalink=angular.lowercase($scope.post.title).
➥replace(/[\s]/g,'-');//generate permalink
        $scope.post.$save(function(){
            $state.go('admin.postViewAll'); //Once saved go to state
➥`admin.postViewAll`
        });
    }

}]);
```

PostUpdateController:

This controller helps update an existing post. It initially loads the post to be updated and allows admin to edit the fields on the UI. When the save button is clicked `$scope.updatePost()` method is called, which uses `$update()` method of `$resource` instance to update it.

```
angular.module('spBlogger.admin.controllers').controller
➥('PostUpdateController',['$scope','Post','$stateParams',
➥'$state',function($scope,Post,$stateParams,$state){

    $scope.post=Post.get({id:$stateParams.id}); //Obtain the Post
➥from backend. Search by Id

    $scope.buttonText="Update"; //Set initial label for button

    $scope.updatePost=function(){
        $scope.buttonText="Updating. . ."; //Once clicked change
➥button text
```

```
        $scope.post.$update(function(){
            $state.go('admin.postViewAll'); //Once updated go to
➥state `admin.postViewAll`
        });
    }

}]);
```

PostListController:

This controller retrieves all the posts from back end and also provides a function
that can delete an existing post.

```
angular.module('spBlogger.admin.controllers').controller
➥('PostListController',['$scope','Post','popupService',
➥'$state',function($scope,Post,popupService,$state){

    $scope.posts=Post.query(); // Obtain all the posts from backend

    $scope.deletePost=function(post){
        if (popupService.showPopup('Really delete this?')) { // Ask
➥for confirmation
            post.$delete(function() {
                $state.go('admin.postViewAll',undefined,{ //once
➥deleted reload the state
                    reload:true
                });
            });
        }
    }

}]);
```

Now, if you remember, we previously created `postService`, which was used by the
`posts` module to show blog posts to the users, in an earlier chapter. We hard coded
some posts into it, so that users see those blog posts when they visit our website.
We also developed two controllers `PostController` and `PostDetailsController`,
which used `postService` to obtain blog posts. Now that we've created the all-new
`Post` service we can modify the controllers to use it. So, here are the updated controllers:

```
angular.module('spBlogger.posts.controllers',[]).controller
➡('PostController',['$scope','Post',function($scope,Post){

    $scope.posts=Post.query(); //obtain all the posts

}]).controller('PostDetailsController',['$stateParams','$state',
➡'$scope','Post',function($stateParams,$state,$scope,Post){

    $scope.closePost=function(){
        $state.go('allPosts');
    };

    $scope.singlePost=Post.get({id:$stateParams.id}); //obtain a
➡single post

}]);
```

Including `angular-resource.js` and Adding the `ngResource` Module

As a last step you should include `angular-resource.js` in `index.html`. After this, add `ngResource` as a dependency to your main module because `$resource` service is defined in this module.

```
angular.module('spBlogger',['ngResource', . . .]);
```

Now, you can access the admin panel at `http://localhost:8000/#/admin`. By default the system shows all the blog posts when you go to the admin panel. Try playing around with the admin panel and create/update a few posts to get an understanding of how everything works. You can always look into the codebase should anything not make immediate sense, as it contains everything we've developed here.

 Authentication and Authorization

We are not looking at authentication or authorization here. Anyone can now access our Admin Panel. This is because, for now, we're more focused on how to perform CRUD operations. For authorization/authentication to work, we'll need some server-side configuration, and we'll get there towards the end of the book.

Unit Testing Our Controllers

At this juncture our controllers aren't all that simple any more. They involve REST interactions and hit remote servers to perform CRUD operations. But during unit testing, we just want to test our controllers and don't want the involvement of real HTTP requests and responses.

Fortunately, AngularJS helps us here, by introducing a mock service called $http-Backend. It helps us configure predefined responses for different requests. So, when our controllers make HTTP requests during unit testing, they go to the mock $http-Backend and, as a result, we get our predefined responses, eliminating the dependency on real HTTP responses so that we can focus on testing just the controllers.

 Using a Fake Back End for Testing

A real $httpBackend exists, which is internally used by $http, of course. But during unit testing we'll use the fake example defined in the angular-mocks.js file and inside ngMock module. We've already asked Karma to load this file in karma.conf.js.

As we're not using the old postService any more, it's a good idea to comment out its test specs or even delete them if you wish. Also note that these tests go into **test/unit/controllersSpec.js**.

In this section we'll be unit testing two controllers: PostController and PostDetailsController.

First up? Let's see how to unit test the PostController. The controller issues a GET request to **http://spblogger-sitepointdemos.rhcloud.com/api/posts** and retrieves all the blog posts. Here is the unit test:

```
beforeEach(module('spBlogger.posts.controllers'));
beforeEach(module('spBlogger.posts.services'));
beforeEach(module('spBlogger.admin.services'));
beforeEach(module('ngResource'));
beforeEach(module('ui.router'));



describe('PostController Test\n', function(){
```

```
    var $httpBackend;

    beforeEach(inject(function(_$httpBackend_) {

        $httpBackend=_$httpBackend_; //store fake $httpBackend
➥ in a variable

        $httpBackend.expectGET('http://spblogger-sitepointdemos.
➥rhcloud.com/api/posts').respond([{title:'Test',_id:1},
➥{title:'Test2',_id:2}]); //respond with 2 post objects

    }));

  it('Should initialize controller with 2 posts',
➥inject(function($rootScope,$controller,Post) {

    var $scope=$rootScope.$new(); //create a new scope

    $controller('PostController',{$scope:$scope,Post:Post}); //
➥instantiate controller

    $httpBackend.flush(); // flush so that responses are actually
➥sent

    expect($scope.posts.length).toBe(2); // Now we should have 2
➥post objects in model
  }));

});
```

Before our `it()` block runs, we retrieve `$httpBackend` and store it in a variable. Note that we're doing this because it's going to be needed in the `it()` block as well. And you should also note that AngularJS Dependency Injection will still work if you prefix/suffix service names with underscores, such as `_$httpBackend_`.

The method `$httpBackend.expectGET()` enables you to define a response to send when a GET request is made to a particular URL. It also ensures that the test will fail if a GET request is not made in the subsequent `it()` block. Furthermore, if you write multiple `expectGET()` then their order is important. The actual requests in our controller (in `it()` block) should be made in that order. But if you don't mind whether the request is made or not, and simply want to configure some predefined responses, you can do so with `$httpBackend.whenGET()`.

expect Methods

There are also several `expect` methods for other HTTP verbs, for example `expect-POST()`, `expectPUT()` etc. For a complete list, do go through the documentation:
`https://docs.angularjs.org/api/ngMock/service/$httpBackend`

Another thing to note is that the HTTP response is asynchronous in nature. Asynchronous code is usually difficult to maintain and follow because the result isn't immediately available. On the other hand, we're all familiar with synchronous code. But, in reality, it's not possible to modify `$httpBackend`'s behavior to respond synchronously. That's why there is a `flush()` method on `$httpBackend`, which allows us to flush a response manually whenever we want. This gives us more control because it lets us know when the result will be available. As a result, we can use it to write our test cases easily.

Once you're ready to test your expectation (for example, `expect($scope.posts.length).toBe(2)`) you should call `flush()` prior to it. By doing this `$httpBackend` sends the predefined response to the `$http` service and you can check your models.

And so, in the above unit test we ensure that our controller, when instantiated, should make a GET request to `http://spblogger-sitepoint-demos.rhcloud.com/api/posts` and in response it sends two objects.

Here is the unit test for `PostDetailsController` whose job is to obtain an `id` from `$stateParams` and retrieve the corresponding post:

```
describe('PostDetailsController Test\n', function(){

    var $httpBackend;

    beforeEach(inject(function(_$httpBackend_) {

        $httpBackend=_$httpBackend_;

        $httpBackend.expectGET('http://spblogger-sitepointdemos.
➥rhcloud.com/api/posts/2').respond({title:'Test2',_id:2});
```

```
➡//respond with a single object

    }));

    it('Should initialize controller with 1 post',
➡inject(function($state,$stateParams,$rootScope,$controller,Post) {

        var $scope=$rootScope.$new();

        $stateParams.id=2;

        $controller('PostDetailsController',{$scope:$scope,
➡$stateParams:$stateParams,$state:$state,Post:Post});

        $httpBackend.flush(); // flush so that responses are
➡actually sent

        expect($scope.singlePost).not.toBe(undefined); //make sure
➡the model is initialized
    }));

});
```

This unit test is same as above, but here we test that our controller issues a GET request to `http://spblogger-sitepointdemos.rhcloud.com/api/posts/2`. In response it gets a single object and the scope model `$scope.singlePost` is initialized with one post object.

Now you can run Karma as usual and check the results. If you tweak the expectations you'll see the tests fail. I also encourage you to go through the `$httpBackend` documentation (given above) and write some test cases for the CRUD controllers yourself.

We've now developed a CRUD app for our Single Page Blogger and added some unit tests as well. The next chapter will focus on one of the trickiest parts of AngularJS—directives.

Chapter **10**

AngularJS Directives

The Directive API is one of the coolest features of AngularJS. Now that you've been developing in AngularJS for some time, you've come across many simple directives, such as ng-repeat, ng-show, ng-model, etc. But when you come to develop real world apps you'll most likely need custom directives. This chapter will teach you how to build these and implement them in our demo app.

What Are Directives, Really?

A directive is something that attaches special behavior to a DOM element and teaches it awesome tricks! Let's take the example of the built-in ng-repeat directive: What this does is attach special behavior to a DOM element by repeating it multiple times. Similarly, ng-show and ng-hide conditionally show or hide an element. Let's think of a few scenarios in which directives could help solve a problem. For example, normal HTML markup can't create a date picker widget. To introduce a custom element like this into HTML you need a directive. In essence, the basic idea behind directives is quite simple: to help to make your HTML truly interactive by attaching event listeners to the elements and/or transforming the DOM.

Directives From the jQuery Perspective

Let's imagine how we attach special behaviors to elements in jQuery. To implement a date picker, first we create a normal HTML input element, like this:

```
<input type="text" class="date-picker"/>
```

Then we change its default behavior through some JavaScript code, which might look something like this:

```
$(".date-picker").datePicker();
```

But when other designers see your code they might not immediately see what this element does. They need to check out the underlying JavaScript code to be sure of its function. But with AngularJS you can create a directive for this element and use it like this:

```
<date-picker></date-picker>
```

In this way, you can create truly reusable components with directives, and this approach to building custom components is definitely neater and more intuitive.

Creating Custom Directives

Directives come in four flavors, as follows:

- As elements: `<date-picker></date-picker>`

- As attributes: `<input type="text" date-picker/>`

- As classes: `<input type="text" class="date-picker"/>`

- As comments : `<!--directive:date-picker-->`

But it's best to try and use directives as elements and attributes whenever possible, as this makes it very clear and easy to see what they do.

Let's examine how a directive is actually written. The following snippet creates a directive which outputs `Hello, World`:

```
angular.module('myApp', []).directive('helloWorld', function() {
  return {
      restrict: 'AEC',
      replace: true,
      template: '<h3>Hello, World!</h3>'
  };
});
```

The first argument to `angular.module().directive()` is the name of the directive. The second argument is a directive definition function that returns an object. This object (called directive definition object) has various properties that are used to configure a directive. We'll cover these options shortly. The function passed as the second argument (the directive definition function) can optionally list dependencies such as `$rootScope`,`$http` etc.

Note that although you use camelCase to name the directive, when using it in the HTML you'll need to separate the words with dashes (-) or colons (:).

You can use the directive in your HTML as follows:

```
<hello-world/>
```

Or:

```
<hello:world/>
```

You can also use it as an attribute:

```
<div hello-world />
```

Or:

```
<div hello:world />
```

If you want to be HTML5 compliant you can prefix your directive name with x- or data-.

```
<div data-hello-world></div>
```

Or:

```
<div x-hello-world></div>
```

While matching the directive name, AngularJS will automatically strip the prefixes `data` or `x` and convert a hyphen/colon separated name to camelCase.

 Using a Prefix

> It's good practice to prefix your directive names with something (maybe your organization name). This is because, if a future HTML version includes an element that uses the same name as your directive, your code will break. Likewise, you shouldn't use the prefix `ng`, as it's already being used by AngularJS.

Now let's see the various configuration options we used in our `Hello World` directive.

- `restrict` – This provides a way to specify how a directive should be used in HTML (remember that there are four ways a directive can be used). In this case we've set it to `'AEC'`, which means the directive can be used as an attribute, a new HTML element or class. The order of the letters doesn't matter. Equally, if you don't want the directive to be used as a class you could, for example, skip 'C'.

- `template` – This specifies the HTML markup that'll be produced when the directive is processed by AngularJS. This doesn't have to be a simple string. The template can be complex, often involving other directives, expressions ({{ }}), etc. In most cases you'll want to use the `templateUrl` property instead of `template`. And so, ideally you should place the template in a separate HTML file and make `templateUrl` point to it. For example, you can use `templateUrl` as follows:

```
angular.module('myApp', []).directive('helloWorld', function() {
    return {
        restrict: 'AEC',
        replace: true,
        templateUrl: 'hello.html'
    };
});
```

- replace – This specifies that the generated template will replace the HTML element on which the directive is applied. In our case we've used the directive as <hello-world></hello-world>. Because the replace property is set to true when the directive is compiled, the output template replaces the markup <hello-world></hello-world>. As a result, the final output is <h3>Hello World!!</h3>. If you set replace to false, the output template will be inserted as a child to the element on which the directive is applied.

The same also applies if you use the directive as an attribute. Let's assume that the above directive is used as an attribute:

```
<div hello-world></div>
```

If you have replace:true then the final outcome will be: <h3>Hello World!!</h3>. Now, if you set replace to false the output will be:

```
<div hello-world>
    <h3>Hello World!!</h3>
</div>
```

Keep Your Directives in a Separate HTML File

It's best practice to keep your directive's template in a separate HTML file and refer to it through the templateUrl property. This keeps your directives and the templates maintainable.

There's one more thing to note. If you use / at the beginning of the templateUrl path, the template file is resolved relative to the web app root. Otherwise, the path is relative to the main view index.html. You may also set the base url in your **index.html** as <base href="/" />. This way the template files will be resolved relative to the web app root automatically if you don't prefix the paths with /.

The Link Function

As we discussed earlier, the template used by your directive can be complex and involve data-binding expressions {{}}. These expressions are meaningless if the directive's template is not compiled against the correct scope. That's why every directive needs a scope. In order to make use of this scope we can take advantage of the `link` function, and this is configured by the `link` property of directive definition object. Inside the `link` function you can set models on the **scope** object, watch models for changes, and add event listeners to DOM elements. If you're performing any DOM manipulation, this is the only place to do so. Let's modify our `helloWorld` directive to make use of the `link` function.

We have the following requirements:

1. Let's allow our users to enter a message, and our directive should display that message alongside our `Hello, World!` string.

2. Our directive should also be able to watch when the message changes.

3. When somebody clicks on the template produced by the directive, the message should be set to "empty".

First, let's define a controller `MainController`, which sets the value of the scope model message to `I Love AngularJS`:

```
angular.module('myApp', []);

angular.module('myApp').controller('MainController',
➥function($scope) {
  $scope.message = 'I love AngularJS';
});
```

Now our directive `helloWorld` can be modified to include a `link` function:

```
angular.module('myApp').directive('helloWorld', function() {
  return {
    restrict: 'AEC',
    replace: true,
    template: '<p ng-click="clearMessage()">Hello, World!
➥{{message}} </p>',
    link: function(scope, elem, attrs) {

      scope.$watch('message', function(value) {
        console.log('Message Changed!');
      });

      scope.clearMessage = function() {
        scope.message = '';
```

```
    }

    elem.bind('mouseover', function() {
      elem.css('cursor', 'pointer');
    });

  }
 }
});
```

Now, you can use it in HTML as follows:

```
<body ng-controller="MainController">
  <input type="text" ng-model="message"
➥placeholder="Enter message" />
  <hello-world></hello-world>
</body>
```

The link function accepts the following parameters:

- scope: The scope object for the directive. By default this is same as the parent's scope. For instance, if you have ng-controller in the markup and our directive is used inside it, then the directive will use the parent controller's scope. This means that you can set models and watchers on this scope inside the link function. But this is not your only option. Directives can also be configured to define their own scope—something we'll cover later in this chapter.

- elem: This is the element on which our directive is applied. This element is already jQLite wrapped. If you remember, jQLite is a subset of jQuery and supports the basic DOM operations you'll habitually need. But what if we require the features of the full jQuery library, instead of jQLite? Well, the secret is that you only need to load the jQuery script before AngularJS in the HTML! That's all. Do this and AngularJS will now wrap elem with jQuery and pass it to the link function.

- attrs: This is a map containing the attributes and their values that are applied to the directive in HTML. For instance, you can attach attributes to your directive element in HTML like this: <hello-world some-attribute></hello-world> and access it in the link function as attrs.someAttribute.

attrs Contains all the Attributes Set for the Element of the Directive

It's important to note that `attrs` contains, not only the attributes that were set for the directive, but also all the attributes set for the element of the directive. This way, even if you use a directive as an attribute itself, you can access all the other attributes on the same element.

There's No Need to Convert elem to a jQuery-Wrapped Element

You might find code in which people convert the `elem` passed to the `link` function to a jQuery-wrapped element by writing `angular.element(elem)`. This is unnecessary. If you're loading jQuery before AngularJS the `elem` argument is already a jQuery element. If you want to know which methods are supported by jQLite refer to the documentation[1].

Now let's see what our modified directive `helloWorld` does:

1. Our directive uses a data binding expression `{{message}}` in the template. When the user types something into the input field this expression changes automatically. This is because our directive's `scope` is same as that of the enclosing controller. Any change to the model `message` on the controller's `scope` is properly reflected in the directive's template.

2. Inside the `link` function, we set up a watcher on the `scope` model `message` so that we know when it changes.

3. We also set up a function `clearMessage()` on the `scope`, which clears the model `message`.

4. Furthermore, we want to change the cursor style to pointer when the user hovers their mouse on the directive's template. For that we set up a `mouseover` event listener on the DOM element through `elem.bind()`.

So that's an overview of the `link` function, which should be used to attach models to the `scope`, set up watchers on `scope` models, add event listeners to DOM elements, etc.

---

[1] https://docs.angularjs.org/api/ng/function/angular.element

The Compile Function

Along with the `link` function, there's also another important function in the directive API: `compile`. This is configured through the `compile` property of a directive definition object.

The `compile` function is used to perform a DOM transformation before the `link` function runs. Note that the compile function doesn't have access to the `scope`, and must return a `link` function. But if there's no `compile` function you can configure the `link` function as usual.

The `compile` function accepts the following arguments.

- `tElement` – The element on which the directive is applied. The prefix t indicates that this is a template element and no `scope` is available yet.

- `attrs` – The map of attributes declared on the element in markup.

The `compile` function can be written like this:

```
angular.module('testModule').directive('testDirective', function() {
  return {
    compile: function(tElem,attrs) {
      //do optional DOM transformation here
      //tElem is jQLite/jQuery wrapped
      return function(scope,elem,attrs) {
        //linking function here
      };
    }
  };
});
```

Most of the time, you'll be working with the `link` function alone. This is because most directives are concerned with registering event listeners, watchers, updating the DOM, etc., and this is done inside the `link` function. Directives such as ng-re-peat, which need to clone and repeat the DOM element several times, use the com-pile function before the `link` function runs. This leads to the question of why two separate functions are needed at all. Why can't we just have one? To answer this, we need to understand how directives are compiled by AngularJS.

Compilation of Directives

When the application bootstraps, AngularJS starts parsing the DOM using the `$compile` service. This searches for directives in the markup and matches them against registered directives. Once all of these have been identified, AngularJS executes their compile functions. As we've touched on before, the compile function returns a link function, which is added to the list of link functions to be executed later. This is called the compile phase. If a directive needs to be cloned multiple times (such as `ng-repeat`), we get a performance benefit, because the `compile` function runs solely for the cloned element. However, the `link` function runs for each cloned instance of that element. That's why the compile function doesn't receive a scope.

After the compile phase is over, the linking phase, where the collected link functions are executed one by one, starts. This is where the templates produced by the directives are evaluated against the correct scope, and are turned into Live DOM which react to events.

Changing a Directive's Scope

By default, a directive gets its parent's scope. But we don't always want that. If we're exposing the parent controller's scope to the directives, they're free to modify its properties. In some cases your directive may want to add several properties and functions to the scope that are for internal use only. For example, if you have a directive that deals with comments, you may want to set some internal variable to show or hide some of its specific sections. If we set these models to the parent's scope we would pollute it.

And so, we have two other options:

■ Use a child scope — This scope prototypically inherits the parent's scope.

■ Use an isolated scope — A new scope that doesn't inherit from the parent and exists on its own.

The scope can be configured with the scope property of the directive definition object. Here's an example:

```
angular.module('myApp').directive('helloWorld', function() {
  return {
    scope: true,  // use a child scope that inherits from parent
    restrict: 'AE',
    replace: true,
    template: '<h3>Hello, World!</h3>'
  };
});
```

The above snippet of code asks AngularJS to give the directive a new child scope that prototypically inherits from the parent scope. You can use this method if you want all the parent scope models to trickle down transparently to the child scope. This enables you to reuse these models and also set additional internal models to the child scope. Figure 10.1 depicts the scenario:

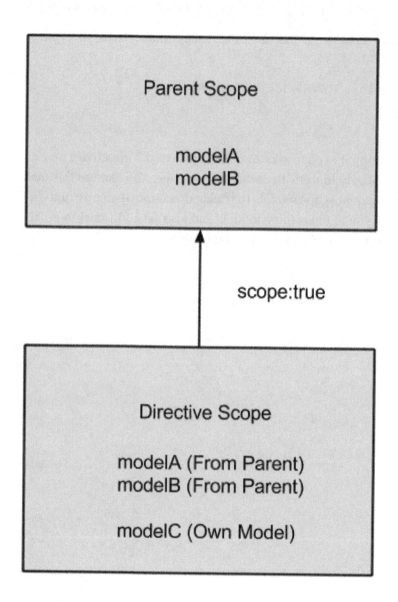

Figure 10.1. Giving the directive a new child scope that prototypically inherits from parent scope

But sometimes you may not need all the parent scope models and may require additional decoupling. Your other option, an isolated scope, is shown below.

```
angular.module('myApp').directive('helloWorld', function() {
  return {
    scope: {},  // use a new isolated scope
    restrict: 'AE',
    replace: true,
    template: '<h3>Hello, World!</h3>'
  };
});
```

This directive uses a new isolated scope that doesn't inherit from its parent. Isolated scopes are good when we want to create reusable components. By isolating the scope we guarantee that the directive is self-contained and can be easily plugged into an HTML app. This protects the parent scope from getting polluted, as it's not accessible inside the directive. In our modified `helloWorld` directive if you set the scope to {} the code won't work any more. Instead, it'll create an isolated scope for the directive and the expression `{{message}}` will now refer to the isolated scope property (not the parent scope), which is undefined. Take a look at Figure 10.2, which depicts an isolated scope.

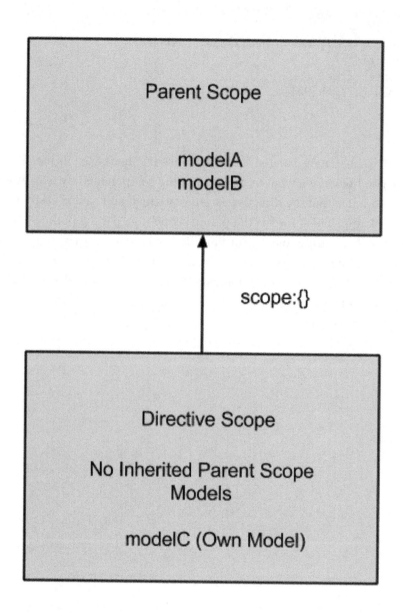

Figure 10.2. Isolated scope

Note that isolating the scope does not mean that you have no access to the parent scope's properties. There are techniques that allow you to access the parent scope's properties and also watch for changes in them. Let's see how to do that.

Binding Between Parent Scope and Isolated Scope Models

Often, it's convenient to isolate a directive's scope, especially if you are manipulating many scope models and attaching models or functions to scope for internal usage. But you may also need to access some parent scope properties inside the directive in order for the code to work. The good news is that AngularJS gives you enough flexibility to selectively pass parent scope properties to the directive through bindings.

Let's isolate our directive's scope and see how we can pass the parent scope model message to it. Our helloWorld directive will look like this:

```
angular.module('myApp').directive('helloWorld', function() {
  return {
    restrict: 'AEC',
    scope: {}, // isolated scope introduced here
    replace: true,
    template: '<p ng-click="clearMessage()">Hello, World!
➡{{message}} </p>',
    link: function(scope, elem, attrs) {
       ..

       ..
       // link function code goes here
    }
  }
});
```

Now, let's see the different options for passing parent scope models to the directive.

Using @ For One-Way Binding

In the directive definition, shown below, we've specified that the isolated scope property message should be bound to the attribute messageAttr, which is applied to the directive in the HTML. If you look at the markup below, you can see the expression {{message}} is assigned to message-attr. When the value of the expression changes, the attribute `message-attr` also changes. This, in turn, changes the isolated scope property, `message`.

```
angular.module('myApp').directive('helloWorld', function() {
  return {
    restrict: 'AEC',
    scope: {
        message:'@messageAttr'
    },
    replace: true,
    template: '<p ng-click="clearMessage()">Hello, World!
➥{{message}} </p>',
    link: function(scope, elem, attrs) {
        ..
        ..
        // link function code goes here
    }
  }
});
```

Now the HTML markup can be written as:

```
<body ng-controller="MainController">
  <input type="text" ng-model="message"
➥placeholder="Enter message" />
  <hello-world message-attr="{{message}}"></hello-world>
</body>
```

@ is used to establish a one-way binding between isolated scope model and a parent scope property. We call this one-way binding because with this technique you can only pass strings to the attribute (using expressions, {{}} or just static values). When the parent scope property changes, your isolated scope model also changes. However, the reverse is not true! You can't change the parent scope model by manipulating the isolated scope model.

Now if you run the code it will work. But there's still a problem. When you click on the directive's template the isolated scope model `message` will be set to "empty", but the parent scope `model message` won't change, due to the one-way binding. As a result, the message in input field won't change. We'll see how to solve this in the next section.

Using = For Two-Way Binding

Unlike @, this technique (=) lets you assign an actual scope model to the attribute rather than just plain strings. As a result you can pass values ranging from simple strings and arrays to complex objects to the isolated scope. Additionally, a two-way binding exists. Whenever the parent scope property changes, the corresponding isolated scope property also changes, and vice versa. As usual, you can watch this scope property for changes.

To use a two-way binding the `scope` property of our directive definition object can be modified as follows:

```
scope: {
    message:'=messageAttr' // notice = instead of @
},
```

The corresponding HTML markup will be:

```
<hello-world message-attr="message"></hello-world>
```

Note that in the above markup we don't use {{}} any more. Rather, we pass the actual scope model; this is because of the two-way binding.

Also you'll notice that, when you click on the directive template, both isolated and parent scope models `message` change, which solves the problem described above.

Using & to Execute Functions in the Parent Scope

It's sometimes necessary to call functions defined in the parent scope from a directive with an isolated scope. To refer to functions defined in the outer `scope` we use &. To demonstrate the concept, let's introduce a function `showMessage()` to our controller's scope and call it from our directive.

Here is the modified controller:

```
angular.module('myApp').controller('MainController',
➥function($scope) {

  $scope.message = 'I love AngularJS';
```

```
    $scope.showMessage=function(){
      console.log('Message Changed');
    }
});
```

Our directive's **scope** property can be modified as following:

```
scope:{
  message:'=messageAttr',
  showMessage:'&showMessageAttr' // Bind with parent scope function
},
```

Now let's call this function every time the model **message** changes. So, the watcher inside **link** function should be rewritten as:

```
scope.$watch('message', function(value) {
    scope.showMessage(); // This will call the function defined by
➡enclosing controller
});
```

The HTML markup looks like this:

```
<hello-world message-attr="message"
➡show-message-attr="showMessage()"></hello-world>
```

The code archive contains code for all the above options. You can download and play around with it to make sure you understand the isolated scope completely.

In case you want to pass arguments to the parent scope function you need to list the function parameters in the HTML as well. For example, assume **showMessage()** declares a parameter **arg** as follows:

```
$scope.showMessage=function(arg){
    console.log('Message Changed with argument'+arg);
}
```

Now, in HTML you need to change the binding as follows:

```
<hello-world message-attr="message"
➥show-message-attr="showMessage(arg)"></hello-world>
```

Next, inside your directive while calling the function you need to pass an object with the argument name and value as follows:

```
scope.$watch('message', function(value) {
    scope.showMessage({arg:'sample argument'});
});
```

Using Matching Isolated Scope Model and Attribute Names

If the isolated scope property and the attribute name is the same you can change the directive definition like this:

```
angular.module('myApp').directive('helloWorld', function() {
    return {
        restrict: 'AEC',
        scope: {
            message:'@' // No messageAttr
        },
        ..
        ..
        //Rest of the code
    }
});
```

The corresponding HTML markup will be:

```
<hello-world message="{{message}}"></hello-world>
```

Notice the isolated scope model and attribute name in HTML match. The above example uses @, but the same holds true for = and & based binding as well.

$parent in Isolated Scopes

Every **scope** object contains a special property called **$parent** which refers to its parent **scope**. The isolated **scope** also has a **$parent** property. But it refers to the enclosing controller/directive's **scope**.

Parent Scope vs. Child Scope vs. Isolated Scope

As an AngularJS beginner one might get confused while choosing the right scope for a directive. By default, a directive doesn't create a new scope and uses its parent's scope. But in many cases this isn't what we want. If your directive manipulates the parent scope properties heavily and creates new ones, it might pollute the scope. Letting all the directives use the same parent scope isn't a good idea because anybody can modify our scope properties. The following guidelines may help you choose the right scope for your directive:

- **Parent Scope** (`scope: false`)—This is the default case. If your directive doesn't manipulate the parent scope properties you might not need a new scope. In this case, using the parent scope is okay.

- **Child Scope** (`scope:true`)—This creates a new child scope for a directive which prototypically inherits from the parent scope. If the properties and functions you set on the scope are not relevant to other directives and the parent, you should probably create a new child scope. With this you also have all the scope properties and functions defined by the parent.

- **Isolated Scope** (`scope:{}`)— This is like a sandbox! You need this if the directive you're going to build is self-contained and reusable. Your directive might be creating many scope properties and functions which are meant for internal use, and should never be seen by the outside world. If this is the case, it's better to have an isolated scope. The isolated scope, as expected, does not inherit the parent scope.

Transclusion

Transclusion is a feature that enables us to wrap a directive around arbitrary content. We can extract and compile it against the correct scope later, and eventually place it at the specified position in the directive template. If you set `transclude:true` in the directive definition, a new transcluded scope will be created which prototypically inherits from the parent scope. If you want your directive with isolated scope to contain an arbitrary piece of content and execute it against the parent scope, transclusion can be used.

Let's say we have a directive registered like this:

```
angular.module('test').directive('outputText', function() {
  return {
    transclude: true,
    scope: {},
    template: '<div ng-transclude></div>'
  };
});
```

And this directive can be used as follows:

```
<div output-text>
  <p>Hello {{name}}</p>
</div>
```

ng-transclude says where to put the transcluded content. In this case the DOM content <p>Hello {{name}}</p> is extracted and put inside <div ng-transclude></div>. The important point to remember is that the expression {{name}} interpolates against the property defined in the **parent scope** rather than the isolated scope.

Differences Between transclude:'element' and transclude:true

Sometimes we need to transclude the element on which the directive is applied rather than just the contents. In these cases transclude:'element' is used. This, unlike transclude:true, includes the element itself inside the directive template marked with ng-transclude. As a result of transclusion your link function gets a transclude linking function pre-bound to the correct directive scope. This link function gets access to a clone of the DOM element that's to be transcluded. You can perform tasks like modifying the clone, adding it to the DOM, and so on.

Have a look at the following example, which repeats a DOM element using this technique and changes the background color of the second instance:

```
angular.module('myApp', []).directive('transcludeDirective',
➦function() {
  return {
    transclude: 'element',
    scope: {},
    restrict: 'AE',
    replace: true,
    link: function(scope, elem, attrs, ctrl, transclude) {
      transclude(function(clone) { //'clone' is the clone of
➥ the directive element
        clone.css('background-color', 'yellow');
        elem.after(clone); //append the clone
      });
    },
    template: '<div ng-transclude></div>'
  }
});
```

Now the directive can be used in HTML as follows:

```
<p transclude-directive>Hello World!</p>
```

Also note that by using `transclude:'element'`, the element on which the directive is applied is converted into an HTML comment. So, if you combine `transclude:'element'` with `replace:false`, the directive template essentially gets `innerHTML`ed to the comment—which means nothing really happens! Instead, if you choose `replace:true` the directive template will replace the HTML comment and things will work as expected. For instance, using `replace:false` with `transclude:'element'` makes sense when you want to repeat the DOM element and don't want to keep the first instance of the element (which is converted to a comment).

The Controller Function and Require

The controller function of a directive is used if you want to allow other directives to communicate with yours. In some cases you may need to create a particular UI component by combining two directives. For example, you can attach a `controller` function to a directive (`outerDirective`) as shown below.

```
angular.module('myApp', []).directive('outerDirective', function() {
  return {
    scope: {},
    restrict: 'AE',
    controller: function($scope, $compile, $http) { // you can
➥inject dependencies here
      // $scope is the proper scope for the directive
      this.addChild = function(nestedDirectiveScope) { // this
➥refers to the controller
        console.log('Got the message from nested directive:' +
➥nestedDirectiveScope.message);
      };
    }
  };
});
```

This code attaches a controller named outerDirective to the directive. When another directive wants to communicate, it needs to declare that it requires this directive's controller instance. This is done as shown below.

```
angular.module('myApp', []).directive('innerDirective', function() {
  return {
    scope: {},
    restrict: 'AE',
    require: '^outerDirective', //We need the outerDirective
➥controller
    link: function(scope, elem, attrs, controllerInstance) {
      //the fourth argument is the controller instance you require
      scope.message = "Hi, Parent directive";
      controllerInstance.addChild(scope);
    }
  };
});
```

The above directives can be used in the markup as follows:

```
<outer-directive>
  <inner-directive></inner-directive>
</outer-directive>
```

require: '^outerDirective' tells AngularJS to search for the controller on the
element and its parent. In this case, the found controller instance is passed as the

fourth argument to the `link` function of `innerDirective`. Inside the `link` function, we send the `scope` of the nested directive to the parent by calling `controller-Instance.addChild()`.

To summarize, you should use `controller` to expose an API for others to communicate with your directive.

Cleaning Up Your Directive

Inside your directive, if you register any listener to the `scope`, it'll be destroyed automatically at the same time as the `scope`. But if you register listeners on a service or a DOM element which isn't going to be destroyed you should manually clean them up. Otherwise you may introduce memory leakages.

When your `scope` is getting destroyed it will broadcast a `$destroy` event. You can listen to it, and perform any final cleanups like so:

```
scope.$on('$destroy',function(){
    // cleanups here
});
```

Let's take an example of a directive, which uses `$interval` service to log a message every five seconds. When the `scope` is going to be destroyed we need to clear this timer.

```
angular.module('myApp',[]).directive('testDirective',
➥function($interval){
    scope:true,
    replace:true,
    link:function(scope,elem,attrs){

        var timer=$interval(function(){
            console.log('message logged');
        },5000);

        scope.$on('$destroy',function(){
            $interval.cancel(timer);
```

```
          }
      }
});
```

IE 8 Precautions

It seems that older versions of IE are not very happy with custom element names.
So, if you want to support IE 8 and use custom element names like <hello-world>
in the markup you need to pre-declare the element names, as follows:

```
<!doctype html>
  <html xmlns:ng="http://angularjs.org" id="ng-app"
➥ng-app="optionalModuleName">
    <head>
      <!--[if lte IE 8]>
        <script>
          document.createElement('hello-world');
          document.createElement('ng-include');
          document.createElement('ng-pluralize');
          document.createElement('ng-view');

          // Optionally these for CSS
          document.createElement('ng:include');
          document.createElement('ng:pluralize');
          document.createElement('ng:view');
        </script>
      <![endif]-->
    </head>
    <body>
      ...
    </body>
</html>
```

This example is taken from from https://docs.angularjs.org/guide/ie. You can visit
this link to discover more about IE compatibility issues. The above trick should be
employed if you use custom element names and still want to support older versions
of IE. But if you use directives as attributes or classes you are good to go. It's worth
noting that AngularJS 1.3 is dropping IE 8 support.

Conclusion

This concludes our overview of AngularJS directives. You can create truly reusable custom components with the directive API. However, we haven't seen any real world use of the directives yet! That's why the next chapter focuses on using them to create a comment system for our demo app.

Chapter 11

Adding a Comment System to Single Page Blogger

Every blogging app has an integrated comment system and obviously our Single Page Blogger would be incomplete without one. We're going to build a simple comment system by creating a custom directive. Let's name this directive `spb-comments`. Here is its initial structure:

```
angular.module('spBlogger.posts.directives',[]).
➥directive('spbComments',function(Post){
    return {
        restrict:'AEC',
        scope:{
            postInstance:'='
        },
        replace:true,
        link:function(scope,elem,attrs){

        },
```

```
            templateUrl:'modules/posts/views/comments.html'
    }
});
```

The code goes into the file: **modules/posts/js/directives.js**.

As you can see, the directive creates an isolated scope. The isolated scope has a property called postInstance. The page that's going use this directive will pass the post object to it. Each post object has an array of comments which will be iterated in the directive's template. The directive also has a dependency on the Post service which is injected via Dependency Injection.

The template of the directive is placed in the file **modules/posts/js/directives.js**. It looks like this:

```
<div class="row">
    <div class="col-xs-12">
        <h3>Comments</h3>
        <br/>
        <textarea cols="40" rows="5" class="form-control"
➥ng-model="comment.content" placeholder="Type your comment here">
➥</textarea>
        <br/>By : <input type="text" ng-model="comment.author"
➥class="form-control" placeholder="Type your name here"/> <br/>
        <input type="submit" value="Add" ng-click="saveComment()"
➥class="form-control btn-success small-button" />
        <hr/>
        <div class="comments-list">
            <div class="single-comment" ng-repeat="comment in
➥postInstance.comments">
                <div class="content">{{comment.content}}</div>
                <div class="info">By: <span>{{comment.author}}
➥</span>
➥| On: <span>{{comment.datePublished | date:'MM-dd-yy'}}</span>
➥</div>
            </div>
        </div>
    </div>
</div>
```

The template provides input fields for users to enter their comments. Each comment has content and author properties. So, we bind the two input fields to the above scope models through `ng-model`. When the `Add Comment` button is clicked we call the scope function `saveComment()`, which saves the comment. The template also lists all the comments for the given post using `ng-repeat`.

Now let's update our directive's `link` function to define the `saveComment()` function that actually saves the comment entered by the user.

```
link:function(scope,elem,attrs){

    scope.saveComment=function(){
        var postID=scope.postInstance._id,
                savedPostInstance={};
        scope.comment.datePublished=new Date(); //Give a date to the
➥comment
        angular.copy(scope.postInstance,savedPostInstance); //copy
➥the post instance in `scope` to a variable `savedPostInstance`
        savedPostInstance.comments.unshift(scope.comment); //push the
➥comment to the savedPostInstance
        scope.postInstance.comments.unshift(scope.comment); //push
➥the comment to the `scope.postInstance` as well
        scope.comment={}; // clear the comment
        savedPostInstance.$update(); //Now update `savedPostInstance`
➥so that the new comment goes to the server.
    }
}
```

You could have just pushed a new comment to `scope.postInstance` and called `$update()` on it. But the problem is that once a resource instance is updated all of its properties, including comments, are cleared and in the view you won't see anything. So, you have to fetch the fresh copy of the updated post from the server again. To workaround this, we first copy the original `scope.postInstance` to a variable called `savedPostInstance` and update it. As a result of the update, the properties of the resource instance `savedPostInstance` are cleared. But it doesn't impact our view as our scope model `scope.postInstance` is still bound to the UI and is updated with a new comment. (Also, note that we push the comment to `scope.postInstance` as well).

Our comments directive uses an isolated scope so that it's self-contained and can be easily plugged into any app as long as we supply a `Post` instance to it.

We use this custom directive in **singlePost.html**, which is present inside **modules/posts/views/singlePost.html**. Here's the code:

```
<div class="comments">
    <spb-comments post-instance="singlePost"></spb-comments>
</div>
```

`singlePost` is the post object obtained from the server. It's assigned to the attribute `post-instance` which is two-way bound to the isolated scope property of the directive.

We're done! Users can now browse through posts and comment on them. Figure 11.1 shows how it looks on my system:

Figure 11.1. Commenting on a post in Single Page Blogger

Unit Testing Our Directive

Now that you've written the directive it's time to unit test it as usual. We'll write a simple unit test to verify that the directive loads the required number of comments upon compilation.

So, here is our test, which goes into **test/unit/directivesSpec.js**:

```
beforeEach(module('spBlogger.posts.directives'));
beforeEach(module('spBlogger.admin.services'));
beforeEach(module('templates')); // This module loads all our
➥templates pointed to by templateUrl.

describe('Directive Test\n', function(){

    it('Should initialize comments div with 2 comments',
➥inject(function($rootScope,$compile) {

        var $scope=$rootScope.$new(); //Create a new scope

        $scope.singlePost={comments:[{content:'test',author:'test'},
➥{content:'test1',author:'test1'}]}; // Fake comments array in a
➥fake post instance

        var template='<spb-comments post-instance="singlePost">
➥</spb-comments>'; // This our markup which uses the directive

        var elem=angular.element(template); // wrap the element with
➥jQuery as $compile service compiles DOM and not a String

        $compile(elem)($scope); // Link it with proper scope

        $rootScope.$digest(); // Fire a digest so that expressions
➥are evaluated

        expect(elem.find('.single-comment').length).toBe(2); //
➥Expect number of comments to be 2
    }));

});
```

When unit testing directives, $compile is your friend. In the above example it compiles the DOM, which uses our directive and links it with a scope. Finally, we fire a $digest() cycle. As we've fed a fake post object with two comments, our directive template should produce two .single-comment elements. We check that with expect(). You can play around with it and change the expected values to see the test fail.

But wait! Does this test work? Not yet! As our directive has a templateUrl property, a separate GET request will be fired to fetch the template. But the $httpBackend doesn't call the expectGET() function and AngularJS complains that an unexpected

GET request was made. To overcome this we need to use a Karma plugin called `karma-ng-html2js-preprocessor` which converts HTML files into JavaScript strings to generate AngularJS modules. As a result, AngularJS won't send a GET for this and will, instead, serve the template from `$templateCache`. In our case our templates are loaded as a module called `templates`. That's why we wrote `beforeEach(module('templates'))` in the beginning.

In order to run this test, we need to::

1. Go to the root of the project `sp-blogger` and run `npm install karma-ng-html2js-preprocessor --save-dev`.

2. Download the updated **karma.conf.js** and replace the old one with this.

Now run `sh scripts/test.sh` and see the tests pass!

Conclusion

In this chapter we not only learned about directives but also implemented a feature using them. The unit testing is simple, but gives you an idea about how directives are unit tested. As you keep working with directives and testing them you will encounter new problems and learn how to tackle them. But for now you can relax as you've just covered one of the trickiest parts of AngularJS. The next chapter will give you a tour of the Dependency Injection framework in AngularJS.

Chapter 12

Dependency Injection In AngularJS

Dependency Injection (DI) is one of the best features of AngularJS. It makes our lives easier by letting us write loosely coupled and easily testable components. The DI framework's in charge of creating components, resolving their dependencies, and passing them to other components when requested. You've already seen many examples of Dependency Injection. This chapter covers two core AngularJS services called `$provide` and `$injector` that work in the background to make Dependency Injection possible.

A Brief Recap

Components may obtain their dependencies in the following two ways:

1. By invoking `new` on a constructor function to obtain their dependency themselves.

2. By using a global variable to look up dependencies.

But sadly these solutions come at a price. If a component invokes `new` on another component, then both are tightly coupled. This makes unit testing very difficult as, to test one component, you'll need the other upon which it depends.

Secondly, if you need a global object to obtain a dependency then that object needs to be passed around throughout your app. But this isn't the best way of doing things, because each component should know as little as possible about other components to improve testability. To avoid these issues, AngularJS does things in a different way: using a **service locator**.

Assume that you have the following constructor function, which is used as a controller:

```
function SimpleController($scope,$rootScope,$http){
    $scope.someModel="Hello, World!";
}
```

The controller declares its dependencies through the method parameters. While instantiating the controller, AngularJS looks for the registered services that match the parameter names and automatically injects them as arguments. Rather than obtaining the dependencies ourselves, we ask the DI subsystem to inject those dependencies for us. We call these dependencies "injectable types" because they can be injected into other components. This hugely improves the testability of your app because, while unit testing a particular component, you can mock up the dependencies and just focus on the component under test.

But how are these injectable components registered? The answer is the $provide service. Let's take a look at how $provide works.

The $provide Service

The injectable types most commonly used in AngularJS are services. As we saw in Chapter 5, every service has an associated provider, and the $provide exposes a method called provider to register one. Take a look at the following example:

```
angular.module('myApp',[]).config(function($provide){
    $provide.provider('alertService',function(){
        this.$get=function(){
            return function(){
                alert('Service in action');
            }
```

```
        }
    });
});
```

You can get hold of the $provide service inside the config block of your module. Then you can call $provide.provider() to register a new provider. Now, in another component, say a controller, you can ask for alertService to be injected as follows:

```
function simpleController(alertService){
    alertService();
}
```

When you ask for the alertService the provider's $get method is called and you receive what it returns.

The $provide service doesn't expose the provider() method alone. It also exposes methods like service(), factory(), value() and constant() to register different injectable types. For convenience these methods also exist on the module level so that you can directly call them on angular.module(). But they do the same thing in the end.

Now let me reveal a secret. Methods such as factory(), value(), constant() etc. all create providers for you implicitly without obliging you to type all the provider related stuff.

Above, we created the alertService through a provider. Now let's see how to do the same using a factory:

```
app.config(function($provide) {
    $provide.factory('alertService',function(){
        return function(){
            alert('Service in Action');
        }
    });
});
```

Or we can call the method factory() on angular.module(),

```
angular.module('myApp').factory('alertService',function(){
    return function(){
       alert('Service in Action');
    }
});
```

This code creates a provider for `alertService` automatically and is the same as writing a `provider` yourself. You can get the created provider as usual inside a `config` block by declaring a dependency on `alertServiceProvider`.You can also achieve the same result using a `value()` service. I recommend you also try that on your own.

This brings up another important question: While calling a constructor function or a normal method, how does AngularJS resolve the dependencies? Well, `$provide` is only half of the story. `$injector` is the service that actually resolves the dependencies. Let's see how!

The `$injector` Service

`$injector` is responsible for actually instantiating the injectable types and resolving the dependencies. The `$provide` service registers the injectable types with `$injector`. Then it's the `$injector` which instantiates these injectables using the code provided by the `$provide` service. While invoking a method or constructor function `$injector` knows how to resolve its dependencies. Let's take a look at the following controller, which has three dependencies:

```
function TestController($scope,$http,customService){
    //controller code goes here
}
```

When this controller is to be instantiated, the `$injector`'s `instantiate` method gets called. It will look something like this:

```
$injector.instantiate(TestController);
```

While instantiating this controller `$injector` will go through the parameters list and call `$injector.get(serviceName)` to obtain the service instance. This is where the corresponding provider's `$get()` method is called to obtain our service instance.

To put it another way, the $injector's get() method knows how to resolve a dependency.

The $injector service also offers another method called invoke(), which takes a function and calls it, resolving the dependencies. If you have a function and it has some dependencies you can write something like this to invoke it via $injector:

```
$injector.invoke(function(customService,$http){
    //some code here
});
```

But this leads to the basic question of how to access the $injector? The answer is simple: Have it dependency-injected into your service/controller. Yes, $injector knows how to inject itself. Actually, AngularJS creates an $injector for your app while bootstrapping. Here is how you can access $injector inside your service:

```
angular.module('myApp').service('customService',function($injector){
    var $http=$injector.get('$http'); //get $http service
    var $rootScope=$injector.get('$rootScope'); //get the $rootScope
});
```

You can also get $injector injected into the config block of your module, like this:

```
angular.module('myApp').config(['$injector',function($injector){
    //use $injector here
}]);
```

Apart from the above techniques you can also have the $injector for selected modules. This is done as follows:

```
var injector=angular.injector(['ng','customModule']);
```

 $injector Will Create Only One Instance of Any Service

$injector will create only one instance of any service. Once the service instance is obtained, its value is cached and used subsequently. Every time you ask for the service via dependency injection you will always get the same instance.

Dynamically Injecting a Dependency

Now that you know how dependency injection works in AngularJS, I'll share a use case of the `$injector` service. As we saw, the `$injector.get()` method finds and returns a service by name. We can use this to obtain a dependency dynamically. Take a look at the following code, which defines a simple controller:

```
angular.module('myApp',[]).controller('SimpleController',
➡['$injector',function($injector){
    $scope.getDependency=function(serviceName){
        var service=$injector.get(serviceName);
        //use service here
    }
    $scope.getDependency('$http');
}]);
```

In the above example, our controller defines a method on `scope` called `getDependency()`. It accepts a single argument, which is the service name to look for, and uses `$injector.get()` to obtain it. So, here you don't need to list the dependencies in the controller's constructor function. Rather, we use `$injector` to obtain the dependencies dynamically. While you may not need this kind of arrangement often, it's good to have it in your toolbox.

Registration of Controllers, Filters, and Directives

So far we have only seen how services are registered. What about controllers, directives, and filters? Well, these components are not registered via `$provide` and, consequently, they aren't injectable. The following list shows how they're registered:

▪ controller: There is a `$controller` service (and `$controllerProvider`), which is responsible for setting up your controllers. The `$controllerProvider.register()` method registers a new controller. When you call the method `angular.module().controller()` to register a controller, `$controllerProvider.register()` actually gets called behind the scenes. We've already seen the usefulness of the `$controller` service during unit testing. You can basically use it to instantiate your controller manually and carry on with your testing easily.

▪ filter: Filters are registered via the `$filterProvider.register()` method. Later if you want to obtain a filter instance in another component you can do so by calling `$filter(filterName)`. Of course you'll need to declare a dependency on the $filter service to use it. We'll look into this in detail shortly when we reach the filters chapter.

▨ directive: AngularJS has a built -in service called $compile. Using it, directives are registered via the $compileProvider.directive() method. With the help of the $compile service you can manually compile an HTML string and then link it with a scope to interpolate the bindings and add the element to DOM. Let's take a look at the following directive:

```
    angular.module('myApp').directive('compileDirective',
➡['$compile','$rootScope',function($compile, $rootScope) {
      return {
        restrict: 'A',
        link: function(scope, elem, attrs) {
          var html = '<div>Hello, World! {{message}}</div>';
          var element = $compile(angular.element(html))(scope);
➡//get the element by compiling and linking it
          elem.after(element); // add the compiled element to the
➡DOM
        }
      }
    }]);
```

The first thing to note is that the $compile service expects a DOM. So, you pass the HTML string to angular.element() to create a jQuery/jQLite wrapped element. After invoking $compile with the newly created element you'll receive a linker. To interpolate the bindings (in our case {{message}}) you need to call the linker function with the proper scope. At this point we have an element that can be added to DOM. $compile service comes in handy while unit testing directives. Without it there's no other way to invoke a directive in unit tests. We've already explored this in the last chapter. If you don't remember it feel free to flip a few pages and go through the unit tests we wrote for our comment directive.

While registering filters, controllers, and directives may not be very relevant to you at present, there's no harm in knowing how different components are registered by AngularJS internally. So, later, if you run into some error, you can easily debug and know what's happening behind the scenes.

Conclusion

To summarize, we can inject dependencies into any function that's invoked via `$injector.invoke()` or `$injector.instantiate()`. On the other hand, only those values can be injected into a function which are registered via `$provide` (We'll later see how filter is a different case).

The following definition functions can get their dependencies injected via dependency injection:

- Service

- Factory

- Provider's `$get` method

- Controller

- Directive

- Filter

And the following are the injectable types which can be injected into other components:

- Service

- Factory

- Provider

- Value

- Constant

This chapter discussed dependency injection in AngularJS. The next chapter takes a look at AngularJS filters.

AngularJS Filters

Sometimes data stored in a web app is in a format that's different from what we want to show to the users. For example, you may store two-digit country codes in lowercase in your database, but wish to display those country codes on a web page in uppercase. This is where AngularJS **filters** come in. Filters, as the name suggests, help to filter or format the data to be displayed to the users.

Most commonly, filters are applied to data binding expressions in the template. But they can also be used inside controllers, services, and directives. This chapter covers filters in AngularJS. Once you have the basics covered, we'll see how to implement and unit test some simple filters in our demo app.

Filter Basics

The most common usage of filters can be found in view templates. Here is how we apply a filter to an expression:

```
{{countryCode | uppercase}}
```

Here, `countryCode` is the `scope` model and `uppercase` is the name of the filter (in this example, `uppercase` is a built-in filter in AngularJS). If you have an expression you'd like to display in uppercase, you simply need to add the `uppercase` filter to it. Note how the expression is separated from the filter by a vertical pipe character (`|`).

Filters can take arguments too! Let's take a look at another built-in filter in AngularJS, the `date` filter:

```
{{currentDate | date : 'yyyy-MM-dd'}}
```

The `date` filter formats a `Date` object as a string representation. As you can see, we've passed a single argument to the filter, which says how to format the date.

Filters can also accept multiple arguments. To pass multiple arguments you simply separate the arguments with a colon (`:`). Take a look at the following snippet, which passes three arguments to an imaginary filter:

```
{{expression | imaginaryFilter: arg1 : arg2 : arg3 }}
```

 Angular's Built-in Filters

> AngularJS ships with many useful and fun-to-use filters out of the box. Here is a list of some important AngularJS filters you'll find useful:
>
> - `currency`[1] : Formats a number as currency
>
> - `number`[2] : Formats an expression as a number
>
> - `date`[3] : Formats a date object into string
>
> - `json`[4] : Formats and shows an object as JSON string

---

[1] https://docs.angularjs.org/api/ng/filter/date

[2] https://docs.angularjs.org/api/ng/filter/number

[3] https://docs.angularjs.org/api/ng/filter/date

[4] https://docs.angularjs.org/api/ng/filter/json

Fun with Custom Filters

You may be wondering what we do if we need a filter that isn't built-in to AngularJS. In this situation, you need to use custom filters, and these are relatively easy to create. Let's see how.

To register a filter you need to call the function `angular.module().filter()`. As usual, the first argument is the name of the filter. The second argument is the filter factory function. For instance, the following snippet creates a filter that restricts the number of characters in a string to 127.

```
angular.module('myApp',[]).filter('limitCharacters',function(){
    return function(input,characterCount){
        return (input.length > characterCount) ?
➥input.substring(0,characterCount) : input;
    }
});
```

The second argument to the `filter()` function is called a filter factory function. This is where we return the actual filter. If your filter has dependencies, you can list those as arguments in this function. In this simple example we don't have any dependencies, but you will need them in future. Now, let's examine the filter function returned from the factory. The first parameter represents the expression on which the filter is applied. The rest of the parameters are the filter arguments, which can be 0 or above (remember, filters can accept arguments). Now, in the template we apply the filter like so:

```
{{content | limitCharacters : 127}}
```

Assume that `content` is the `scope` model, which contains a long string. As you can see `limitCharacters` is applied on the expression with the help of a vertical pipe (|). We also want to pass an argument to the filter specifying how many characters to limit.

Chaining Multiple Filters

In the example above, we restricted the number of characters in a string to a certain length. But, what happens if we have another requirement, such as wanting to make the characters uppercase as well? Well, you can chain filters; the output from the first filter will become the input to the next filter, and so on. Let's tweak the previous example to apply an `uppercase` filter immediately after the `limitCharacters` filter, so that they're chained:

```
{{content | limitCharacters : 127 | uppercase}}
```

In this example, the `limitCharacters` filter will be applied first, and then `uppercase` will be applied to the result from first filter.

 Ordering of Chained Filters

The ordering of the filters may have a dramatic effect on the performance of your app. For example, if you have a very long string you should first limit its size and then uppercase it—not the other way around. Similarly, it's a bad idea to first sort, and then filter your data, because a a quantity of data will need to be ordered for no good reason.

Using Filters in Controllers, Services, and Directives

So far we've seen how to use filters in the view templates. But the good news is that filters are injectable and you're allowed to use them inside the controllers, services, and directives via dependency injection. The trick is that you need to add a suffix `Filter` to the filter name while listing it as an argument for dependency injection. For example, if you want to use the previously created filter `limitCharacters` in your controller, you should inject `limitCharactersFilter` in the controller. Here's how we do that:

```
angular.module('myApp',[]).controller('TestController',
➥function($scope,limitCharactersFilter){
    $scope.content=limitCharactersFilter
➥('This is less than 127',127);
});
```

The first argument to the filter is the input to which the filter should be applied. After that you can pass the optional arguments. As we're applying the filter inside the controller there's no need to keep it in the template. So, in the template itself we only need to write the following expression:

```
{{content}}
```

You can inject the filter in exactly the same way inside services and directives.

Next, let's meet some really interesting filters you'll encounter in day-to-day programming.

 Why the Suffix?

You're probably wondering why we need the extra suffix `Filter` while injecting the filter into our controller? In the last chapter, I noted that filters are not registered through the `$provide` service. Instead they're registered with `$filterProvider`. If we directly passed `limitCharacters` as an argument to our controller, Angular's DI system would look for a provider named `limitCharactersProvider` and try to inject the service `limitCharacters`. The suffix `Filter` tells the DI system that it should first look for the provider and, if it's present, use it. Otherwise it must strip the suffix `Filter` and look for a corresponding filter and inject that. So, if the service name is `exampleFilter`, say, (you should never actually name your services like this) then DI will first look for `exampleFilterProvider` and, if it finds it, use it. Otherwise, it'll look for a filter named `example` and try to inject that.

Meet a Filter Called `filter`

There's a built-in filter in AngularJS called `filter` that takes an array of items and returns a sub-array based on a filtering condition. `filter` is most commonly used in conjunction with `ng-repeat`.

To understand the concept here let's create a small app that lists a group of friends' details. Here is our controller, with some hardcoded example data:

```
angular.module('myApp',[]).controller('FriendsController',
➥function($scope, $filter) {
  $scope.friends = [{
    name: 'Sandeep',
    phone: '7432453412',
    country: 'IN'
  }, {
    name: 'John',
    phone: '8647323423',
```

```
      country: 'US'
    }, {
      name: 'Alex',
      phone: '5453562353',
      country: 'NZ'
    }, {
      name: 'Martin',
      phone: '2376454323',
      country: 'US'
    }, {
      name: 'Ian',
      phone: '8645432364',
      country: 'AU'
    }, {
      name: 'Rob',
      phone: '8967654567',
      country: 'UK'
    }];
});
```

And, this is our template, which lists all the friends with their details:

```
<body ng-controller="FriendsController">
    <h3>Your Friends are:</h3>
    <ul>
      <li ng-repeat="friend in friends">
        {{friend.name}} ({{friend.phone}}, {{friend.country}})
      </li>
    </ul>
</body>
```

Now, let's assume that you want to filter through the list to look up all of your friends whose names contains a particular string ('sa', for example). This is where `filter` shines. You can attach it to `ng-repeat` whereupon it'll filter through the list and return only the relevant results. Let's add an input field to the above template so that the list refreshes itself based on the filter text typed into the field. Here's the modified template:

```
<body ng-controller="FriendsController">
    <h3>Your Friends are:</h3>
    Filter: <input type="text" ng-model="filterText"/>
    <ul>
```

```
        <li ng-repeat="friend in friends | filter: filterText">
            {{friend.name}} ({{friend.phone}}, {{friend.country}})
        </li>
    </ul>
</body>
```

Note that we are referencing a scope model `filterText` in the `filter` clause inside `ng-repeat`. The model `filterText` is bound to an input field so that it's updated whenever we type something into it. As `filterText` changes, the list is automatically refreshed based on the filter. Note, however, that this approach accepts a match against any property of the object in the list. To match against a specific property in the object you can change the `filter` clause as follows:

```
<li ng-repeat="friend in friends | filter:{name:filterText}">
    {{friend.name}} ({{friend.phone}}, {{friend.country}})
</li>
```

Now this arrangement should filter only those friends whose `name` property matches the filter text.

While a partial match is sufficient, sometimes you might need a strict match. This means, in the above example if we type j or J as the filter text there should be no results. But if we type the complete name John it should yield one record. The second argument to `filter` is a boolean value indicating whether or not we want a strict match. We can, again, modify our template to introduce a checkbox that toggles this boolean value and use this as the second argument with `filter`.

```
<body ng-controller="FriendsController">
    <h3>Your Friends are:</h3>
    Filter: <input type="text" ng-model="filterText"/>
    Strict: <input type="checkbox" ng-model="isStrict"/>
    <ul>
        <li ng-repeat="friend in friends | filter:{name:filterText}
➡:isStrict">
            {{friend.name}} ({{friend.phone}}, {{friend.country}})
```

```
        </li>
    </ul>
</body>
```

Now if you select the checkbox you'll enter into the strict mode. Similarly, de-selecting the checkbox will bring you back to the normal mode.

Meet the `orderBy` Filter

`orderBy` is another filter that's used in conjunction with `ng-repeat`. This is useful when you want to order a list of items by a certain parameter. Let's arrange the list of our friends by the `name` property, in ascending order. The modified `ng-repeat` looks like this:

```
<li ng-repeat="friend in friends | filter:{name:filterText}:strict
➥ | orderBy:'name'">
    {{friend.name}} ({{friend.phone}}, {{friend.country}})
</li>
```

Now what about descending order? Just modify the `orderBy` filter like this: `orderBy:'-name'`.

Meet the `limitTo` Filter

The third important companion of `ng-repeat` is the `limitTo` filter. As its name suggests, it limits the list items to a specified number. Suppose you want to see the details for five friends only. In that case you can use `limitTo` as follows:

```
<li ng-repeat="friend in friends | filter:{name:filterText}:strict |
➥orderBy:'name' | limitTo:5">
    {{friend.name}} ({{friend.phone}}, {{friend.country}})
</li>
```

We've nearly covered everything. But there's one small trick left. You can obtain your filters in a different way. Let's see how.

Using the `$filter` Service

There is also a built-in service called `$filter`. If you don't want to list the individual filters as arguments you can just inject the `$filter` service and use it to obtain the registered filters. Here is how our previously created controller looks like, modified to use $filter:

```
angular.module('myApp',[]).controller('TestController',
➡function($scope,$filter){
    var limitCharactersFilter=$filter('limitCharacters'); //This
➡gives us the filter. Notice no Filter suffix!
    $scope.content=limitCharactersFilter
➡('This is less than 127',127);
});
```

Using Filters in Single Page Blogger

Let's add two more requirements for our Single Page Blogger app to demonstrate the use of filters. We'll start by looking at a permalink filter.

Permalink Filter

As you already know, we generate the permalink for a post using its title. To do that we lowercase the title entered by the admin and replace all the spaces with hyphens (-). For example, if the title for a post is "Lorem Ipsem Post" the permalink will be: http://localhost:8000/#/posts/44/lorem-ipsum-post. Generating these permalinks is a good example of using a filter that we can use in both our view template and controller. The objective here is simple: while the admininstrator is typing in the title field, we can show them what the permalink will look like.

First, let's create a filter called permalink inside the file modules/admin/js/filters.js:

```
angular.module('spBlogger.admin.filters',[]).
➡filter('permalink',function(){
    return function(title){
        return title===undefined ? '' : angular.lowercase(title).
➡replace(/[\s]/g,'-');
    }
});
```

The filter is quite simple. If the user has not typed anything into the title field it's undefined, in which case we simply return an empty string. Otherwise, we convert the title to lowercase and replace all the spaces with dashes -. Now we need to display it on the view so that administrators see the permalink updated whenever they type into the title field. Open up the file **modules/admin/views/_form.html** and place the filter just below title input field. Here is the code:

```
<input type="text" name="title" ng-model="post.title"
➥ng-required="true" class="form-control" id="title"
➥placeholder="Title">
<span>Permalink:<i>/posts/[id]/{{post.title | permalink}}</i></span>
```

As usual, we invoke our filter with the vertical pipe. As the model `post.title` changes the filter is re-evaluated and the view is updated with the new permalink.

That's it! But we can also use this filter elsewhere. You might remember that `Post-CreationController` also calculates the permalink value. I'll leave it up to you to inject the filter into the controller and use it to calculate the permalink . Just make sure to inject `permalinkFilter` and *not* `permalink`.

Now, let's write the unit test for this filter. As this is a filter test it should go into **test/unit/filtersSpec.js**. Here's the code you need:

```
describe('filter', function() {

  beforeEach(module('spBlogger.admin.filters'));


  describe('Permalink Filter Test\n', function() {

    it('Should Replace all spaces with hyphens and convert to
➥lowercase', inject(function(permalinkFilter) {
      expect(permalinkFilter('I had 3 spaces')).
➥toEqual('i-had-3-spaces');
    }));

  });

});
```

The test is pretty straightforward. Here we just inject `permalinkFilter` and test it with a sample input as usual.

Now you can run **scripts/test.sh** or **scripts/test.bat** to execute the tests.

Wordcount Filter

A helpful feature of many blogging apps is the ability to show the word count of a post while it's being written or edited. Let's add that to our app using filters.

Here is the code for the filter wordcount from the file **modules/admin/js/filters.js**:

```
angular.module('spBlogger.admin.filters').
➥filter('wordcount',function(){
    return function(input){
        return input===undefined ? 0 : input.split(/\s/g).length;
    }
});
```

If the admin has not typed any content the count is 0. Otherwise we break at every space to count the words. Now the filter can be used in the template **modules/admin/views/_form.html**:

```
<span>{{post.content | wordcount}} words</span> <br/>
```

Lastly, we need to test this filter as well. So, here is the snippet for the unit test that goes into test/unit/**filtersSpec.js** :

```
describe('Wordcount Filter Test\n', function() {

    it('Should count the number of words as 3',
➥inject(function(wordcountFilter) {
        expect(wordcountFilter('Three words here')).toEqual(3);
    }));

});
```

As usual, you can run **scripts/test.sh** or **scripts/test.bat** to see the test results.

Conclusion

Filters give you great power in terms of formatting data. In this chapter we covered the basics of filters and explored some of the built-in filters. We also learned how to create custom filters and saw three important filters that work with ng-repeat. Finally, we saw how to build two simple filters for our demo app and unit test them.

Next up, we'll move on to look at animation in AngularJS.

Chapter

14

AngularJS Animation

Animation is an important part of any web app that wants to create a rich user experience. With the release of AngularJS 1.2 creating animations has become even easier. If you have an existing AngularJS app, all you need to do is add CSS classes to your elements to provide a hook for the animations. AngularJS automatically adds or removes these classes at various points in the lifecycle of several directives. You can write CSS rules against these classes and get started with animation in no time.

Animations can be written using CSS3 transitions, CSS keyframe animations, and JavaScript code. This chapter will teach you how to create animations using all three techniques. To finish, we'll also add a simple animation to our demo app.

 A Primer on Animation Types

We can create animations in AngularJS using three techniques:

▪ **CSS3 Transitions**: Normally, when you change a CSS property the result is instantaneous (say, when you change the color of a `<div>` from white to red, for example). CSS3 transitions[1] provide an easy way to make this change happen gradually over a period of time.

- **CSS3 Keyframes**: CSS3 keyframe animation[2] lets you control the intermediate steps in animation by introducing **keyframes**. This provides a much greater level of control over the animation than using simple transitions.

- **JavaScript Animation**: JavaScript animation is achieved by gradually moving DOM elements, changing element styles, etc. jQuery provides a simple-to-use interface to apply animations to your web app. We can use it in our AngularJS app, too. But do remember CSS3 animations are much faster than JavaScript animations and should be used whenever possible.

Getting Started

Animation is not a core part of AngularJS. To get started, you need to include the script **angular-animate.js** in your main page. Head over to the Angular Seed Master you downloaded earlier and navigate to **app/lib/angular/angular-animate.js**. This is the script you need to include in your project, and it creates a module called `ngAnimate`. In order to use animations you need to declare a dependency on the module `ngAnimate` as follows:

```
angular.module('myApp',['ngAnimate']);
```

Animation with CSS3 Transitions

Let's see how to apply a simple fade-in/fade-out animation using the `ng-if` directive and CSS3 transitions. Assuming you have downloaded and installed `ngAnimate` let's start with a simple template:

```
<div ng-init="isShown=true">
    <input type="checkbox" ng-model="isShown" />Show

    <div class="my-animation-class" ng-if="isShown">
      <h3>Enter/Leave Animation</h3>
```

---

[1] http://www.w3.org/TR/css3-transitions/
[2] http://www.w3.org/TR/css3-animations/

```
    </div>

</div>
```

Here, we have an ng-if directive attached to a div that inserts a template based on the model isShown. Let's say we want to apply an animation while the template is being added or removed. This can be done with simple CSS3 transitions. The ng-if directive automatically adds a couple of CSS classes to the element during its lifecycle. When AngularJS inserts the template a class ng-enter is added. You can use this class to write your starting animation. Once the template has been added another class called ng-enter-active is added to the element, which marks the end of the transition. You can use this class to complete the animation.

I have added a class my-animation-class to the element and we'll write all CSS transitions using this class as a base.

```
.my-animation-class.ng-enter {
  -webkit-transition: 0.5s linear all;
  -o-transition: 0.5s linear all;
  -moz-transition: 0.5s linear all;
  opacity: 0;
  background: green;
}
.my-animation-class.ng-enter.ng-enter-active {
  opacity: 1;
}
```

The starting animation is written using the class .my-animation-class.ng-enter as a hook. We make the opacity 0, set the background as green, and trigger a transition for 0.5s. The good news is that ngAnimate is aware of the transition-delay property (in this case, 0.5s) and automatically adds the class ng-enter-active, which acts as the end point for our animation.

In this case we simply make the opacity 1. Once the animation is over, both the classes ng-enter and ng-enter-active are automatically removed. As a result of the transition we see a fade-in effect while the template is being added, due to ng-if.

Now, let's say that we also want to show an animation when the template is being removed. When this happens, the ng-if directive also adds two more CSS classes called `ng-leave` and `ng-leave-active`. We can use these classes to start and stop the animation when the template is being removed. Here is the CSS to do that:

```css
.my-animation-class.ng-leave {
  -webkit-transition: 0.5s linear all;
  -o-transition: 0.5s linear all;
  -moz-transition: 0.5s linear all;
}
.my-animation-class.ng-leave.ng-leave-active {
  opacity: 0;
}
```

Going Further

`ng-if` is not the only directive that automatically adds and removes `ng-enter` and `ng-leave` CSS classes during its lifecycle. The following table shows the different directives that use these classes:

Event	Start CSS Classs	End CSS Class	Directives
enter	.ng-enter	.ng-enter-active	ngIf,ngView
enter	.ng-enter	.ng-enter-active	ngInclude,ngRepeat
leave	.ng-leave	.ng-leave-active	ngIf,ngView
leave	.ng-leave	.ng-leave-active	ngInclude,ngRepeat
move	.ng-move	.ng-move-active	ngRepeat

You write the animations in a similar way as described above for each of the directives.

AngularJS also supports animation based on the addition or removal of CSS classes. The following table provides a summary:

Event	Start CSS Classs	End CSS Class	Directives
hide	.ng-hide-add	.ng-hide-add-active	ngShow,ngHide
show	.ng-hide-remove	.ng-hide-remove-active	ngShow,ngHide
addition of class	.CLASSNAME-add	.CLASSNAME-add-active	ngClassclass={{classname}}
removal of class	.CLASSNAME-remove	.CLASSNAME-remove-active	ngClassclass={{classname}}

Let's see how we can change our previous example to use `ng-show` and animate it. The modified template is as follows:

```
<div ng-init="isShown=true">
    <input type="checkbox" ng-model="isShown" />Show

    <div class="my-animation-class" ng-show="isShown">
      <h3>Show/Hide Animation</h3>
    </div>

</div>
```

Now we are using `ng-show` to show and hide the template. When the template is being shown the class `ng-hide-remove` is added initially, while `ng-hide-remove-active` is added to mark the end of the transition. Similarly, when the template is being hidden, the `ng-hide-add` and `ng-hide-add-active` classes are added. As a result, we can use these classes to apply some CSS3 transitions:

```
.my-animation-class.ng-hide-remove {
  -webkit-transition: 0.5s linear all;
  -o-transition: 0.5s linear all;
  -moz-transition: 0.5s linear all;
  opacity: 0;
  background: green;
}
.my-animation-class.ng-hide-remove.ng-hide-remove-active {
  opacity: 1;
}
.my-animation-class.ng-hide-add {
  -webkit-transition: 0.5s linear all;
  -o-transition: 0.5s linear all;
  -moz-transition: 0.5s linear all;
}
.my-animation-class.ng-hide-add.ng-hide-add-active {
  opacity: 0;
}
```

Support in Older Versions of IE

CSS3 transitions are not supported in IE9 and earlier. If you want to support these browsers, you might use jQuery animations instead. We'll see how to do that shortly. But do bear in mind that CSS3 transitions are always faster and should be used whenever possible.

Animation Using Keyframes

We've seen how to write animations using CSS3 transitions, but `ngAnimate` also supports animations using CSS3 keyframes. Let's see how to refactor the show/hide animation we discussed earlier using keyframes. The process is very similar; the only difference is that you don't need to write any CSS against `ng-hide-remove-active`. Your CSS code will target the class `.ng-hide-remove` and the animations will be managed within `@keyframes` blocks. Here's the CSS to support keyframe animations (The template remains same as before):

```css
.my-animation-class.ng-hide-remove {
  -webkit-animation:0.5s fade-in;
  animation:0.5s fade-in;
}

@keyframes fade-in {
  from { opacity:0;background:green; }
  to { opacity:1; }
}

@-webkit-keyframes fade-in {
  from { opacity:0; background:green;  }
  to { opacity:1; }
}
```

The above code displays an animation when the `div` is being shown. I'll leave it up to you to write an animation for when the template is being hidden.

 Support in Older Versions of IE

Like CSS3 transitions, keyframe animation also doesn't work with IE9 and below.

Animation Using jQuery

If you need more control over the animation and want to support older browsers you can always use JavaScript for animation. Let's see how we can use jQuery for animating our previous example involving the `ng-if` directive. Here's the template:

```
<div ng-init="isShown=true">
        <input type="checkbox" ng-model="isShown" />Show

        <div class="my-animation-class" ng-if="isShown">
          <h3>Enter/Leave Animation</h3>
        </div>
</div>
```

To attach animations through jQuery you need to create an `animation` component
by calling the `angular.module().animation()` function. The following code shows
the creation of such a component:

```
angular.module('animationDemo', ['ngAnimate']).
➥animation('.my-animation-class',function(){
  return {
    enter: function(elem,done){

      elem.css({
        background:'green',
        opacity:0
      });

      elem.animate({
        backgroundColor:'white',
        opacity:1
      }, done);

    },
    leave:function(elem,done){
      elem.css({
        opacity:1
      });

      elem.animate({
        opacity:0
      }, done);
    },

    move : function(element, done) { done(); },

    beforeAddClass : function(element, className, done) { done(); },
    addClass : function(element, className, done) { done(); },

    beforeRemoveClass : function(element, className, done)
```

```
➥{ done(); },
    removeClass : function(element, className, done) { done(); }
  }
});
```

As you see, the first argument to the `.animation()` function is the name of the CSS class present on your target element. In our case, it's `.my-animation-class`. The second argument is a factory function that returns an object that possesses various properties to attach animations. As we are using `ngIf`, we can use the `enter` and `leave` properties to apply animations.

Inside `enter`, we first set the opacity to 0 and change the background color to green. Next, we call `jQuery.animate()` to make a transition. Also note the `done()` function is passed to `animate()` to mark the end of transition. The same is true of the `leave` transition, but, in terms of opacity, we do the reverse.

There's also support for other types of animation through properties such as `move`, `beforeAddClass`, `addClass`, `beforeRemoveClass`, `removeClass` etc. In our example, we only need `enter` and `leave` animations so we can omit these properties. Later on we'll see how to utilize other properties.

Note that you need to load jQuery before AngularJS in order for the animation to work. Bear in mind, also, that you should always use CSS3 animations in your app so that modern browsers can take advantage of them. Then, in your JavaScript animation component, you can detect the browser and conditionally write animations so that users of older browsers get a fallback to jQuery animation.

Animation Using ngClass

So far we've seen the three ways of writing animations and, in every method, CSS classes have played the major role in attaching them. You might remember `ng-class` conditionally attaches classes to the element based on the `scope` model value. It's even easier to employ this to write our animations. Let's see how we can animate elements with the `ng-class` directives.

As we saw in the previous table, animation hooks look like `.CLASSNAME-add`, `.CLASSNAME-add-active` &, `.CLASSNAME-remove`, and `.CLASSNAME-remove-active`. Think of `CLASSNAME` as the name of the class that's added or removed by `ng-class`. So, when `ng-class` adds a new class to the element, the animation you wrote against

.CLASSNAME-add will be triggered. The end of the animation is marked by .CLASS-NAME-add-active. The same is true for .CLASSNAME-remove and .CLASSNAME-remove-active.

Take a look at the following snippet, which displays a 100x100 div. Let's say that, on hover, its size should expand to 200x200 and then return back to its original size:

```
<div class="my-animation-class" ng-class="{'growing-div':grow}"
➥ng-mouseover="grow=true" ng-mouseout="grow=false"></div>
```

When a user hovers on the div, a class growing-div is attached to it. ng-class also adds the class growing-div-add for starting the animation. When this happens, the transition written against .growing-div-add will be triggered. Similarly the transition written against growing-div-add-active will be triggered when the animation needs to be stopped. This is where we increase the size of the div.

Here is the code for the transition:

```
.my-animation-class {
  height: 100px;
  width: 100px;
  background:green;
}
.my-animation-class.growing-div-add {
  -webkit-transition-property: height, width;
  -webkit-transition-duration: 1s;
}
.my-animation-class.growing-div-add-active {
  width: 200px;
  height: 200px;
}
```

Now, when you hover on the div its size will grow and then come back to normal. However, if you want the div to retain its size as long as the user hovers on the div, you can use the following CSS transition:

```
.my-animation-class.growing-div{
  -webkit-transition-property: height, width;
  -webkit-transition-duration: 1s;
}
```

```
    width: 200px;
    height: 200px;
  }
```

I encourage you to try `.CLASSNAME.remove` and `.CLASSNAME.remove-active` animations on your own to make it so that when the div returns to its normal size the
transition is smooth.

Now if you wanted to achieve the same effect using JavaScript, you could use the
following:

```
angular.module('animationDemo', ['ngAnimate']);

angular.module('animationDemo').animation('.my-animation-class',
➥function(){
  return {
    addClass : function(elem, className, done) {
      if(className==='growing-div'){
        elem.animate({width: '200px',height:'200px',duration: 1000,
➥queue: true}, done);
      }
    },
    removeClass : function(elem, className, done) {
      if(className==='growing-div'){
        elem.animate({width: '100px',height:'100px',duration: 1000,
➥queue: true},done);
      }
    }

  }
});
```

In our previous discussion of JavaScript animation, we saw the `enter` and `leave`
functions. Now let's see two more functions: `addClass` and `removeClass`. The `ad-
dClass` function will be called when `ng-class` adds the class to the element.
`className` detects the class being added, and writes the transition accordingly.
Similarly, `removeClass` is called when the class is removed. We use jQuery animation
here to ensure the transition is smooth when the div returns to its original size.

You can comment out the CSS rules and add this code to see it working. No other change is needed. Again this uses jQuery's animation, so you need to load jQuery before AngularJS.

Animation with Custom Directives

We've seen how to use animations with directives such as ngIf,ngShow,ngClass, etc. What if we wanted to use animations with our own directives? The good news is that ngAnimate provides a useful service called $animate which can be used to roll out animations with custom directives. To use $animate, you need to inject it into your directive's factory function. It defines the following functions, which can be invoked within your directive to trigger the appropriate animations:

- enter(elem,parent,after,callback) : Appends the child element into the parent node or after the *after* node and then runs enter animation.

- leave(elem,callback): Runs leave animation and removes the element from DOM.

- move(elem, parent, after, callback): Moves the element into the parent node or after the *after* node and runs the move animation.

- addClass(elem,className,callback): Runs the addClass animation and adds the specified class to the element.

- removeClass(elem,className,callback):Runs the removeClass animation and removes the specified class from the element.

Let's create a directive that uses $animate for animations. We'll develop a simple directive which will generate and display a random number on a button click. If the generated number is more than 0.5, the number should shake.

The directive code is pretty straightforward:

```
angular.module('animationDemo', ['ngAnimate']).directive('shakeDiv',
➥function($animate, $timeout) {
  return {
    link: function(scope, elem, attrs) {
      scope.generateRandom = function() {
        scope.randomValue = Math.random().toFixed(2);
```

```
            if (scope.randomValue > 0.5) { //if >0.5 add the class
                $animate.addClass(elem.find('.my-animation-class'),
➥'shake');
                $timeout(function() {
                    $animate.removeClass(elem.find('.my-animation-class'),
➥'shake');
                }, 1000);
            }
        }
    },
    template: '<input type="button" ng-click="generateRandom()"
➥value="Generate Random Value"/><h2 class="my-animation-class">
➥{{randomValue}}</h2>'
    }
});
```

The name of our directive is shakeDiv. It has two dependencies: $animate and
$timeout. It has a simple template that consists of a button and an <h2> element
which displays the generated random number.

On the button click scope.generateRandom() is called; it generates a random value.
If the value is more than 0.5, we call $animate.addClass(elem.find('.my-anima-
tion-class'), 'shake') to trigger addClass animation where we perform a shake
effect. Next, we use $timeout service to remove the class after 1s. We do this so
that the shake effect doesn't last forever.

Now the CSS3 keyframe animation for the shake effect is as follows:

```
.my-animation-class {
    -webkit-animation-duration: 1s;
    animation-duration: 1s;
    -webkit-animation-fill-mode: both;
    animation-fill-mode: both;
}

@-webkit-keyframes shake {
    0%, 100% {-webkit-transform: translateX(0);}
    10%, 30%, 50%, 70%, 90% {-webkit-transform: translateX(-10px);}
    20%, 40%, 60%, 80% {-webkit-transform: translateX(10px);}
}
@keyframes shake {
    0%, 100% {transform: translateX(0);}
    10%, 30%, 50%, 70%, 90% {transform: translateX(-10px);}
```

```
    20%, 40%, 60%, 80% {transform: translateX(10px);}
}
.my-animation-class.shake {
    -webkit-animation-name: shake;
    animation-name: shake;
}
```

Adding Simple Animation to Single Page Blogger

Let's see how to apply animation to Single Page Blogger. We'll add an animation to the comments section. Currently, when you add a new comment to a post it appears suddenly. Now let's make comment appearance smooth by adding a fade-in transition.

If you open up the template for comments **modules/posts/views/comments.html** you'll find the following `<div>` that is repeated through `ng-repeat`:

```
<div class="single-comment" ng-repeat="comment
➡in postInstance.comments"></div>
```

Now you should recall `ng-repeat` adds a class `.ng-enter` when a new item is added to the list. It also adds `.ng-enter-active` when the animation should end. So, you can simply open up **app.css** and add the following CSS rules for animation:

```
.single-comment.ng-enter{
    -webkit-transition: 1s linear all;
    -o-transition: 1s linear all;
    -moz-transition: 1s linear all;
    opacity: 0;
}
.single-comment.ng-enter.ng-enter-active{
    opacity:1;
}
```

Note that **.single-comment** is the name of our target element class. Now, if you open a post and add a new comment you can see a fade-in effect! That's it.

It's almost too simple to add animations to an existing AngularJS app. There are many more places in Single Page Blogger where you can add animation. For example, when the `ui-view` content changes it adds `ng-enter` and `ng-enter-active` classes. You can start with this and gradually move to other places.

Don't Go Overboard with Animation

Don't go overboard with animations. Use them sparingly and they'll have a much bigger impact.

Remember to Install ngAnimate in the App

For animation to work in Single Page Blogger, you need to have installed `ngAnimate`.

Conclusion

In this chapter we explored the different ways of applying animations in AngularJS. You'll have noted that addition and removal of CSS classes play the major role in animation. You can write either CSS rules or JavaScript code that fires transitions or animations based on the classes. In a nutshell, AngularJS enables us to write animations using CSS3 transitions, CSS keyframe animation, and JavaScript. You can also roll out animations within your own directive using `$animate` service. I hope you've enjoyed reading about animations. The next chapter will discuss deployment.

Chapter 15

Deployment and Internationalization

You're nearing the end of the book, and are well on your way to becoming an Angular ninja. But there is a tiny gotcha! We've been busy developing functionality for our app right from the beginning, but how do we deploy our app for the world to see it? And what about people from different locations who speak different languages? Can they understand our website content? Well, this chapter answers these questions and readies your AngularJS app ready for deployment.

To begin with, let's see how we can deploy our app.

Deployment

Here's an overview of best practice deployment:

1. Open up **index.html** from our demo app (**/sp-blogger/index.html**), scroll to the bottom, and you'll see our source code is divided into many JavaScript files. The problem with loading multiple script files is that they block parallel execution. In addition to this, there's a limit on the maximum number of parallel resource downloads for the same domain. When the browser encounters a `<script>` tag the rendering stops and it starts executing the script. This done, it then moves

to the next `<script>` and so on. Of course, you can set the `async` attribute on `<script>` element, which will enable multiple scripts to be downloaded asynchronously. However, this gives the server a lot more work to do. The solution to these issues is to concatenate all the scripts into a single file so that the browser can download the whole lot in a single HTTP request. This clearly improves the performance and reduces your app's response time.

2. Simply concatenating files is not enough, though. To improve the performance further we need to reduce the script size so that the browser can quickly download it.

3. We need to repeat steps one and two for CSS files as well; in other words, we also need to link and compress CSS files.

4. Finally, it's a good idea to keep source code and deployable code in separate directories to make it easy to deploy the app.

It's a huge pain to do all these tasks manually each time we prepare our app for deployment. And so, we'll use a tool called **Grunt**[1]. Grunt is a task runner that automates recurring tasks for us, and it's available as a Node module. Let's see how we can use Grunt in our demo app.

First of all, we need to download and install the `grunt-cli` node module globally. To do this run the following command from terminal:

```
npm install grunt-cli -g
```

This will add the `grunt` command to your system path so you can invoke it from any directory. Next, you need to install the actual `grunt` module locally in your app. So now go to your app root directory `/sp-blogger` and run the following command:

```
npm install grunt --save
```

Grunt will now look for a special file `Gruntfile.js` in the root directory in order to read the tasks. Let's add this file to the root of our app and list all the tasks in it. Figure 15.1 shows the presence of **Gruntfile.js** in our app.

---

[1] http://gruntjs.com/

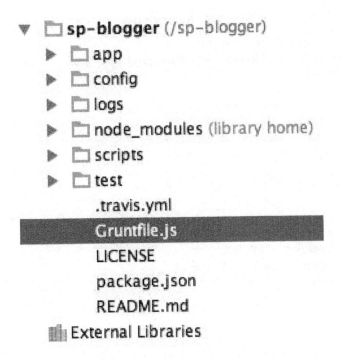

Figure 15.1. Grunfile.js in place

Next up, we need to download a selection of Grunt plugins that automate a variety of tasks. These are node modules and need to be installed via npm. Before doing that let's take a look at each of the tasks:

1. **grunt-contrib-concat**: Concatenates multiple JS files into one.

2. **grunt-contrib-uglify**: Minifies the JS files.

3. **grunt-contrib-cssmin**: Minifies CSS files.

4. **grunt-usemin**: Replaces the references to non-optimized files with the optimized and concatenated file.

5. **grunt-contrib-copy**: Copies the source files into the deployable directory.

6. **grunt-contrib-clean**: Cleans the output deployable directory.

We need to update the devDependencies in **package.json** with the above module names. The content of **package.json** becomes:

```
{
  "name": "Single Page Blogger",
  "description": "A Single Page Blogging app built with AngularJS",
  "devDependencies": {
    "karma": "~0.10",
    "karma-chrome-launcher": "^0.1.2",
    "karma-jasmine": "^0.2.2",
    "karma-junit-reporter": "^0.2.1",
    "karma-ng-html2js-preprocessor": "^0.1.0",
    "phantomjs": "~1.9",
    "protractor": "~0.17.0",
    "grunt-contrib-concat": "~0.3.0",
    "grunt-contrib-uglify": "~0.2.7",
    "grunt-contrib-cssmin": "~0.7.0",
    "grunt-usemin": "~2.0.2",
    "grunt-contrib-copy": "~0.5.0",
    "grunt-contrib-clean": "~0.5.0"
  }
}
```

Now we simply run `npm install` from our app's root directory to install the modules.

No Need to Install the Modules if You're Using the Code Archive

If you're using the book's code archive, it already has these modules installed, so you won't need to run `npm install`.

Finally, you need to create a directory **/sp-blogger/dist** in which our distribution release will be placed.

Now open up **Gruntfile.js** and take a look inside to understand what really happens in deployment:

1. `grunt.initConfig` provides options for configuring different tasks.

2. `clean: ["dist", '.tmp']` tells grunt to clean up `dist` and `.tmp` directories before copying resources.

3. The `copy` task configuration specifies which directories to copy to the **dist/** directory. In our case we only copy **app/** and **script/web-server.js** to the output directory.

4. `useminPrepare` and `usemin` specify the main files that contain references to various scripts. In our case the files are app/**index**.html and dist/**app**/index.html. The script and CSS files included in **app/index.html** will be concatenated and minified.

5. `uglify` configuration gauges whether or not to compress the files.

As described previously, Grunt task plugins are installed via npm. And so, we need to register these tasks with the following code in **Gruntfile**.js:

```
grunt.loadNpmTasks('grunt-contrib-clean');
grunt.loadNpmTasks('grunt-contrib-copy');
grunt.loadNpmTasks('grunt-contrib-concat');
grunt.loadNpmTasks('grunt-contrib-cssmin');
grunt.loadNpmTasks('grunt-contrib-uglify');
grunt.loadNpmTasks('grunt-usemin');
```

Finally, we need to tell Grunt what to do when we type grunt in the terminal. What we really want is to run the above tasks one after another, like so:

```
grunt.registerTask('default', [
    'clean', 'copy', 'useminPrepare', 'concat', 'uglify', 'cssmin',
➥'usemin','adjustBuiltLinks'
]);
```

Now, open up **app/index.html**. We need to tell Grunt about the files we want to concatenate and minify. For CSS files, we use the following comment block:

```
<!-- build:css app/built/app.min.css -->
<link rel="stylesheet" href="lib/bootstrap/bootstrap.css">
<link rel="stylesheet" href="css/app.css">
<!-- endbuild -->
```

This means the two CSS files mentioned will be concatenated and minified and the result will be placed in **dist/app/built/app.min.css**.

Similarly, for these scripts we write the following:

```
<!-- build:js app/built/app.min.js -->

<script src="lib/jquery/jquery.js"></script>
```

```
<script src="lib/bootstrap/bootstrap.js"></script>
<script src="lib/angular/angular.js"></script>
<script src="lib/angular-ui-router/angular-ui-router.js">  </script>
<script src="lib/angular/angular-resource.js"></script>
<script src="lib/angular/angular-sanitize.js"></script>
<script src="lib/angular/angular-animate.js"></script>

<script src="js/app.js"></script>
<script src="js/controllers.js"></script>
<script src="js/directives.js"></script>
<script src="js/filters.js"></script>
<script src="js/services.js"></script>

<script src="modules/admin/adminModule.js"></script>
<script src="modules/admin/js/controllers.js"></script>
<script src="modules/admin/js/filters.js"></script>
<script src="modules/admin/js/directives.js"></script>
<script src="modules/admin/js/services.js"></script>

<script src="modules/posts/postModule.js"></script>
<script src="modules/posts/js/controllers.js"></script>
<script src="modules/posts/js/filters.js"></script>
<script src="modules/posts/js/directives.js"></script>
<script src="modules/posts/js/services.js"></script>

<!-- endbuild -->
```

And so, ultimately, the script files will be concatenated and minified and stored in **app/built/app.min.js**.

Now, let's start the deployment. Go to **/sp-blogger** and just type `grunt` and hit enter. Once the process finishes, open up **dist/app/index.html** and you'll notice that it contains only a single CSS and JavaScript file. The **index.html** content looks like this:

```
<!doctype html>
<html lang="en" ng-app="spBlogger">
<head>
  <meta charset="utf-8">
  <base href="/">
  <title>The Single Page Blogger</title>
  <link rel="stylesheet" href="built/app.min.css"/>
</head>
```

```
<body>
  <div class="container">
    <br/>
    <div class="jumbotron text-center">
        <h1>The Single Page Blogger</h1>
        <p>One stop blogging solution</p>
    </div>
    <div ui-view class="main-content">Loading . . .</div>
    <div class="row footer">
        <div class="col-xs-12 text-center">
            <p>The Single Page Blogger</p>
        </div>
    </div>
  </div>
</body>

    <script src="built/app.min.js"></script>
</html>
```

Congratulations! You've completed the deployment. Now, to verify it, run the following in terminal:

```
cd sp-blogger/dist/app
```

And then:

```
node ../scripts/web-server.js
```

This will start the server and you can open up `http://localhost:8000` as usual in the browser. Now your app is optimized and its performance improved.

Source Maps for Debugging

An issue with the approach described here is that we're running different code in development and production modes. The code in production is optimized, as it's minified and concatenated. There's a chance that you may find a bug in the production mode that doesn't occur in development mode. To address this, you can run Grunt every time you change code, and always work in production mode so that you're sure that the code works in production.

To make debugging easier, you can start using Source Maps[2]. A source map is basically a mapping between the production code and the original development code you authored. So, if you encounter some error in the minified version you can easily locate its exact position in the original code.

Whenever you make significant changes and need to redeploy the app to the cloud you simply need to run `grunt` and go to the **dist/** directory to pick up the release.

So that's deployment. I encourage you to go through the grunt documentation to learn more about the tool and different tasks.

Finally in this chapter, let's make our app accessible to users from around the world. To do this we need to add **internationalization** support. Let's see how we can do that in AngularJS.

Internationalization

To add internationalization to our demo app we'll use a very easy-to-use third-party module called angular-translate[3]. You don't need to download the script as I've already placed it in the demo app. The path to the file is **/sp-blogger/app/lib/angular/angular-translate.js**.

To demonstrate `angular-translate` let's add German-language support to Single Page Blogger. First, we need to load the script in **index.html** so that AngularJS can find the module. Here is how we include the file:

```
<script src="lib/angular/angular-translate.js"></script>
```

The next step is to add a dependency on the module `pascalprecht.translate` defined by `angular-translate`. So, we go to `sp-blogger/app/js/`**app.js** and add the above module in the dependencies list. It now looks like this:

---

[2] http://www.html5rocks.com/en/tutorials/developertools/sourcemaps/
[3] http://angular-translate.github.io/

```
angular.module('spBlogger',['ngSanitize','ngResource',
➥'ngAnimate','ui.router','pascalprecht.translate',..]);
```

Note that I omitted our custom modules listed towards the end for the sake of brevity.

Now, we need to add a `config` block to our main module `spBlogger` and inject `$translateProvider` to add translations to it. The following code shows how it's done:

```
angular.module('spBlogger').config(['$translateProvider',
➥function($translateProvider){

    $translateProvider.translations('en', {
        TITLE: 'The Single Page Blogger',
        SUBTITLE: 'One Stop Blogging Solution',
        COMMENTS: 'Comments',
        BY:'By',
        ADD:'Add'
    });

    $translateProvider.translations('de', {
        TITLE: 'Single Page Blogger',
        SUBTITLE: 'Die Komplettlösung für Ihr Blog',
        COMMENTS: 'Kommentare',
        BY:'Von',
        ADD:'Hinzufügen'
    });

    $translateProvider.preferredLanguage('en');

}]);
```

We use `translateProvider.translations` to store the translations against a key. Here we added translations for English and German. But if you want to support more languages you can keep adding more translations using the same method. Finally, `$translateProvider.preferredLanguage('en')` sets the preferred language to English.

Next, we'll add a toggle button to `index.html`, which will allow users to switch between languages. The following markup creates this:

```
<div class="btn-group btn-toggle">
        <button class="btn btn-xs btn-default"
➥ng-class="{en:'active'}[languagePreference.currentLanguage]"
➥ng-click="languagePreference.switchLanguage('en')" >English
➥</button>
        <button class="btn btn-xs btn-primary"
➥ng-class="{de:'active'}[languagePreference.currentLanguage]"
➥ng-click="languagePreference.switchLanguage('de')">German</button>
</div>
```

Note that we're using Bootstrap's CSS classes to create toggle buttons.

The next thing we need to do is add a function `languagePreference.switchLanguage()` to $rootScope. This takes the language key and switches to the specified language. For that we modify the `run` block in our module `spBlogger` as follows:

```
angular.module('spBlogger').run(['$state','$rootScope','$translate',
➥function($state,$rootScope,$translate){

    $state.go('allPosts');

    $rootScope.languagePreference={currentLanguage:'en'};

    $rootScope.languagePreference.switchLanguage=function(key){
        $translate.use(key);
        $rootScope.languagePreference.currentLanguage=key;
    }
}]);
```

The function `$translate.use(key)` takes a key and loads the translations written against it. In addition, we use the property `$rootScope.language.currentLanguage` to apply the `active` class, conditionally, to the toggle button in the view.

Now we need to open up **index.html** and replace the static hardcoded strings with something like:

```
{{'KEY' | translate}}
```

So, the following expressions can be added to `index.html` to represent title and subtitle of the website.

```
<h1>{{'TITLE' | translate}}</h1>
<p>{{'SUBTITLE' | translate}}</p>
```

Now let's open up `modules/posts/views/comments.html` and replace the text `Comments` and button label `Add` with:

```
<h3>{{'COMMENTS' | translate}}</h3>
```

And:

```
<input type="submit" value="{{'ADD' | translate}}"
➥ng-click="saveComment()" class="form-control btn-success
➥small-button" />
```

We're all set! Of course, should you wish, you can add more translations and internationalize additional sections.

To test this you can go to `localhost:8000` in the browser and switch the language by clicking on the toggle button. As soon as you switch you can instantly see the labels change to the chosen language. Cool, isn't it?

Figure 15.2 and Figure 15.3 show how the app looks in German :

Figure 15.2. Single Page Blogger in German

Figure 15.3. The comments section, internationalized

Supporting Many Different Locations

When the number of translations grows in terms of size it's not feasible to keep them in a single JavaScript file. You need to break the translations into separate external files organized by location and load them asynchronously. The good news is that `angular-translate` has excellent support for this. Check out the documentation[4] for more details.

Conclusion

We're almost at the end of the book! First we saw how to optimize our app for deployment with `grunt` and now we've gone international with `angular-translate`. But to be a true ninja you need to understand how to authenticate the users of your app, and so that's the topic of the final chapter.

---

[4] http://angular-translate.github.io/docs/#/guide/12_asynchronous-loading

Chapter **16**

Authentication and Authorization in AngularJS

Authentication and **Authorization** are two important parts of any web application. Authentication is a process during which a client needs to prove its identity to the server. Authorization, on the other hand, is used by the server to determine if the user has permission to view a particular resource. In this chapter you'll learn how to implement user authentication and authorization in our demo app.

Before getting started, let's go through our problem statement. We want to implement an authentication/authorization mechanism where only administrators can publish, edit, or delete posts. To authenticate themselves, the users must provide a username and password and we'll check if it's valid. If so, we'll redirect the administrator to the admin panel route where he or she can perform CRUD operations. Otherwise the user will be asked to log in again. We'll also check if the user is logged in every time an admin route loads so that nobody can access the admin route directly.

The main issue we have is that any security constraints we put in on the client-side can easily be circumvented. Securing our resource URLs from unauthorized access is a server-side affair and hence we need to take care of this first. Then, on the client side, we can use AngularJS to provide a better user experience by asking the users to log in to access secure routes. Remember that the view templates and code for secure routes can still be accessed by the end users. But as long as your API endpoints are secured and protected this shouldn't be a problem. With these points in mind, let's implement authentication in our demo app.

Adding Login Functionality

If you remember, our API endpoints for interacting with posts for Single Page Blogger look like the following. I have omitted the hostname in the URLs, which is : `spblogger-sitepointdemos.rhcloud.com`.

URL	HTTP Verb	Request Body	Result	Protected
`/api/posts`	GET	empty	Returns all posts	No
`/api/posts`	POST	JSON String	Create new post	Yes
`/api/posts/:id`	GET	empty	Returns single post	No
`/api/posts/:id`	PUT	JSON String	Updates existing post	No
`/api/posts/:id`	DELETE	empty	Deletes existing post	Yes

Additionally, I have now added security constraints to the endpoints. The last column, `Protected`, indicates if the URL is protected. We have two secure endpoints—that is endpoints involving POST and DELETE actions. You need to authenticate yourself to access these. The other endpoints use PUT and GET requests that are available for public access. The PUT request should really be protected also, as it changes the state of server resource just like POST. But as we're allowing the public to comment on the posts and thereby update them let's keep it open for now for the sake of simplicity.

Also, we have another endpoint `/login` that'll authenticate the users, and this expects a JSON string containing `username` and `password` as the POST body. If the login succeeds it responds with a JSON response, which represents the admin. Otherwise it'll send a "401 unauthorized" response. Similarly, to log out a user we have another endpoint called /`logout`. It responds to a POST request and logs out the currently logged-in user.

Now, let's take a look at what we need to do on the AngularJS side of things:

1. Create a state `login` which shows a login screen to the user.

2. Once we have a username and password we'll make a POST request to the remote server endpoint /`login`, which will check the validity.

3. If the username/password combination is valid it will send a JSON response representing the user. Otherwise it'll send a 401 status code.

4. Once the login is successful we'll take the user to the admin panel. In our case the admin state name is `admin`. So, the admin user will be redirected to here.

5. In case of unsuccessful login, we will show an error message and ask the user to re-authenticate.

6. To logout we simply send a request to the remote server URL /`logout` and redirect the user to the `login` state.

Firstly, let's define a state `login`, as follows:

```
$stateProvider.state('login',{
    url:'/login',
    controller:'LoginController',
    templateUrl:'modules/admin/views/login.html'
});
```

This is defined in the file **app/modules/admin/adminModule.js**. Here is the template used in this state:

```
<div class="row">
    <div class="col-sm-6 col-md-4 col-md-offset-4">
        <h1 class="text-center login-title">Login to Admin Panel
➥</h1>
        <div class="account-wall">
            <form class="form-signin" ng-submit="login()">
                <div ng-show="invalidLogin"
➥class="alert alert-danger">Invalid username/password</div>
```

```
                    <input type="text" class="form-control" p
laceholder="Username" ng-model="credentials.username"
ng-required="true"/>
                    <input type="password" class="form-control"
placeholder="Password" ng-model="credentials.password"
ng-required="true"/>
                    <button class="btn btn-lg btn-primary btn-block"
type="submit">{{buttonText}}</button>
                </form>
            </div>
        </div>
</div>
```

This is a simple form that asks for a username and password. These values are stored in two scope models called `credentials.username` and `credentials.password` respectively. When the Login button is clicked the form is submitted and our function `login()` runs, which starts the authentication process. This is how the function is defined in our controller `LoginController`:

```
angular.module('spBlogger.admin.controllers').controller
('LoginController',['$scope','authService',
'$state',function($scope,authService,$state){

    $scope.buttonText="Login";

    $scope.login=function(){

        $scope.buttonText="Logging in. . .";

        authService.login($scope.credentials.username,$scope.
credentials.password).then(function(data){
            $state.go('admin.postViewAll');
        },function(err){
            $scope.invalidLogin=true;
        }).finally(function(){
            $scope.buttonText="Login";
        });
    }
}]);
```

Before initiating the login, we change the button text to `Logging in` so that the user gets feedback that the process has started. Then we use a custom `authService` (you'll see shortly) to login. If authentication succeeds we load the state `admin.postViewAll`.

In case of unsuccessful login we set a scope model `invalidLogin` to true so that the user can see an error message. And finally in either case we change back the button text to `Login`.

The final login screen looks like Figure 16.1.

Figure 16.1. The login screen

Now, let's create a custom service called `authService` that deals with authenticating the user:

```
angular.module('spBlogger.admin.services').factory('authService',
➥['AUTH_ENDPOINT','LOGOUT_ENDPOINT','$http','$cookieStore',
➥function(AUTH_ENDPOINT,LOGOUT_ENDPOINT,$http,$cookieStore){

    var auth={};

    auth.login=function(username,password){
        return $http.post(AUTH_ENDPOINT,{username:username,
➥password:password}).then(function(response,status){
            auth.user=response.data;
            $cookieStore.put('user',auth.user);
            return auth.user;
        });
    }

    auth.logout=function(){
```

```
        return $http.post(LOGOUT_ENDPOINT).then(function(response){
            auth.user=undefined;
            $cookieStore.remove('user');
        });
    }

    return auth;

}]);
```

Here are the endpoint URLs for login and logout respectively:

```
angular.module('spBlogger.admin.services').value('AUTH_ENDPOINT',
➥'http://spblogger-sitepointdemos.rhcloud.com/login');
angular.module('spBlogger.admin.services').value('LOGOUT_ENDPOINT',
➥'http://spblogger-sitepointdemos.rhcloud.com/logout');
```

All the above go into **app/modules/admin/js/services.js**.

authService.login() function takes a username and password and makes a request to AUTH_ENDPOINT. If the login is successful, it stores the user info in authService.user as well as $cookieStore so that it's available across page reloads. By the way, $cookieStore is defined in a separate module called ngCookies. So, we need our main module to depend on this and include angular-cookies.js script.

Now let's see the logout() function. It simply sends a POST request to LOGOUT_ENDPOINT and, upon success, clears both authService.user and $cookieStore's user.

To add $cookieStore support you need to include the following script in app/**index**.html:

```
<script src="lib/angular/angular-cookies.js"></script>
```

If you're using the code archive, I've already placed the script in the appropriate directory in the codebase so you don't have to download it.

As usual, here's how to declare the dependency on ngCookies:

```
angular.module('spBlogger',['ngCookies', . . .);
```

I have omitted the other dependencies for brevity. This goes into **app/js/app.js**.

Now we'll add a controller to the state `admin`. This will help perform the logout action. So, here is the controller with the `logout()` function:

```
angular.module('spBlogger.admin.controllers').controller
➡('AdminController',['$scope','authService','$state',
➡'user',function($scope,authService,$state,user){

    $scope.logout=function(){
        authService.logout().then(function(){
            $state.go('login');
        });
    }
}]);
```

The state `admin` should also be updated to include this controller:

```
$stateProvider.state('admin',{
    url:'/admin',
    abstract:true,
    controller:'AdminController',
    templateUrl:'modules/admin/views/admin-home.html'
});
```

Now if you open up `http://localhost:8000/#/login` you can see the brand new login page. The username and password are **admin** and **admin**. If you provide the correct values you'll be taken to `http://localhost:8000/#/admin`. In case of incorrect values you'll see an error message as shown below.

Figure 16.2. An invalid login

But if you logout and try to access `http://localhost:8000/#/admin` directly you'll be able to do so. That's because we haven't implemented access control yet! So, let's do it now.

Authorization

Our objective in this section is to prevent direct access to the `admin` state. Non-authenticated users shouldn't be able to access the URL `localhost:8000/#/admin`. Although they may access the view template for this state directly in the browser (by loading `http://localhost:8000/modules/admin/views/admin-home.html`) our API endpoints are already secure.

In UI Router, we have the concept of the `resolve` property in the state definition. This `resolve` property is an object that lists several dependencies that should be resolved before the controller is loaded. We can introduce one such dependency to our `admin` state—the `authService.user` property. If it's set it means the user is logged in and we are good to go. Otherwise, we cancel the state loading and redirect the user to the `login` state.

So, our modified `admin` state looks like following:

```
$stateProvider.state('admin',{
    url:'/admin',
    abstract:true,
    controller:'AdminController',
    resolve:{
        user:['authService','$q',function(authService,$q){
            return authService.user || $q.reject
➥({unAuthorized:true});
        }]
    },
    templateUrl:'modules/admin/views/admin-home.html'
});
```

Note the user property inside resolve. If we find the authenticated user in auth-
Service we return it. Otherwise we return a promise that always rejects (with er-
ror.unAuthorized=true) which, in turn, prevents the state from loading and triggers
a $stateChangeError event.

 Listing Dependencies

> You can list a dependency in the controller AdminController as user and, if
> the state loads successfully, it'll have the value authService.user.

Now, what we do is listen for a $stateChangeError event on $rootScope. If the
error.unAuthorized is set to true we know the user is trying to access admin
without authenticating first. So, we redirect to the login state. Here's how it looks:

```
angular.module('spBlogger.admin').run(['$rootScope','$state',
➥'$cookieStore','authService',function($rootScope,$state,
➥$cookieStore,authService){

    $rootScope.$on('$stateChangeError', function(event, toState,
➥toParams, fromState, fromParams, error) {
        if(error.unAuthorized) {
            $state.go("login");
        }
    });
});
```

```
    authService.user=$cookieStore.get('user');

}]);
```

We also retrieve the user from $cookieStore when the app loads and set it to auth-Service.user. This'll be useful in case of page refresh.

Now what if an authenticated user accesses the login state? Should we ask them to log in again? No. We'll send the user directly to the admin state. For that we add a resolve property to the login state and check for authService.user. If it's set we reject the state loading with error.authorized=true. Here's the code:

```
$stateProvider.state('login',{
    url:'/login',
    controller: 'LoginController',
    resolve:{
        user:['authService','$q',function(authService,$q){
            if(authService.user){
                return $q.reject({authorized:true});
            }
        }]
    },
    templateUrl:'modules/admin/views/login.html'
});
```

Now we listen to $stateChangeError and check whether error.authorized is true. In that case we redirect to admin state. Here is the code:

```
    $rootScope.$on('$stateChangeError', function(event, toState,
➡toParams, fromState, fromParams, error) {

        if(error.unAuthorized) {
            $state.go('login');
        }
        else if(error.authorized){
            $state.go('admin.postViewAll');
        }
    });
```

Remember our client-side AngularJS app runs on http://localhost:8000 and the Node.js back-end is on the cloud. As we're performing a cross-origin communication here we need to tell $http to send the session ID with the request (By default AngularJS won't send the session ID) so that we'll stay authenticated. If the API endpoints belong to the same server as your Angular app, this step won't be needed. Inside the `config` block of our main module we write the following code to allow sending credentials with the request:

```
$httpProvider.defaults.withCredentials = true;
```

Congratulations! We now have a login system ready for our Single Page Blogger. And this marks the end of the book as we've just released the ninja version of our app. Good work! All that remains is to follow our build process with `grunt` to obtain the deployable.

Where To Go Next?

While we've discussed most of the aspects of AngularJS there's a lot you can do to improve your AngularJS knowledge, including further reading and refining our demo app.

Things to Do Now

To improve your skills and explore new things in AngularJS you may want to get acquainted with the following:

1. AngularJS is great for creating awesome real-time apps. To create real-time apps you need a real-time back-end. This is where Firebase comes in handy. You can use Firebase[1] with your AngularJS app to store and sync data. Although Firebase is a paid service you can use the free hacker plan for testing purposes. I wrote a tutorial on Firebase[2] for SitePoint.

2. Clone the AngularJS Github repository[3] to your system and play with it. After all, reading code greatly improves your skill set. And who knows you might start contributing as well!

3. Read the documentation[4]. You'll find lots of useful examples there.

---

[1] https://www.firebase.com/
[2] http://www.sitepoint.com/creating-three-way-data-binding-firebase-angularjs/
[3] https://github.com/angular/angular.js
[4] https://docs.angularjs.org/guide

4. Go to the Angular UI Router[5] official website and check out the documentation.

5. Subscribe to the AngularJS[6] and ng-conf[7] YouTube channels for useful videos.

6. Head over to SitePoint for some cool AngularJS tutorials[8].

7. Have a look at all the nice things built with AngularJS.[9]

8. Subscribe to AngularJS questions on Stackoverflow[10] and take advantage of the active community.

9. If you're interested in mobile apps you may take a look at Ionic[11], which uses AngularJS to create hybrid apps.

Improving Our Demo App

Single Page Blogger is still very basic, but it could be greatly improved. Here are a few feature ideas; you can add these to take your app to the next level:

1. When a post is being loaded, display a loading icon and hide it when the post is shown. Hint: Show the loading icon through `ng-show` on `$stateChangeStart` event and hide it on `$stateChangeSuccess` event. These events are triggered at the `$rootScope`.

2. The access control feature we implemented in this chapter is a basic one. You can improve it by adding role-based access control. Upon login the user info you obtain should have a list of permissions. Depending on these permissions the user can perform operations. For example, the admin can perform all the CRUD operations while an editor can only create and edit posts.

3. The footer currently says "The Single Page Blogger". Create a new service that returns a version number and use it to show this in the footer. Hint: Use a directive and service.

---

[5] http://angular-ui.github.io/ui-router/

[6] https://www.youtube.com/user/angularjs

[7] https://www.youtube.com/user/ngconfvideos

[8] http://www.sitepoint.com/?s=angularjs

[9] https://builtwith.angularjs.org/

[10] http://stackoverflow.com/tags/angularjs/info

[11] http://ionicframework.com

4. Add more languages and translations to our app.

Host it Yourself : Back-end

As you know the back-end Node.js application that powers Single Page Blogger is hosted in the cloud. It means all the readers of this book are sharing the same MongoDB instance to store the posts. If this is not what you want, you can host the app yourself. There are two codebases available for download:

1. The main Single Page Blogger codebase that you've been using throughout this book

2. The Single Page Blogger Node.js back-end. This has been deployed to Openshift cloud so that you don't have to host it locally.

But if you are familiar with Nodejs and MongoDB and already have these installed you can host the back-end on your machine. Assuming you have got Node.js and MongoDB installed, just follow the steps below to install the back-end on your machine:

1. Download and unzip **sp-blogger-backend.zip**. It'll create a directory named **sp-blogger-backend**.

2. Go to the above directory in the terminal and type `node ./bin/www`. This should start a server on `localhost:8080`. Ensure you've already started MongoDB before running the command.

3. Now you should configure your AngularJS app (`sp-blogger`) to use the local endpoints instead of the remote ones. So, use the following configurations in **app/modules/admin/js/services.js**:

```
angular.module('spBlogger.admin.services').value('API_ENDPOINT'
➥,'http://localhost:8080/api/posts/:id')
angular.module('spBlogger.admin.services').value('AUTH_ENDPOINT'
➥,'http://localhost:8080/login');
angular.module('spBlogger.admin.services').value('LOGOUT_ENDPOINT'
➥,'http://localhost:8080/logout');
```

4. Now access your app as usual with the URL `http://localhost:8000` and this'll now use the local endpoints.

That's it! I hope you enjoyed reading this book. Keep rocking in AngularJS!

CPSIA information can be obtained at www.ICGtesting.com
Printed in the USA
LVOW03s1539220615

443393LV00031B/208/P